UNCIVIL
RIGHTS

Teachers, Unions, and Race in the Battle for School Equity

JONNA PERRILLO

The University of Chicago Press

Chicago and London

JONNA PERRILLO is assistant professor of English education at the University of Texas at El Paso.

The University of Chicago Press, Chicago 60637
The University of Chicago Press, Ltd., London
© 2012 by The University of Chicago
All rights reserved. Published 2012.
Printed in the United States of America

21 20 19 18 17 16 15 14 13 12   1 2 3 4 5

ISBN-13: 978-0-226-66071-4 (cloth)
ISBN-13: 978-0-226-66072-1 (paper)
ISBN-10: 0-226-66071-0 (cloth)
ISBN-10: 0-226-66072-9 (paper)

Library of Congress Cataloging-in-Publication Data

Perrillo, Jonna.
    Uncivil rights : teachers, unions, and race in the battle
for school equity / Jonna Perrillo.
        p. cm.
    Includes bibliographical references and index.
    ISBN-13: 978-0-226-66071-4 (cloth: alkaline paper)
    ISBN-10: 0-226-66071-0 (cloth: alkaline paper)
    ISBN-13: 978-0-226-66072-1 (paperback: alkaline paper)
    ISBN-10: 0-226-66072-9 (paperback: alkaline paper)
1. Educational equalization—New York (State)—
New York—History—20th century.   2. African
Americans—Education—New York (State)—New
York—History—20th century   3. Racism in education—
New York (State)—New York—History—20th century.
4. Teachers—Political activity—New York (State)—
New York—History—20th century.   5. Civil rights
movements—New York (State)—New York—History—
20th century.   6. Teachers—Civil rights—New York
(State)—New York—History—20th century.
7. Teachers' unions—New York (State)—New York—
History—20th century.   I. Title.
    LC213.23.N45P47 2012
    379.2'6097471—dc23
                                                2011043368

♾ This paper meets the requirements of
ANSI/NISO Z39.48-1992 (Permanence of Paper).

For my family

Contents

Acknowledgments

Writing is often solitary work, but I have been fortunate to have many friends and colleagues who have helped me enormously along the way. No one did more in this regard than Jonathan Zimmerman. Jon is a perceptive and diligent reader, a tireless advisor, and a great friend. He is one of my best advocates, not just in work but in life, and I thank him for his wealth of suggestions and constant encouragement and devotion to my success. I have benefited tremendously from the insightful feedback of a host of other colleagues as well, especially Diana D'Amico, Zoe Burkholder, Daniel Perlstein, Kate Rousmaniere, Barbara Beatty, Robert Gunn, Carley Moore, Nicole Wallack, Jim Fraser, Diana Selig, Michael Topp, Chuck Ambler, Sarah Bennison, and the members of the Boston History of Education Consortium. All of these people helped me to develop an idea — or many ideas — over the years I wrote this book, and I thank them for it.

In addition, I am grateful to the University of Texas at El Paso for awarding me a University Research Initiative grant to support my work at the Kheel Center at Cornell University. I am honored that the American Federation of Teachers and the Walter P. Reuther Library selected me as the Albert Shanker Educational Research Fellow in 2010 and thereby funded my research at Wayne State University. With any historical research, the advice and assistance of archivists can make all the difference in what evidence can be found in a short period of time. Dan Golodner at the Reuther Library knows everything about every teacher union, and I am thankful for his long-standing assistance and engagement in my work. Patrizia Sione and her entire staff at the Kheel Center made a short visit incredibly productive for me, and I am grateful. Gail Malmgreen at the Tamiment Library at New York University helped me over many years. David Ment at the New York City Board of Education archives was also generous with his time and expertise, and I very much enjoyed our conversations.

The teachers of the West Texas Writing Project have taught me more than anyone about the challenges contemporary teachers and students together face. As a group, they are a model of teacher professionalism and dedication to one's craft; I am especially grateful to Dory Munder, Richard Helmling, Manuel Aldaco, Nellie Ugarte, Michelle Villalobos, Letty Mendez, Chrissy Beltran, April Stene, Hillary Hambric, and Elsa Trevino for conversations and work partnerships that enabled me to develop my ideas more fully. At the National

Writing Project, Pat Fox, Joye Alberts, and Nick Coles aided me in better understanding the connections between my scholarship and my work as a director.

In addition, I am grateful to David Ruiter for helping me to structure my work life most productively in the book's final stages. Kate Mangelsdorf's and Doug Meyer's mentorship and support enabled me to accomplish more in my teaching and administrative work, which invariably made me a more enthusiastic writer. Nadine Garcia made it possible for me to revise my original manuscript as carefully as I had hoped.

Cristobal Silva, Liz Camp, and Jack Dougherty all gave me valuable advice as I prepared this for submission. Carley Moore proved, as always, to be a fantastic and devoted friend as she helped me with the cover. Adam Nelson read my manuscript for the University of Chicago Press with precision and generosity. He not only helped me to fine-tune some of my ideas in the book's final stages but also taught me much about how to be a first-rate reviewer. Elizabeth Branch Dyson is a dream to work with; I cannot imagine a more conscientious or helpful editor. We began this collaboration as unfamiliar colleagues, but I hope we are ending it as friends. Promotions Director Levi Stahl answered my every query with lightening speed and taught me a great deal about the publication process. I thank Sharon Brinkman for patiently detecting inconsistencies and errors I read over many times.

Stacey Sowards is as generous as friends come, and because of her help, I had more Saturday afternoons to write. In El Paso, many colleagues and friends have influenced my thinking and, simply, made my life better. I am especially grateful to Rosa, Jeff, Richard, Stacey, Marion, Deane, Tom, and Joanie for making El Paso home. In New York, I thank Katie, Lawrence, Carley, Matt, Nicole, Bob, and Madeline and Albert Wallack for opening their homes to me and helping me to feel as though I never left.

Finally, I thank my family, whose confidence in me and my pursuits has shaped me in ways that likely exceed my own understanding. My grandparents, Angelo and Edith Perrillo, once students of New York City schools themselves, sparked my initial interest in this project. My father Robert, my earliest role model of an academic, taught me from a young age to value diligence and hard work, both of which I needed to embrace to write this book. He has celebrated my every achievement, and I hope this book makes him proud. My mother Johanna juggled work and parenthood when I was a child; over the last several years, she has assisted me in doing the same. I am beyond thankful to her for her help, every time I asked, and for being, truly, a tireless mother and grandmother. My aunt Fredericka provided me with moral support and the comforts of home as I set the groundwork for this book. The Childresses and the Gunns cheered me on throughout my writing. I thank my sister Kerry for bountiful packages and for serving as a needed sounding board for my parenting questions and hypotheses.

Robert Gunn is many things to me, including husband, friend, colleague, writing partner, and advocate. He is also one of my best readers. I am forever grateful for his unfailing generosity, dedication, and interest as we talked about this book over the years. Robert, thank you. Franny was born ebullient, sociable, and empathetic. As a result, she has made the inevitable conflicts that arise for all working parents and children easier for both of us to weather. Henry's early sense of wonder reminds me daily of the joy that learning can and should be for all young people. My children will forever be my best achievement. Although I began this book before they came along, its completion means so much more to me because they did.

Introduction

"To some the teacher is in the best strategic position to further move-ments for a new social order," New York City teacher union leader Henry Lin-ville wrote in 1935. The problem, as Linville saw it, was that "the great majority of teachers would probably insist that their point of view, as well as their inter-ests, are in keeping with the economic and social *status quo*, if, indeed, they are interested in the great social questions of the day."[1] Within five years, Linville's assessment of teachers as socially conservative would appear out of date. As the early civil rights movement and World War II pushed educators to respond to America's race problem, many city teachers wholeheartedly adopted inter-cultural programs in the schools and an opportunity to fight prejudice. Em-bracing an image of themselves as "conscripts in the battle" against "intol-erance, greed, hatred, and indifference," teachers wrote enthusiastically of a new emphasis on race relations in their classrooms and of their goal to change students' and parents' prejudices and "make them conform to the American spirit."[2] This emphasis on a changed society was not to last, however. By 1955, a year after *Brown v. Board of Education* forced the integration of schools in the South, many teachers were fighting job assignments to the city's segregated black schools. When asked to put their social beliefs on the line, teachers chose not to work in minority schools where the facilities and resources were inadequate, class sizes were larger, and many students, they believed, pos-sessed "language handicaps, cultural differences, and cultural deficiencies" that created "a lack of interest in learning, and indeed a resistance to school."[3] Teacher strikes in response to school reform efforts led by black parents and community activists in the 1960s only furthered the gap between grassroots efforts to reform minority schools and teachers' sense of their professional well-being. At the height of the civil rights movement, it appeared that Henry Linville had been right about teachers.

Uncivil Rights traces the tensions between teachers' rights and civil rights in New York City from the Great Depression to the present, examining teachers' participation in creating a progressive "social order," their investment in the status quo, and the relationship of both to their professional self-interests. This story of teachers in the nation's largest school district has been over-looked in historical scholarship, but it is essential for understanding the con-nection between teacher professionalism and civil rights that is central to No Child Left Behind (NCLB), legislation that has not only impacted the shape of public education in our own day but also has marked the most radical federal government intervention in public education since the 1960s. When NCLB was ratified in 2001 with enthusiastic bipartisan support, a wealth of evidence indicated that minority students continued to receive an unequal education almost fifty years after *Brown*. Lawmakers on both sides of the aisle and education organizations, including teacher unions, wanted to be part of an effort to improve minority schools. Since that time, students, parents, educators, and some politicians have come to see that the design and implementation of the Act are deeply flawed. Minority children are not achieving more as a result of the accountability measures NCLB has put into place. Teachers have not fared well either, as their expertise has been subordinated to schools' efforts to meet state mandates. Studies show that many minority schools have turned to standardized curricula, teaching to the test, and eliminating programs in the arts and other disciplines that do not appear on state exams in an effort to improve students' scores. At the same time, racial segregation, the unequal distribution of resources, and teacher turnover rates in minority schools match or surpass pre-*Brown* statistics.[4] Both teachers' rights and civil rights have lost out in our schools, and *Uncivil Rights* will explain why.

In investigating moments of conflict—and collaboration—between teachers and black civil rights activists, *Uncivil Rights* traces the historical relationship between two social movements that are often studied separately: teachers' struggle for professional agency—especially for the freedom to teach where, what, and how they deemed best—and black Americans' quest for an equal education. Examining these movements in tandem reveals a troubled relationship among the most important stakeholders in public schools—students, teachers, parents, and the local communities schools serve—and it identifies the causes of that trouble. Although teachers' rights and civil rights need not be viewed as conflicting categories, they often were made so, both by teachers, who came to see civil rights efforts as detracting from or competing with their own goals, and by civil rights efforts and mandates that regulated and at times deprofessionalized teachers' work in minority schools. In uncovering this history of conflict, I focus especially on the role that teachers and teacher unions played in creating it. I do so not to assign blame to teachers or to generalize their political views but instead to use their changing conceptions of professional rights and the mechanisms they used to articulate those rights as a vantage point for understanding three important and interconnected problems: (1) a historical tension between teachers' professional objectives and civil rights campaigns that at times challenged those objectives; (2) a continuing, if nevertheless changed, tension between teacher professionalism and civil rights in our own time; and (3) the limitations of rights rhetoric as a framework for designing productive and successful schools and school cultures.

As Thomas Sugrue has noted, pervasive de facto segregation in New York City housing and employment led many white New Yorkers, like Northern whites more largely, to "liv[e] blissfully unaware of racial inequality or of their role in perpetuating it" because they could easily ignore its subjects.[5] City teachers, at least 90 percent of whom were white throughout the period this book covers, were different from average white New Yorkers. They had the opportunity to witness racial inequality firsthand through teaching assignments, through civil rights groups' reports that publicized inequities in minority schools, and through other teachers' written accounts of working in such schools that were published in education journals and the union press. Most importantly, and unlike many Northern whites, teachers were often compelled to confront their own role in creating racial inequalities. This confrontation led some teachers to commit to a pedagogy focused on social justice, but it led more to view their professional well-being as threatened in schools where they needed to work harder and under more difficult circumstances than did their colleagues in white schools.

Teacher unions had existed in New York City since 1916, but they remained marginal organizations in the mid-1950s. Membership in the social democrat Teachers Guild totaled approximately twenty-four hundred teachers in 1955, capturing just a fraction of the city's forty thousand teachers.[6] Its rival, the communist-oriented Teachers Union, had once listed over seven thousand members, but those numbers quickly diminished during the red scares of the 1950s. Until the 1960s, New York City teachers preferred to belong to any one of approximately seventy different groups and organizations, including some that divided them by location or teaching level, such as the Bronx Boro-Wide Teachers Association and the High School Teachers Association, or by special interest, such as the Unemployed Teachers Association. While some of these associations were powerful and others not, they all lacked the stigma that the term "union" implied. Although the issues the Teachers Union and Teachers Guild fought affected a wide swath of educators, most teachers associated unions with political radicals or factory workers rather than with professionals. Many of the teachers who had founded the Teachers Union in 1916, and those who joined both unions before World War II, were first-generation Americans whose parents were unionized laborers. But for most teachers throughout the 1930s, 1940s, and 1950s, including those who were also first-generation Americans and first-generation professionals, teaching's appeal included its opportunity to distinguish themselves from laborers rather than to ally themselves with them. "Plain snobbery," Teachers Guild president Rebecca Simonson charged, prevented teachers from joining unions and "taking reasonable steps to promote their own welfare."[7]

The resistance to teaching assignments in minority schools in the second half of the 1950s offered teacher unions a golden opportunity to recruit more people to their organizations. Parent groups in Harlem had been studying and critiquing the education their children were receiving throughout the 1930s, including the low percentage of experienced teachers working in Harlem schools, but they only gained influence as the number of minority schools grew throughout the city. In 1955, the Public Education Association (PEA) conducted a report on the state of the city's junior high schools. Studying majority white schools and majority black schools, the group concluded that of all the inequities between the two, teacher quality was the most drastic and significant. The PEA stopped short of recommending that more experienced and talented teachers be required to teach in or be transferred to minority schools, realizing that incentives would draw more satisfied and willing faculty than would mandates. But when Superintendent William Jansen asked for one thousand teachers to volunteer to work in minority schools in response to the report, only twenty-five responded.[8] The Board of Education, which had been experimenting with involuntary teacher transfers since World War II, turned to them in 1955 as their most substantial plan for improving the schools. The Teachers Union supported the policy. The Teachers Guild, which had protested the transfer of teachers on a case-by-case basis for over ten years, organized around the issue. Involuntary teacher transfers, the Guild contended, "limit[ed] the freedom of teachers to select the schools where they can do their best work."[9] In arguing for the right to choose their workplace, teachers relied on a number of inarguable facts, including that teaching in underfinanced schools with larger class sizes and insufficient classroom resources was more demanding work than teaching elsewhere. They also called on the cultural myth that racial prejudice caused black Americans, including children, to possess inferiority complexes that made them difficult to teach. Teaching assignments in minority schools, Guild unionists contended, were not fair and equal.

In its resistance to a system of rotating teachers through minority schools, the Guild found an issue that capitalized on many teachers' anxieties in postwar New York City. While the black population in the city rose by 62 percent between 1940 and 1950, the white population only rose by 3 percent. White flight, the exodus of Southern blacks to the urban North, and the segregated nature of the city's neighborhoods and schools guaranteed that more white teachers would be teaching in minority schools, in Harlem and elsewhere in the city. By

1966, one in every three public school students in the city was black, and the number of segregated schools had only grown.[10] Teachers across the political spectrum described feeling as though they were "stepping into a lion's den" when assigned to black schools, feelings exacerbated by a lack of significant relationships with black Americans.[11] In addition to resisting what they saw as more difficult jobs in minority schools, teachers also feared that they would have less freedom to teach how and what they wanted in classrooms that were being monitored by activist parents and community organizations. This concern only grew in the 1960s as black parents and activists formed community control boards to study and improve their neighborhood schools. The goals of such boards—including gaining more influence in the hiring decisions in schools and enforcing the inclusion of a multicultural curriculum designed by minorities—further threatened many teachers' sense of professional agency. White teachers feared being critiqued on what and how they taught, including how they disciplined students; by the mid-1960s, one teacher lamented, "All a teacher has to do is stand up to a [black] pupil and he is in lots of trouble."[12]

In response to these anxieties, the Teachers Guild and the United Federation of Teachers (UFT), which the Guild would transform into in 1959, developed a postwar strategy that focused on insulating teachers from civil rights demands. This strategy culminated in the fall of 1968 with the infamous Ocean Hill-Brownsville strikes, which shut down the city's schools for over two months. Once fearful of being transferred to minority schools to teach, teachers now struck in response to a community control board's effort to transfer nineteen educators to another district. Recent scholarship has examined these events in terms of black power and the militancy of late 1960s social movements, but the strikes take on new meaning when examined through a longer view, what Jacqueline Dowd Hall calls "the long civil rights movement" and what was by this time a nearly forty-year effort to improve minority schools.[13] If teachers in the 1940s and 1950s sought to appease black parents while nevertheless ignoring their most important requests, many teachers at the end of the 1960s were unwilling to do even this much; the distance between the movements had grown too great.

Teachers' problematic fight for professional freedom is one that reverberated throughout the nation, influencing teachers and teacher unions in other parts of the North, changing the character of American organized labor, and coming to influence our own political period. By the time of the Ocean Hill-Brownsville strikes, fifty-three thousand of the city's fifty-seven thousand teachers were members of the UFT. This explosive growth in membership suggests that the union's focus on protecting teachers' freedom had a powerful appeal. In what *New York Times* education reporter Fred Hechinger called the urban conflict of "teacher power versus community power," teachers won.[14] By the early 1970s, the UFT had effectively dismantled community control boards, disempowering minority parents and education activists. As the largest local in the nation, the UFT frequently dictated the policy of the national organization, the American Federation of Teachers, and, as a result, had a newfound influence in federal politics. Teachers inspired other public employees to organize and to strike, earning New York the moniker "Strike City" and transforming municipal unions into the new lifeblood of the American labor movement. City teachers' relationships to race progress movements were seminal to all of these developments.

Although more than four decades have passed since the Ocean Hill-Brownsville strikes, our own political period resonates with the tensions that evolved between a growing teacher union movement and a flourishing civil rights movement and with the legacy of the events *Uncivil Rights* recounts. NCLB, which is recognized as the largest federal effort to improve public schooling since the Johnson administration's Elementary and Secondary Education Act of 1965, has prioritized teacher quality and accountability. While black parents in the 1990s responded to many of the same problems with their children's schools that they critiqued a half-century earlier, many called for greater accountability in measuring the success of schools and school reform efforts. But the mechanisms NCLB lays out for assessing the quality of education that minority students receive—and the quality of teachers in minority schools—have exacerbated rather than lessened the differences between low-income, minority public schools and middle-class, white ones. Struggling schools with some of the greatest needs for creative, individualized teaching have become centers for a booming business in standardized curricula, packaged and sold as mechanisms for quality control in the classroom. Preparing students to perform well on their exams has extracted the most time away from other classroom objectives among low-achieving students. And, especially resonant with the history *Uncivil Rights* traces, parents have been provided with little more than standardized testing data to assess the quality of education being offered in their children's schools.

If NCLB is disturbing in its outcome for minority students and parents, it is no more inspiring for teachers. Postwar teachers opposed the growing influence of noneducators on their work in the classroom, but the 1950s and 1960s hardly compare with the regimentation teachers experience in their work in minority schools today. State exams, curricula mandates, and an ever-changing cycle of initiatives to improve student performance in schools at risk of losing state funding have left teachers with little control over how and what they teach. Altogether, the solutions that politicians, state education boards, education administrators, and corporations have devised and the messages implicit in those solutions have prioritized the opinions and decisions of interest groups outside of the profession over the professional knowledge of those within it. In deprofessionalizing teachers in the schools that need high-quality teachers the most, reforms have had the frequent, regrettable effect of making teaching poor and minority students a professional liability.

This dual disempowerment of teachers and students in part stems from what Arnold Fege describes as the "inability to imagine a nationwide system in which educators, parents, and communities work collaboratively to improve schools."[15] Even on the most local levels, within individual neighborhoods, this collaboration has been difficult. These challenges have not stemmed solely from government edicts or Board of Education regulations; just as important has been the relationship among teachers, teacher unions, and minority communities and their difficulties in working together. Our own times speak to the legacy of the story of New York City teachers and their relationship to civil rights efforts: when teachers' rights and students' rights are in conflict, both are bound to lose.

While teachers ran to unions after World War II for protection from minority communities seeking greater influence in improving their schools, they were also drawn to unions by a new, postwar focus on group rights and group identity. Nationally and in New York, teacher unions and associations were intertwined with other social movements from their beginnings, including the larger labor movement, the early women's movement, and the early civil rights movement. In the interwar period, both the Teachers Guild and the Teachers Union focused on bread-and-butter issues that challenged women teachers in particular, issues of academic freedom and freedom of speech that resulted from both world wars, and oral teaching examinations that were widely understood to penalize teachers with "ethnic" accents. Throughout much of the 1950s, the Teachers Union publicly exposed the shockingly low percentage of black teachers in the city and petitioned to train and hire more. Teachers Union members fought to integrate schools, build new facilities in minority neighborhoods, and rid schools of racist textbooks (including one written by New York City's school superintendent at the time); they created forward-thinking black history materials to be used in schools that were purchased by libraries and educational institutions across the nation. At the same time, the Guild and the UFT recruited black teachers from the South to teach in the city's schools, presented plans to integrate the schools, and, in the summer of 1964, sent the largest single contingent of Northern teachers to teach in the Mississippi Freedom Schools. Teachers' reports and writings on these

events—in their union newspapers, education journals, and private corre-
spondence—reveal that their civil rights efforts provided them with a genuine
sense of excitement, conviction, and purpose. In addition to serving as insulation for teachers, then, unions also had the capacity to serve as organizations
within which teachers could perform important social and political work to
reform race relations and schools simultaneously.

This work also exposed teachers to a new language of human rights they
then used to fight for their own gain. Unionists wrote about the "oppressed
teacher" in the 1920s and 1930s, but when they did, they referred to someone
who was underpaid, overworked, and subordinate to the whims of her school
administrator. The fight for teachers' rights in the interwar period was a fight
for better working conditions and compensation, and freedom from administrative dictums over their classrooms. In contrast, the oppressed teacher of
the 1950s and 1960s was plagued by what teachers perceived to be a more expansive cast of characters; the civic partnerships created within the civil rights
movement, along with changes in the wider culture, meant that the teacher's
responsibilities were now "spelled out for her by judges, psychologists, psychiatrists, social workers, business men, and religious leaders." Even parents
appeared to have more control over teachers' professional lives than they did.
The resulting fight for teachers' rights included a fight for better working conditions—especially smaller classes, reduced bureaucratic chores, and greater
authority in discipline procedures—and to be made "free . . . to do the job they
[were] trained to do."[16] While civil rights activists fought for the right to an equitable education for their children, teachers increasingly framed their struggle as one about freedom *from* the influence of black parents and activists.

Borrowing from the concepts and strategies of the black civil rights movement was not unusual but, in fact, was integral to the development of other social movements in the late 1960s and 1970s, including feminism, the Chicano
and American Indian movements, ethnic revivalism, disability rights advocacy,
and, as this book shows, professional rights movements. Matthew Frye Jacobson writes that the language of civil rights created "a shift in public language
for all," one that served to construct a sense of "'natural' alliance, 'natural'
conflict, solidarity, prior right, competition, or betrayal" among groups shar-
ing a social identity.[17] A rhetoric of alliance or solidarity encouraged over fifty
thousand teachers, invariably of a wide range of political views, to value their
shared interests and concerns over their differences, and, at times, to subordinate their personal political convictions to the actions of a larger professional
movement. This phenomenon, as much as individuals' limited views about racial others, can help us to understand how and why teachers voluntarily participated in important civil rights movement events at the same time they fought

the interests of the actual black students and parents they were assigned to serve. Or, otherwise stated, it explains how teachers worked for and against the advancement of equality for black Americans through their unions, a contradiction with which some members, black and white, struggled.

But, as Jacobson contends, in creating a sense of allegiance, the language of rights also denotes a necessity to identify competitors, those who seek to deny a group their rights for their own gain. Mary Ann Glendon argues that a connected, if not identical, sense of antagonism is essential to rights talk, a rhetoric she likens to a language of entitlement and "of no compromise." The powerful role of the courts in the postwar "rights revolution" and the enormous cultural value of the *Brown* case, she contends, points to a greater societal value for events that "seemed to wipe out ancient wrongs with the stroke of a pen" over acts of legislation such as the Civil Rights Voting Act that, by their very creation and passage, required political compromise.[18] While, in fact, contemporary studies of the *Brown* case tend to focus on the political compromises it entailed, Glendon's argument about the appeal and usefulness of contest over compromise is nevertheless helpful for a richer understanding of why, as the civil rights movement progressed, teachers believed their work needed protection from the agendas of activists and parents who were not trained educators and how it served them to voice their professional dissatisfactions as injustices.[19] One on hand, conflicts among teachers, parents, and education activists resulted from a perceived schism of interests and a coordinating struggle for a limited share of power. African American parents' fight in the 1940s and 1950s for more experienced and better trained teachers in their children's schools, for example, threatened to affect the teachers with greater seniority who typically had more control over their own teaching assignments. At the same time, a framework of contest or competition gave teachers a means to distinguish their professional, disciplinary knowledge of how to teach children from black parents' and activists' experiential knowledge of black children. Teachers claimed that their professional authority—grounded in academic training—enabled them to assess students' academic potential and performance. But parents often drew very different conclusions about both. If the language of rights and entitlement enabled teachers in developing black parents into opponents, it also helped them to justify the distance between their frequent perceptions of black students as uninterested and unmotivated and parents' perceptions of those students.

It is important to note as well that although teachers, like others, drew on the civil rights movement in their struggle for professional agency, and although this borrowing was common to other identity groups, the ends to which they framed their struggle became fundamentally different from that of black parents and activists. The efforts of civil rights activists were aspirational: parents and community leaders wanted better schools, including more knowledgeable and experienced teachers and more opportunities made available for their children in those schools. If their children had the same quality of education as white children, they believed, their lives beyond school would also improve. The efforts of teachers, however, became increasingly reactionary or focused on what Isaiah Berlin terms as "negative liberty," a view of freedom that seeks to outline and protect "the area in which a man can act unobstructed," as compared with "positive liberty," a view of freedom that emphasizes "being one's own master" and "bearing responsibility for [one's] choices."[20] The civil rights work of teachers and teacher unions proved that they could be visionary and could create work and plans for future work that could promote social change. But as their efforts for their own professional rights increasingly focused on minority parents and community advocates in the late 1950s and 1960s, the battle for teachers' rights became one over what they could not achieve under given circumstances and over whom they did not want to influence their work. Given the unchanging problems of the physical conditions of and resources in minority schools, as well as many teachers' views about "culturally deficient" black children, it was difficult for teachers to articulate how their work would be different, or how their students' lives would improve, if they were left free to teach without outside influence.

The fight for teachers' rights, then, was a movement often driven by anxiety, including teachers' concern that their professionalism was being undermined and underestimated and that the challenges they faced in the classroom were being read as performance failures. At times, they were right. It was easy for teachers to substantiate their anxieties with evidence—in fact, they were seen, by parents and by organizations such as the PEA, to be failing black children. Armed with evidence, these everyday anxieties came to drive union policy and teacher unions' relationships with the minority communities they served. Too often, however, the ramifications of these anxieties—including growing tensions and divisions between teacher unions and racial minority communities—have been misunderstood by union critics to be inevitable, even natural, products of teacher unions as political organizations or the result of socially conservative teacher union leaders, who themselves became professional bureaucrats and politicians as union membership rapidly expanded in the 1960s and 1970s. For this reason, historians often examine leaders in their scholarship about teacher unions. Albert Shanker, president of the UFT from 1964 to 1984, has made an especially compelling subject because he was charismatic in the mold of many of the most influential labor leaders and because his frequently antagonistic style of leadership came about just as conflicts between teachers and community control boards were heightening.[21] In contrast to these other studies, *Uncivil Rights* focuses as much as possible on the observations and actions of ordinary teachers. The growing divide between teachers and the minority communities they served may not always have been aided by the leadership of either group, but it was fostered by many individual teachers and their experiences in the classroom and by many ordinary parents increasingly disappointed by their children's experiences in those same classrooms. For this reason, it is vital to examine not only how leaders shaped union agendas but how teachers influenced those agendas just as much.

Both teacher unions and the black civil rights movement took new shape in the political context of the 1930s, and so this book begins there. Chapter 1 traces the beginnings of a parent-based civil rights movement for equal education in Harlem and shows how this early movement had a vital impact on teacher unionism. A 1935 riot in Harlem and the resulting organization of parents and activists forced unionists to respond to some of its social and political causes, including overcrowded schools, the systematic placement of African American students in vocational programs, the high percentage of unlicensed and substitute teachers working in neighborhood schools, and the low number of African American teachers in the city as a whole. As the mayor, parents groups, and the black press publicly exposed these problems, New York City teachers, including unionists, became divided in their response. While the 1935 break of the Teachers Union into the communist Teachers Union and the socialist Teachers Guild has been traditionally understood as a product of competing political ideologies, this chapter shows that race politics were central to these competing views. As Teachers Union members dedicated themselves to teaching in Harlem schools and supporting local parents and community organizers, the Guild argued that teachers must "defend the law" and align themselves instead with education administrators. By World War II, both unions held positions on Harlem schools that were connected to and representative of their larger ideologies about teachers, political action, and the roles of the schools in building "a new social order."

World War II pressured Americans to address their own race problems at home; to do their part, city teachers made a greater effort to address racism in the schools. Chapter 2 focuses on teachers' race progress efforts, beginning in 1942, and the way in which they did and did not influence other union policies about schools and race. The Teachers Union created bibliographies and other materials for teaching black history and petitioned for a black resident to be appointed to the Board of Education. The Teachers Guild focused on improving vocational education for black students. Both unions advocated the adoption of interculturalism, an early form of multicultural education that focused on eliminating prejudice. Both unions also developed relationships with Harlem organizations to press the Board of Education to reduce class sizes, hire more teachers, and adopt plans to integrate Harlem schools. At the same time, studies by the Board of Education revealed that most teachers were still averse to teaching in minority schools and that the Guild aided its teachers who wished to be transferred out of "difficult" schools. Even in this harmonious, politically active period, then, teachers considered their job quality or job satisfaction to be in conflict with teaching minority students.

Chapter 3 traces the transformation of teacher unions between 1950 and 1960 that resulted from teacher assignment campaigns. As postwar civil rights campaigns in the city grew, organizations such as the Urban League and parent study groups increasingly focused on teacher quality as the major obstacle to the fair and equal education of black students. Teachers Union efforts supported these investigations into teacher quality and supported Board of Education plans to transfer experienced teachers to minority schools. At the same time, the Guild became ever more determined to organize teachers and consolidate the city's multitudinous existing teacher organizations into one movement. To do so, Guild campaigns focused on the "oppressed teacher," one who lacked morale because she also lacked any agency in the education bureaucracy. The issue of teacher transfers to minority schools was symbolic of this lack of agency. The oppressed-teacher argument served to depoliticize conversations at the same time that it drew on human rights rhetoric and that race politics in the city schools were becoming all the more difficult to ignore. In 1959, the Guild consolidated with other teacher organizations to form the UFT, a larger, more powerful teacher union that would come to symbolize the growing division between teachers' rights and civil rights.

Chapter 4 explains how simultaneous changes in unionists' conceptions of teachers' rights and black New Yorkers' strategies for improving their neighborhood schools culminated in the 1968 Ocean Hill-Brownsville strikes. The success of membership campaigns in the 1950s meant that the UFT was no longer composed of the most liberal teachers but instead comprised a membership who possessed a range of political views. In 1963, members of the Teachers Union voted to join the UFT because their post–cold war marginalization left them without influence on their own. The demise of a radical union in which teachers could fight for race progress serves as an especially powerful barometer of teachers' relationship to the civil rights movement at a time when the movement was most visible and powerful. At the same time that UFT membership was increasingly politically conservative, tensions between newly established community control boards and teacher unions escalated.

Tired of broken promises of integration, black parents and activists fought for greater community control over who taught and what was taught in minority schools. Unionized black teachers who were not necessarily supporters of black power nevertheless found the city's unions to fail African American students and teachers and formed black teacher groups within the UFT. By 1970, relations between teachers and the minority communities they served seemed irreparably damaged.

The 1960s marked both a period of more visible efforts for school reform on the part of black parents and a growing tension between these parents and black teachers. As chapter 5 outlines, teacher union campaigns in the 1970s and 1980s can be understood as a product of this visible effort and of teacher unions' need to put forth a more publicly responsive image. Albert Shanker, president of the UFT and, as of 1974, the American Federation of Teachers, was essential to this process. In his development of a weekly column in the *New York Times* and in his support of the Reagan administration's report on school failure, *A Nation at Risk*, Shanker worked to put forth a more consolidated message about teacher professionalism than had existed in the 1970s, one that simultaneously asserted that teacher unions were more powerful than they had been before the 1960s and, at the same time, more accountable for upholding high professional standards. Teachers' responses to this argument about accountability varied but were also tangential to a teacher power movement that more effectively produced political power for teacher unions than it heightened individual teachers' authority in their schools and their communities.

Finally, the conclusion of *Uncivil Rights* examines the recent efforts that teacher unions have made to address the quality of education in minority schools, the limits they have faced in their efforts, and the ways in which the historical tension between teachers' rights and civil rights has shaped our own political period. The agenda midcentury teachers developed to advance their own professionalism—including resistance to teacher transfers—undermined their moral authority in local communities; the legacy of this agenda enabled the design of federal legislation that focuses on teacher quality as the primary obstacle to minority student success. The failure of NCLB to improve education for minority students and the historical events this book traces indicate that it is important that we rethink the centrality of rights talk to school reform projects and instead see the empowerment of teachers and students as mutually beneficial goals, not just in rhetoric but in reality.

CHAPTER 1

Building a "New Social Order"

Teachers, Teacher Unions, and Equity in the Great Depression

On the afternoon of October 21, 1936, fourteen-year-old Robert Shelton was standing in a hallway of Harlem elementary school P.S. 5, sent by his parents to wait for his sister. While this much is certain, the events that followed are not. According to the school's faculty, Robert was told by a teacher not to loiter in the hall, and when he began to cause a disturbance in response, the principal, Gustave Schoenchen, was called. Schoenchen brought Robert to his office, and when the boy picked up a ruler and threatened to hit him with it, the 250-pound, one-armed principal struggled to subdue him. According to Robert's parents, their son was beaten without provocation, called "vile names" by the principal, and ordered to wash blood off of his face or Schoenchen would "beat [him] into unconsciousness." Pictures of a shirtless, bespectacled Robert Shelton were published in the city's black press, showing the boy with bandages on his head, abdomen, and arm. But the physician who had treated Robert at Harlem Hospital stated that he had not applied any of the bandages in the photograph, nor were they necessary. If the events at P.S. 5 were unclear, they nevertheless resonated with Harlem parents and some teachers, who knew that black children were often the victims of white hostility, including in the public schools they attended. By the time of Schoenchen's trial, an organized delegation of Harlem parents, civic organizations, and New York City Teachers Union members had picketed the school for months, demanding the principal be fired and be replaced with someone "who has shown in practice an understanding of the needs of the people of Harlem."[1] On the streets and in their union press, Teachers Unionists protested for three months that "Schoenchen must go. And with him must go the attitude that 'anything is good enough for Harlem.'"[2] In January 1937, the Board of Education transferred the principal to a school in Queens. But the perceived attitude that Harlem schools deserved less than the city's other schools remained.

This chapter begins with the Schoenchen episode because it serves as an illuminating moment in what this chapter and book are about: the critical role that race and race progress movements played in shaping teachers' views of professionalism and professional rights in the nation's largest school district. The case was important for what it signified to Harlem residents and to some liberal teachers: that public schools, which might have promised black students a respite from racial discrimination, often embraced and perpetuated it. This stark fact indelibly influenced the development of both New York City's black civil rights movement and teachers' professional movements in the 1930s, shaping their agendas and setting the course for school reform efforts for the remainder of the century. While both social movements predated the Depression, they grew and acquired a changed sense of consequence in the context of economic collapse. Black New Yorkers faced greater unemployment numbers than any other demographic group in the city, while teachers, who already faced deep salary cuts, were compelled by the Board of Education to contribute an additional 5 percent of their earnings to support needy children.[3] In response to what the Depression had revealed about the nature of opportunity and exploitation in American society, black city residents and city teachers, independently from and collectively with each other, sought to create what Teachers College professor George Counts named in 1932 "a new social order." Counts, along with his colleagues John Dewey, William Heard Kilpatrick, Harold Rugg, and others, named themselves the social reconstructionists. As a group, they argued that public schools were central to social reform and that in the process "teachers must abandon their easy optimism" and "deal more fundamentally, realistically, and positively with the American social situation than has been their habit in the past." The reward for teachers in this effort, Counts explained, was not just ethical but political in character. If teachers "could increase sufficiently their stock of courage, intelligence and vision," he estimated, they "might become a social force of some magnitude."[4]

Nowhere in the city was the potential of teachers tested more than in what had become its segregated black schools, the majority of which were located in Harlem. Between 1920 and 1930, the black population in the city had more than doubled. "To assimilate the children of so large a Negro population into a city school system that would recognize no distinction of race or color is a problem of the first magnitude," contended State Commissioner of Education Frank Pierrepont Graves in 1931. In fact, the "implication for the organization of school, for the recruiting and assigning of teachers," he assessed, already produced "one of the most difficult problems the city face[d]."[5] Graves concluded that the challenge of educating black youth stemmed from a growing black population, but many signs indicated that the situation was more complicated, made so in part by educators who frequently measured students by their race. Serving as a background to the Schoenchen story, and making it believable, if not familiar, to many Harlem residents were what had become the indisputable facts about the neighborhood's public schools and the everyday inequities that affected all black children in Harlem. "After Schoenchen, what?" asked one *New York Amsterdam News* editorial; the principal, it reminded its readers, "was only the beginning." Everyday, "less obvious evils" still existed in Harlem schools, including racial segregation, district gerrymandering, the tracking of black students into vocational schools and programs, and "the dumping of principals and teachers into Harlem as 'punishment' for their derelictions elsewhere."[6] Schoenchen was emblematic of many larger problems documented to exist in the Harlem schools, including a faculty who neither understood black children nor held interest in teaching them.

As much as the events at P.S. 5 revealed about the status of young black students, however, they also served as an important backdrop for a changing teacher union movement. Just one year earlier, New York City's unionized teachers had divided into two distinct unions: the communist Teachers Union and the social democrat Teachers Guild. Many of the teachers who now belonged to the Guild had once helped to forge the Teachers Union, Local 5 of the American Federation of Teachers, under the leadership of John Dewey in 1916. The 1935 split has been described by historians as a product of political divisions between a younger, procommunist group of teachers who would remain Teachers Unionists and an older, more professionally established, anticommunist group of teachers who would form the Guild.[7] Beneath the surface arguments about political orientation, however, existed a more complex difference in thinking about the most important professional rights for teachers and the best, most productive means by which to achieve those rights. Although a range of political factions had formed within the Teachers Union shortly after World War I, by the early 1930s, the differences were acute, and infighting consumed much of the union's agenda, from its stand on salary differentials to its financial contributions to the Scottsboro defense. It was no longer possible to maintain, Teachers Union president Henry Linville lamented in 1933, that the Union could regain "the blessed state of harmony which many members have longed for."[8] In October 1935, after a failed attempt to persuade the American Federation of Teachers to expel communist teachers from the Teachers Union, Linville left with approximately eight hundred other members to form the Guild. Dewey, more politically moderate than Counts, transferred his allegiances to the Guild as well.

The Schoenchen case and a developing civil rights movement gave all of New York City's unionized teachers an opportunity by which to more sharply define their agendas and their image, for themselves and for other interest groups whose favor they sought. In the fall of 1935, the Teachers Union had founded a Harlem committee. Committee members and other Teachers Unionists participated in the demonstrations against Schoenchen that took place for four months following the incident. This included a public trial of the Board of Education that the Teachers Union helped to stage in January 1937, with Reverend Adam Clayton Powell serving as judge. Robert Shelton, Teachers Union representative Bella Dodd, and neighborhood parents testified to the poor conditions of Harlem schools and the treatment of black students within them. The "jury," which included Charles Huston of the National Association for the Advancement of Colored People (NAACP), Lester Granger of the Urban League, Frank Crosswaith of the Negro Labor Committee, and A. Philip Randolph of the Brotherhood of Sleeping Car Porters, deliberated and found the Board guilty.[9] As with the other parties represented at the trial, for the approximately three thousand Teachers Unionists, the Schoenchen episode was indicative of a second-class citizenship impressed on Harlem children and, in turn, the teachers who taught them. This sense of shared oppression led Teachers Unionists to build alliances with parent groups and civil rights organizations and to see its own success as dependent on collaboration with "the most prominent, intelligent, and reliable citizens of the communit[ies]" Harlem teachers served. The Union, members asserted, was one of more than fifty organizations that united in the protests.[10] In its alliances with black students and parents, the Teachers Union, even if only representing a fraction of the city's thirty-six thousand teachers, worked to make the quality of black schools a civic and civil rights issue and not solely a Harlem problem.

The Teachers Guild also reported on the Schoenchen case in their press, although not because its members took part in the protests. Instead, the Guild opposed the image that the Teachers Union's actions put forth of city teachers. Guild Bulletin articles reported that "P.S. 5 was mass picketed for days. Demonstrations were conducted by white leaders, with a following of Negro children from the school. Speeches were made condemning the principal." Rightfully, the Guild recounted, the police were called in response. Most important to the Guild was that the Teachers Union "identified itself with the elements that headed these demonstrations." While the Guild disapproved of both the Teachers Union's demonstrations and its partnership with activist elements, the episode offered the Union a means by which it could clearly distinguish its differing view of teacher activism and professionalism. The Guild did not condone the content of the accusations lodged against Schoenchen, but neither did it believe them to be true. The "process of orderly inquiry into all charges before the courts, as well as before the Board of Education" had revealed significant doubts about the Sheltons' claims against the principal. Teachers, the Guild argued, should "defend the law [in Harlem] and everywhere" by responding rationally to what the inquiry revealed; they should not walk the streets with signs because the case conveniently supported their larger political platform.[11]

While the Teachers Union trial appeared to Guild members to make due process into a spectacle, the Guild's faith in the courts and the ability of democratic institutions to uphold civil rights were central to its own actions and its alliances. The union's twelve hundred members "represent[ed] the constructive movement amongst New York City teachers with whom all teachers outside the [Teachers] Union can work," Guild president Henry Linville explained in June 1937. Such a movement also depended on political partnerships, and Linville boasted of the Guild's "friendship [with] the Board of Education, the Board of Superintendents, and the Board of Examiners."[12] Just as the Teachers Union's relationship with Harlem parents and civil rights groups signaled its beliefs in the connection between professionalism and social justice, so did the Guild's relationship with the city's education administrators convey a definition of professionalism in which teachers served as key players in the workings of a larger educational bureaucracy rather than as outsiders to it.

As the two unions' outlooks suggest, central to the story of teacher professionalism and self-advocacy in the 1930s is black Americans' contemporaneous identification of public schools as a site for civil rights struggles and advances. As Jacqueline Dowd Hall has convincingly argued, too often the civil rights movement is equated with "a single halcyon decade," the 1960s, and "to limited, noneconomic objectives." This equation frequently occludes what happened before World War II nationally, including the frequent exclusion of black Americans from New Deal reforms, municipal school zoning laws that promoted segregation, and bank redlining policies designed to do the same for housing—all developments that would come to irrevocably shape public education for urban minority students. Understanding black resistance to these discriminatory acts as a part of rather than anticipatory of a civil rights movement, Hall contends, affords us a "more robust, more progressive, and truer story," one that can also offer a stronger context for the efforts of Harlem parents and activists in the 1930s.[13] Black parents, whose children sat at the intersection of multiple forms of discriminatory practices that impacted the quality of their schooling, were forced to decide which forms of inequity were most important to contest and who would serve as their most important allies. For many Harlem activists, partnering with white unionized teachers offered the promise of school reform from the inside out.

The Teachers Union's and Guild's responses to the Schoenchen case illustrate how in an interwar embrace of a "new social order," teachers and teacher unions discovered that their own burgeoning professional movements would need to contend with the state of black schools and the objectives of developing civil rights efforts to reform them. To be sure, the 1930s marked a critical decade for education politics in New York City for all of the reasons it was important nationwide, including the influence of the Depression on public school finance and the problems that an increasingly feminized profession faced at a time when many men were out of work.[14] But the decade also served as a pivotal moment in a lesser known story, one about teachers' challenging of and contribution to an increasing disparity between white and black schools in the urban North. Just as the Schoenchen case played a part in black city residents' larger movement for better schools, it also compelled city teachers—over 98 percent of whom were white in the interwar period—to articulate their responsibilities to the black students and communities they served in a way that they had not had to do previously. This was most true for unionized teachers, who possessed a public, organized voice. By the end of the Schoenchen case, the two unions were set on distinct courses for determining their role and participation in minority school reform and for advocating for their own profession. In response to the issues Harlem schools raised, city teachers would better define and articulate their sense of purpose and self-definition.

Harlem, Dixie

Even as Guild members doubted the veracity of the accounts lodged at Gustav Schoenchen, the larger problems at the heart of the case—including corporal punishment and the disaffection between white educators and black community members—were familiar to many Harlem residents. These classroom and school-bound problems took on even greater significance in the context of an urban school system that marginalized black students as a whole. Black leaders' responses to the case echoed many parents' frustrations with how minority schools had developed within a rapidly expanding urban public school system. Between 1900 and 1930, the New York City public high school student population had grown from 11,705 to 210,000.[15] More students attended high school in New York City in 1920 than had in the entire nation in 1880; together, the city's thirty-seven thousand teachers served more students in 1930 than did teachers in Los Angeles, Cleveland, St. Louis, Baltimore, Boston, Pittsburgh, San Francisco, and Milwaukee combined.[16] This precipitous growth was caused by several factors, including an increased number of youth attending school for longer periods of time and a tremendous influx of immigrants and migrants into New York in the three decades preceding the Depression.[17] Harlem felt the effects of this influx as much as any other part of the city. From

1900 to 1930, New York's black population had grown from seventy-two thousand to 186,000 and would nearly double again by 1940; approximately two-thirds of the city's black population lived in Harlem during the Depression.[18] By 1930, only one in five black New Yorkers was born in the city. Half to two-thirds were born in the South and had migrated North; the rest were migrants from the West Indies and Caribbean.[19] Like the rest of the city, then, black Harlem contained a diverse and rapidly growing population.

These demographic changes called for the rapid redesign of urban public schools from the previous century, one that frequently codified differences in education quality for white and black students. By 1930, public schools in New York City were structured much as they would be for the rest of the century. Common schools had been replaced by a three-tiered system of elementary, junior high, and high schools that themselves were organized into differentiated curricular tracks. Specialized vocational high schools trained students for jobs in a range of industries, but many academic high schools offered vocational courses as well. The rate of school segregation had increased as quickly as Harlem's black population had grown in the decades leading up to the Depression; area schools that were 6–69 percent black in 1913 served a 97–100 percent black student body by 1934.[20] Although the neighborhood had twenty-one elementary schools, it had only one academic and two vocational high schools, and black students were usually assigned to the lowest tracks in all.[21] As early as 1915, in her study for the Public Education Association, Frances Blascoer found that over 60 percent of "normal" black students in the New York City public schools were overage for their grade. For "exceptional" black students—those who had been identified by teachers and administrators as truant, behaviorally difficult, or "mentally defective"—over 80 percent of students measured as overage.[22] In some cases, principals openly admitted that they limited the number of black students allowed in their schools and in some of the higher skilled vocational tracks because if the student body "were to grow into anything like an equal proportion of white and black pupils . . . the white [students] would not come to the school and it would become a school for colored [students] only."[23]

These institutional and structural differences between black and white schools were compounded by other differences in staff and student relations and in pedagogical technique. Most of the city's principals, State Commissioner Graves found, were trained to oversee the administration of the school staff and made little effort to improve relationships between teachers and pupils or between the school and the surrounding community.[24] This inattention to community relations was all the more consequential when the school staff and the neighborhood residents shared little in common, as was often the case in Harlem. In addition to the specifics of the incident at hand, the Schoenchen case had revealed a lack of trust between the principal and the residents of the surrounding community that was familiar to many Harlem schools. Principals in majority-white schools were much more likely to object to double sessions (a practice that cut the hours in the academic day to serve two shifts of students), singular courses of study, and other measures that regularly defined Harlem schools. Teachers appeared to have more leeway and less accountability in black schools, perhaps because of principals' focus on administration and order. While "the chief basis for classification [of pupils] in most schools is the teacher's opinion," one Board of Education study found, in high-performing white schools, teachers tended to support their personal assessments with standardized test scores, whereas in low-performing black schools, they did not.[25] That is, while teachers in black schools called on intuition, teachers in white schools relied on data; together, the two kinds of schools represented two different models of teaching at work.

Black parents and civil rights organizations, while consistently aware that the schools black youth attended suffered from poor resources and insufficient space, shifted their beliefs about the sources of such inequalities over the decade. As David Ment has proved, in the early 1930s, the NAACP and other civil rights groups believed that racial segregation in Harlem schools was the product of housing and employment discrimination rather than a purposeful strategy on the part of the Board. The city's Board, the Children's Aid Society contended in 1932, practiced "fair treatment" and "no race discrimination."[26] This conclusion derived from a philosophy that schools were fair so long as any differences between them were created incidentally. But not all Harlem leaders found this assessment to go far enough in detecting the ways in which schools perpetuated racial discrimination. Poet Langston Hughes, who would later consult with the Teachers Union on several projects, argued that middle-class blacks who attended "mixed" schools learned to unconsciously equate whiteness "with all the virtues," including "beauty, morality, and money."[27] In addition, the Depression revealed as much as any event that school segregation was connected to other forms of disparity, and by mid decade the politics of integration grew more heated and more central to school reform struggles. In 1936, the Board's budget designated that 168 new schools be constructed throughout the city. Only one of the schools was to be built in Harlem.[28] These decisions had been made by the Board and clearly signaled a lack of dedication to the welfare of black students. So too did the Board's suggestion in 1937 that Wadleigh High School, an all-girls school and Harlem's only integrated high school, be moved to another part of Harlem because it was located in a neighborhood, former superintendent John Tildsley described, "where gentlewomen do not like to pass." Instead, the Wadleigh building was reassigned to house a vocational school specifically for black students.[29] A situation that was insufficient for white female students and teachers, the Board's decision indicated, was acceptable nevertheless for black youth.

Just as important to changing the sentiments of civil rights activists, however, was an indicting report written by a special commission to Mayor Fiorello LaGuardia in 1936. In March 1935, a riot broke out in Harlem after a black Puerto Rican youth was accused of shoplifting a knife from a local store. When police refused to address shoppers' questions about the boy, false rumors quickly circulated that the teenager had been beaten to death by police. Outraged residents took to the streets within hours and directed their frustrations toward neighborhood businesses, smashing windows, looting goods, and creating over two million dollars in property damage. In the end, a Harlem teenager was fatally shot by police.[30] The riot brought national attention to Harlem's political and economic problems. Directly following the incident, LaGuardia appointed the commission of seven black and six white civic activists and social scientists—including E. Franklin Frazier and Oswald Garrison Villard—to investigate its causes. The report the commission soon wrote out of its investigation, considered to be too damning to be published until it was leaked by the New York Amsterdam News in July 1936, focused on many areas in which Harlem residents experienced discrimination and unequal treatment, but the issue of schools and youth rang an especially powerful chord.[31] In short, the committee had found that the quality and conditions of Harlem schools had contributed greatly to a general sense of unrest and malaise that had "set the scene" for the riot. "The school system is at all times a vital part of the life of any community," the committee explained to the mayor, but "in this one, it has become peculiarly important and almost decisive in its influence upon the lives of children."[32] Rather than serving as institutions of racial uplift, Harlem public schools only confirmed a sense of second-class citizenship for black city youth.

Conditions in the Harlem schools were by any definition deplorable. Its school buildings were the oldest in the city and far too small for the number of students they now served. Four schools had no outside space for students to play in; one typical school lunchroom had 175 seats for one thousand students. All lacked sufficient numbers of books and other classroom resources, including faculty and staff. A lack of psychologists and guidance counselors in schools that often needed them more than others meant that black youths "on the verge of delinquency" were often dismissed from school for minor infractions. An insufficient number of teachers led to larger classes and to most of Harlem's schools to operating on a dual- or triple-session schedule, leaving students to attend school for only part of the day. These conditions created a cycle of inequity that was sustained throughout a child's education. Because "poorly equipped and crowded junior high schools of Harlem do not give them adequate preparation for entrance into a senior high school," the mayor's report concluded, black students were tracked into remedial programs and vocational schools.[33] In all of these ways, the commission argued, the state of the neighborhood schools compounded Harlem youths' chances of living adult lives of unemployment and crime. "Practices of racial discrimination, overcrowding in classrooms, antiquated facilities, and dilapidated buildings must be reckoned as contributing elements" to the riot, echoed commission member and Committee for Better Schools in Harlem chairman Reverend John W. Robinson. "Harlem is part of New York City," Robinson reminded Board members. "It is not in Dixie."[34] Yet, as with the report, many of the improvements that black parents and activists had been asking for since the beginning of the decade—including more counseling and medical services, improved school plants, restrooms for teachers, and a free lunch period for teachers in which they were not required to supervise students—only underscored the distinctions between black and white schools.[35]

What the commission found was not news to teachers who taught in Harlem. The same distinctions that defined education for black students also came to shape many Harlem teachers' sense that they, too, were treated differently than their colleagues in more affluent white schools. Harlem teachers often lacked any kind of professional space outside of their individual classrooms, served more students, and taught more classes than teachers in other city schools, and, because of the high concentration of substitute teachers in the neighborhood's schools, frequently were paid less to do so. In the fall of 1935, Teachers Unionist Alice Citron, a Harlem elementary school teacher, and Lucille Spence, the only black teacher at Wadleigh High School, had cofounded the Harlem Committee of the Teachers Union, dedicated to addressing the issues of Harlem students, schools, and teachers.[36] Teachers did not have to belong to a special committee to observe the problems the mayor's report documented. But the commission described the Harlem Committee teachers as especially helpful because so many others were afraid to talk openly about what they saw. The fact that teachers would not testify before the commission "except in private and with complete assurance their identity would remain secret" suggested that there existed in Harlem schools a "feeling of professional insecurity and a system of suppression, not to say terrorism, unworthy of any city, much less of the American metropolis."[37] This insecurity, the commission implied, came from a faculty that saw Harlem children being treated unequally through the inadequacy of the schools they were given to attend and who themselves faced less professional working conditions.

Within this tense atmosphere, black teachers, like black students, faced unique obstacles because of their race. The number of black teachers in the period is difficult to ascertain. The *New York Amsterdam News* reported in 1934 that of the city's thirty-five thousand teachers, 250 were black; four years later, it reported that 650 black teachers worked in the system.[38] Licensing practices that often discriminated against black educators—practices that the city's only black principal, Gertrude Ayer, had to fight herself and brought to public attention—make this gain of four hundred teachers unlikely.[39] These practices included the use of oral exams instituted specifically to weed out teacher candidates with foreign or "Southern" accents. Black teachers applying for teaching positions through the Works Progress Administration (WPA) complained of being hired only for Harlem schools and given clerical or custodial positions, if offered any position at all; in addition, WPA administrators were reported to discriminate against candidates with degrees from Southern colleges, claiming that "a Negro college in the South is not really a college."[40] Yet the number of black teachers in the city was difficult to assess because the Board claimed a color-blind hiring practice and did not keep track of the racial and ethnic makeup of its teaching force at the same time that it worked to prevent black teachers from being licensed. Nor is the experience of black teachers easily understood. While the mayor's commission reported that "overwhelming testimony" pointed to "the cordial cooperation between colored and white teachers," it also held a closed hearing of black teachers in April 1935. Because they feared retribution from the Board, "Negro teachers would not dare tell their stories otherwise," the city's press reported.[41] Even if relationships between white and black teachers were generally positive, such accounts suggested, relationships between black teachers and white administrators frequently were not.

Ultimately, however, with such a relatively small number of black teachers in the city schools, black students' educational experiences were much more dependent on the quality and attitudes of white teachers. Although the mayor's report explicitly stated that its analysis of Harlem teachers did not constitute "criticisms directed at white teachers as a group," many of the problems that it found were inseparable from issues of race. While young Teachers Unionists made up an important part of the teaching corps in Harlem schools, they did not constitute the majority. Instead, the mayor's commission found that "a disproportionate number of older white teachers are to be found in the Harlem schools." Such teachers taught in the schools not because of a political commitment toward black children but because they had begun their careers in these schools, dating back to a period in which the schools' student populations were mostly white. Although such teachers believed that "the influx of Negroes has brought new problems," they admitted to the commission that they were more interested in waiting out the rest of their careers where they were rather than beginning anew in a different school. Whereas overcrowded and underresourced classrooms in Harlem schools "often require the physical vigor and energy which only young men and women are able to exert," the commission reported, these teachers, counting the clock until retirement, often lacked the necessary skills for working with minority children. This, in turn, left older teachers "impatient and unsympathetic towards the children."[42]

Such attitudes were important beyond the consequences they held for students' experiences in individual classrooms. Rather, they enabled the systematic discriminatory practices that characterized Harlem schools. If the segregation of black youth to particular schools in Harlem was created by housing segregation and carefully drawn district lines, the further marginalization of black students within individual schools was a product of educators' beliefs about them. At Wadleigh High School, one of the neighborhood's few racially mixed schools, the faculty chose to hold its annual school picnic at a resort that did not allow the black students to swim in the pool. Teachers had not reported the restriction, the mayor's commission found, because "it offer[ed] a means of discouraging Negro girls from going on the outing."[43] Commission members were equally troubled by what they saw when they visited Wadleigh. "Was it a mere accident that a visitor to one of the elementary schools saw the white girls dressed in nurses' uniforms while the Negro girls were dressed as waitresses?" the report asked. While 75 percent of the school's black students were assigned to dressmaking, domestic science, and other low-ranking vocational classes, not a single black student was placed in the school's college preparatory classes.[44] Witnessing these kinds of discriminatory practices, ones that the commission somehow distinguished from "overt acts of discrimination," motivated it to make its strongest claims about white teachers in Harlem. The kinds of racist practices that students experienced at Wadleigh and at other schools in Harlem, the report stated, are "subtle to the extent that the Negro is ignored or regarded as non-existent." Because many of the white teachers who taught in Harlem "know nothing of Negroes except in the role of servants, clowns, or criminals," they were able to exclude black students from school activities and to train them for menial, low-paying jobs without questioning themselves or their professionalism.[45]

While accounts like those of Wadleigh High suggest that the relationships between black students and white teachers were often shaped by racist viewpoints that many white New Yorkers held, these relationships were also facilitated by school politics in which teaching assignments to Harlem were seen as a comment on a given teacher's professional status. Black teachers often testified that they did not want to be placed solely in black schools but instead wanted to be considered qualified to teach any child.[46] Most white teachers also sought positions elsewhere. The Board's neglect of Harlem schools, the Teachers Union contended, caused "teachers to dread assignments to these schools where the conditions are so bad that teaching becomes police duty, where physical violence is not uncommon, since these neglected children, crowded into dingy buildings, resent the teacher along with the entire regime." Even though individual Teachers Unionists sought to teach black children, the Union as a whole was willing to maintain that Harlem students were different than middle-class white students because of differences in their physical environment. Feeling unable to effect change under these conditions, the Union argued, "teachers seek transfers from these school, so that the turn-over is larger than anywhere else in the system."[47]

Moreover, teachers' attitudes toward their students, which were clearly unprofessional in the case of many who taught at Wadleigh High School, were central to a complicated discourse about teacher professionalism and teacher attitude in the 1930s. In contrast to prewar teaching, when education experts would have seen attitude as unempirical and therefore superfluous to teacher professionalism, now education experts argued that teachers' feelings toward their students were central to the quality of teaching they provided. Importantly, this shift was enabled in part by the work of social scientists who studied the learning conditions of black students. In particular, Otto Klineberg, a Columbia University professor of psychology who would later testify in the 1954 *Brown v. Board of Education* case, made an impact in his study of the intelligence tests conducted on Southern black and on three thousand Harlem residents. Klineberg showed that Southern-born blacks tested lower than Northern-born blacks and, consequently, presented a challenge to city educators who were teaching a growing number of migrants. But he also found that the gap between the two groups narrowed as the migrants attended Northern schools for longer. From this information, he concluded that Southern blacks were not innately intellectually inferior but were made so by a lack of schooling. The progress of Southern blacks in Northern schools, he explained, while offering "no complete proof" that an "improvement in background can bring them up to the White level," also failed to present evidence "to conclude the opposite."[48] In his contention that intelligence was a product of a person's quality of education rather than genetic abilities, Klineberg challenged beliefs that had shaped public school design for over fifty years.[49]

Klineberg's eminent study was one of a number of works by psychologists and social scientists that reflected a shift in thinking about race and intelligence and a movement from thinking about students' abilities as genetically predetermined to considering them shaped by their social environment. The shift held important ramifications for teachers as well as for students. Following World War I, intelligence testing had created a unique vocabulary of rankings, as well as a plethora of surveys, case studies, and statistical analyses that marked education literature as a professional literature and classified teachers' knowledge as a discipline. While the testing industry was founded on the marginalization of ethnic and racial minority students, it had more positively altered conceptions of the profession by implying that teachers were no longer "natural" caretakers but professionals equipped with the scientific methods and theories by which to best understand and serve children.

With the changed thinking about the psychology of learning and intellectual aptitude, education experts and administrators began to focus on the teacher's personality as an important professional tool, one that could potentially counteract the despair brought about first by World War I and then by the Depression. The ideal teacher of the Progressive Era was thought to be efficient, industrious, and loyal, able to organize and discipline larger classes than ever before. The ideal teacher in the interwar period was to be all of those things, as well, but administrators added tact, cooperation, kindliness, cheerfulness, and adaptability to the list of qualities they sought in their faculty.[50] On the whole, the people who trained and evaluated teachers stressed a focus away from the failed science of Progressive Era education; the new, interwar era view of professionalism asked teachers to go beyond the "cold and impersonal . . . scientific method," in the words of one administrator, and to instead remember that "much of human conduct is warm and impulsive."[51]

This attention to personality came to influence teachers' professional training and the ways in which they were evaluated by administrators. Teachers were expected to set a psychological model for students through their classroom performance, for, as one principal wrote to the city's high schools teachers, "We all know that pupils will imitate the good and bad habits of teachers; that the nervous teacher is apt to make his class nervous; that the calm, restful teacher will generally have a quiet and orderly class."[52] The interwar teacher was to be composed and confident without being too assertive. Clyde Miller, Teachers College professor and the Board's director of teacher assignments in the schools, lectured that the most important possession for new teachers was not disciplinary knowledge but "a pretty face, a ready smile, [and] a well-shaped body attractively clothed."[53] Such theories, in addition to demeaning Miller's large number of women students, indicated that teacher professionalism was as much about attitude as it was about skill. The Board agreed; New York City teachers' manuals reinforced an attention to self-presentation and advised their readers on vocal control, personal appearance, how to carry themselves in the classroom, and how to arrange their desk drawers—all actions principals would assess as part of merit exams that qualified teachers for promotion.[54] In addition to teachers' positive attitude toward their work, however, the Board hoped teachers would hold an equally positive attitude toward their students, and it announced that teacher training should emphasize "the development of positive teaching personalities" and "methods of establishing wholesome pupil-teacher relationships." This training was to be contrasted with the singularly academics-focused training of the Progressive Era. "When a teacher is found to be having problems in understanding or sensing child problems," the Board argued, "that teacher, for example, ought not to be taking a course in Greek, no matter how much it might lead to her personal development. She should be taking a course which bears some relation to her improvement in her job."[55]

Teachers across the city questioned the new emphasis on attitude as a panacea in the classroom for a variety of reasons. High school teacher Abraham Gedulig, for example, asked, "Our text-writers urge the necessity of personality in the teachers. But what if the pedagogical procedures drive the little personality we have out of us, and leave us colorless and dry?" Despite the development of more student-centered education theories, teachers were still encouraged by their principals to substitute less substantive, easier-to-grade quizzes for exams and to outline lectures on the chalkboard rather than engage in undirected conversation.[56] Teachers who wanted to be more inventive often described being limited by the architecture and resources of the classroom. "I think I am in a prison where everything is nailed down to the floor," announced one such ambitious teacher. "How can you teach 'creative thought' or 'creative composition' to 35 or 40 souls who are chained down to the ground?"[57] Such an image suggested that both teachers and students were denied the most basic freedoms in the city's schools.

While this conflict existed across a wide swath of teaching situations, it was particularly acute for Harlem teachers.[58] By 1938, a report created by Harlem principals for the Board showed that little had changed in the city's black schools since the mayor's 1936 report. Despite the construction of two new buildings, Harlem schools remained the oldest in the city and lacked auditoriums, gymnasiums, playgrounds, libraries, and sufficient lunchrooms and restrooms, presenting unique challenges to the teachers who worked within them. Of sixteen Harlem schools studied, one was run on quadruple session, eight on triple session, and four on double session, leading to less instruction time for students but more for teachers. The constant use of split shifts meant ten thousand students were in school for only 80 percent of the day and thereby left "free to get into all sorts of mischief for an extra hour each day, on the streets or in undesirable haunts."[59] The principals characterized the students in their schools as "highly emotional, unstable . . . quick-tempered . . . and prone to the use of fists," a condition that was certainly exacerbated, if not created, by overcrowded schools. In several schools, male students were charged with sexually harassing women teachers. "There seems to be no limit to the possibilities of disrespectful, bold, even brazen or obscene remarks to teachers," the principals reported. Rather than effecting a cheerful attitude as some education experts and administrators recommended, Harlem teachers voted with their feet. Some neighborhood schools faced a 35 percent teacher turnover annually. The faculty rosters at Harlem junior high schools, often considered the most difficult teaching assignment in the city, frequently listed up to 40 percent substitute teachers.[60]

The call for teacher optimism also failed to address the living conditions that black students were said to face and the ways in which these conditions influenced their school performance. Neither teachers nor some of the experts who trained them were eager to rid themselves of the specialized, learned methodologies that had contributed to the transformation of teaching from an occupation to a profession.[61] To replace the "science" of intelligence testing, experts such as Counts, Dewey, and Klineberg helped the profession to adopt a social science emphasis on the effect of social environment on learning. In this process, black children's neighborhoods and home lives became all the more important for explaining educators' frequent assessments of their students as intellectually impoverished and socially maladjusted. Not surprisingly, this shift, designed to be more politically neutral, came with its own problems.[62] On the whole, Harlem youth were depicted by educators and some social scientists to possess greater than average experience with divorce, sex, drugs, and violence. Of sixteen hundred Harlem families studied in 1935, seven hundred were found to be one-parent homes.[63] Living in apartments that often housed multiple families and adults who engaged in an "almost continuous performance of noisy quarreling and fighting" and expressed "intense worry over the lack of money and of despair over the future," Harlem children sought escape in tenement roofs and dark hallways. There they encountered "temptations to engage in the most immoral of practices."[64] Many social scientists and educators alike assumed that black students' home lives prepared them for academic failure.

For teachers in Harlem schools in the 1930s, regardless of their political persuasions and personal beliefs, professional training frequently failed to prepare them for their encounters with their students. As city educators described them, Harlem youth were coming to school not as emotional blank slates but feeling "touchy, quarrelsome, [and] often sullen."[65] For students who faced the kinds of lives of crime, poverty, and amorality that Harlem students were described to experience, the teacher's outlook battled against a myriad of large-scale social problems. Many administrators doubted that teachers could radically transform their black students. "Don't feel that you have to accomplish miracles," urged one such high school administrator. "Don't feel anyone is expecting it of you, and don't expect it of yourself. Try for the minimum. . . . Hold that as a goal, but if you don't attain it with some of our deviates, be satisfied."[66] Such messages were problematic not just in what they assumed about deviate black students but also in the lack of professional guidelines they offered to teachers in minority schools. Because the typical guidelines did not seem to apply to them, teachers of low-performing students were frequently left without a vision of professionalism for themselves.

Altogether, the state of Harlem schools in the 1930s set a full agenda for black school reform activists, from school districting and racial segregation to insufficient school facilities to failing teachers. What was clear to many Harlem residents and teachers as a result is that the problem of teacher quality in minority schools was not just the product of individual attitudes and professional capabilities but was enabled by an education system that shuttled some of the city's least experienced teachers to Harlem and then provided them with vastly different education circumstances in which to work. While the unequal environment in which Harlem students and teachers found themselves in the 1930s made teacher success more difficult, it also offered unique challenges to teacher professionalism. This general quandary made the challenges Harlem teachers faced important to teachers who did not teach in black schools but whose professional agency rested nevertheless on public beliefs about what constituted good teaching and who was to be held accountable for students' academic success. How teachers chose to address these challenges would become central to their own arguments about professional equity.

Teacher Professionalism and the Social Order

In the spring of 1932, a Teachers Union luncheon ended hastily, in an act that would anticipate the upcoming fragmentation of the union and the disagreement between its members over the Schoenchen episode. The luncheon had been organized to give teachers a chance to hear from NAACP president Walter White, who spoke on the issue of employment discrimination. At some point, Union member Evelyn Burroughs spoke out, compelling her colleagues to take stronger action on behalf of the Scottsboro Nine. Legislative committee chair Abraham Lefkowitz responded that while black unemployment constituted a "desperate situation," Burroughs and others took advantage of the Union's commitment to this situation to advance their own, communist pet projects. President Henry Linville charged Burroughs and her supporters with "discourtesy" and brought the luncheon to an early end. The *New York Times'* report on the incident gave more attention to Burroughs and the quarrels that followed than it did to White's presentation, and said nothing about what the Union planned to do about unemployment. To Linville and others who shared his views, such a news report was just the point, as acts of political theater threatened to overshadow the Union itself. Within four years, the Teachers Union would have split into two, largely because of this perceived threat.[67]

If their approach to civil rights was different, the workplace agendas for both unions throughout the 1930s were frequently identical. Both the Teachers Union and the Guild rejected purely personality-driven philosophies of teaching and found a new sense of mission in working to redefine teacher professionalism in the 1930s. Both unions supported the Teachers Union's contention that maintaining one's optimism was difficult "in crowded classes of 45 or more pupils, some undernourished, some maladjusted, many requiring individual attention." Both agreed, as the Union maintained, that "[g]ood health and buoyant spirits are essential in a teacher, but so is an educational system that will foster them."[68] In fact, the 1935 split of the Teachers Union was produced less by a difference in agenda than by different visions of *how* to protect teachers from an inadequate educational system and to create schools that would leave them enthusiastic and satisfied. Central to these differences were contrasting views of who and what constituted the professional teacher, given that the image of a person who willed herself into enthusiasm for her job was not a sufficient definition for either union.

But as the luncheon debacle reflected, social politics had always played a role in the work of city teacher unionists, even as they disagreed on what constituted appropriate engagements with social issues. The first constitution for the Teachers Union of the City of New York, drafted in March 1916, had set forth four major objectives for teacher unionists: to provide the means for the legal protection of teachers' interests, to protect teachers against oppressive supervision, to make schools more efficient by promoting good teaching and good teachers, and to obtain equal suffrage between the sexes.[69] While the constitution held a clause recommending that the Union work with parents' associations, it was effectively a labor brief focused on protecting teachers from discrimination or oppressive work conditions. Yet the Union's need to protect its own workers was often tied to social and political issues. Early in the century, it battled restrictions on pregnant women teachers and the Lusk Laws, state laws that in 1918 facilitated the termination of public employees who held radical political views. Both campaigns appealed to early Teachers Unionists because they threatened to affect a wide swath of teachers; in both cases, the Union's causes were helped by broad, changing tides in political sentiment and by connections to larger social movements, including suffrage campaigns.[70] Importantly, the strategies the Union employed in both campaigns—including writing letters and petitions and passing resolutions—did little to risk individual members' professional security or sense of professionalism, even though other conservative teacher organizations saw unionists as radical nevertheless.[71]

The growing organization and advocacy of black activists in the 1930s compelled unionists to determine anew their desired role not just in social politics but in social justice more largely and in the connection between students' interests and their own. The conflicts that resulted were as complicated and drawn out as they were in part because all unionists identified themselves as left of center on the political spectrum. Both Teachers Unionists and early Guild members, most of whom began as Unionists, often described growing up in homes where their parents subscribed to leftist newspapers such as the *Forward*, the *Day*, the *New York Call*, and *The Daily Worker*.[72] The frequent presence of these publications in their homes reflected the high number of teachers who came from working-class, prounion backgrounds.[73] While teaching had long stood as a profession by which working-class women, in particular, could rise into the middle class, Teachers Unionists' and Guild members' personal experiences with unionism may have distinguished them from the vast majority of city teachers who did not join either union and who saw all unionists as radical.[74] In addition to their atypical prounion sentiments, New York City teacher unionists shared a perception of themselves as more liberal on the political and social issues of their day than most other teachers.

In fact, their dissimilar attention to race issues appeared to have little impact on either union's sense of relationship to the political center. This was not unusual for the time; addressing racial inequity did not become part of the mainstream American liberal agenda until World War II.[75] New Deal reform, Gary Gerstle has argued, prioritized economic reform over issues of race and culture and "expressed little interest in remaking individuals or in uniting all Americans into a single moral community" as Progressive Era liberals had. Instead, the Communist Revolution of 1917, the xenophobia and nationalism of World War I, and the failure of capitalism in the Depression shook many liberals' faith in "moral" or "cultural" reform, spurring them to seek out "a rational and controlled democratic politics" and to devise movements that "allowed enlightened elites to manage the common people's quest for freedom."[76] More than the Teachers Union, the Guild—with its penchant for reform through

democratic institutions, its belief in due process, and its desire for partnerships with education administrators—typified liberalism in the period.

As a result, even as the unions differed in their beliefs about how teachers
should participate in social issues, members across unions both saw themselves and each other as progressives, a category that was often amorphous
and difficult to define. As they saw it, teacher unionists frequently agreed in
their political beliefs but differed significantly in their view of the role those
political beliefs should play in a professional movement. The teachers who
sided with future Guild president Henry Linville in the split, as he explained in
1930, "approve[d] of the policy of radicals in raising important issues"; they
just objected to "making a political platform of Teachers Union meetings for
that purpose." The central purpose of any teacher union, Linville and his supporters believed, was "to work for teachers in their jobs."[77] Teachers Unionists
frequently agreed with this assessment of their differences. "The objectives of
the Guild," a Teachers Union report explained, were much like its own, "including the ultimate goal of a 'new social order.'" This new social order was a
product of people who looked "more consciously and more critically at social
problems" and who realized that the solution lay "in a new attitude toward
the world," something that both sets of unionists believed distinguished them
from the majority of teachers. All unionists, they believed, were drawn to the
profession "because of these conceptions regarding progress" and, more specifically, because of their shared belief that teachers, in molding children into
democratic citizens, had an especially important role to play in bringing about
social progress.[78]

And yet their relationship to racial issues was one of the most salient and
important differences between the two unions during the Depression. This
difference stemmed from the unions' unique convictions about the connection between teaching, professionalism, and politics and was distinct, at least
part of the time, from teachers' racial identities; both black and white teachers saw assignments to Harlem schools as pigeonholing, if not always for the
same reasons.[79] If members had long held these differences, however, their
disagreements were more difficult to overlook in the context of a burgeoning black civil rights movement that compelled them to consider the connection between teachers' interests and the interests of others, including black
students. Because of this larger philosophical question about interests, each
union, in responding to the particular political issue of racial equity, also defined its larger identity and sense of mission. For example, Teachers Unionists
Alice Citron, Celia Zitron, Mildred Flacks, Lucille Spence, and many others not
only made a career of working in black schools but rose to leadership positions because of this work. The import of the Harlem Committee as a vehicle

for leadership development within the Union illustrates how civil rights, far from the superfluous project it appeared to Linville and to Guild members, was intimately tied to the organization's structural design. This design in itself likely appealed to teachers who saw teaching as social and political work rather than as strictly academic in nature.

Moreover, Unionists capitalized on a difference in commitment to racial politics, even as they claimed that the two unions' members shared many of the same views. As much as Teachers Unionists dedicated themselves to ideas about race progress, the Union's relationship to civil rights movements aided it in portraying itself as more active, energetic, and authentic than the Guild. "There are many liberal teachers in the Cit[y] who are keenly interested in a new social order," Union president Charles Hendley argued, but they did not act upon that interest similarly. Hendley reinforced a view of the Union as torn apart by generational differences as much as by substantial political ones. "The old administration did not understand the new personnel of the Union," he argued. "It could not adjust itself to the young, restless elements that had a strong tendency towards radicalism."[80] The Guild's "more orderly and dignified campaign for realizing its objectives," the Teachers Union chided, caused it to find the "hurly-burly of young vigorous democracy . . . intolerable."[81]

In its assertions and distinctions, the Teachers Union portrayed itself as an organization that could not afford to settle with a brand of unionism most suitable to an older generation of teachers out of touch with the times. Nor, however, did the Teachers Union find any compelling need to do so, as its own messages and methods appeared to attract more new teachers. "Cooperation with the Guild is not necessary," a Teachers Union group boasted in 1936. "The Union has grown by 3,000 since last year. In the past year, more teachers have joined the Union than those who joined from 1917 to 1935."[82] The Teachers Union rightly saw that it held an advantage in appealing to young, novice teachers, whereas the older, established teachers that the Guild sought were also unlikely to change their views on unionism. In attracting the teachers who prioritized issues of social progress as highly as workplace conditions, Teachers Union president Charles Hendley contended, the organization drew the most "alert and courageous teachers" among the city's corps.[83]

Essential to Teachers Unionists' view of how to create a new social order was the issue of community and, more specifically, defining what constituted a professional, educational community. Their interest in this issue predated the split of the Union. "The idea of educational nuns living in their school cloisters, oblivious to, or tacitly, though sorrowfully, accepting the suffering of millions of our fellow citizens, has no place in [our] society," a Teachers Union editorial had concluded in 1933. Eager to revise the image of the schoolmarm who toiled alone, oblivious to social context, Unionists argued for a vision of the teacher as "a social or community leader dedicated to the philosophy of change and seeking to develop a cooperative spirit which is tolerant to every constructive social idea."[84] Such a philosophy made teachers partners with and leaders of a larger community of public school stakeholders at once. Progressive teachers who "conceive of a new social order and strive to make adjustments for it," Charles Hendley argued, "must find support in progressive parents." For Hendley, this support went beyond the traditional reasoning that joining with progressive or radical citizens would create more effective and supportive political movements. Instead, he argued, "cooperation between parents and teachers renders untenable a position of neutrality by the teacher on the vital issues of his time." If the schoolmarm worked free of political convictions because she was cut off from the political world, Hendley suggested, the "live teacher," who worked as part of a larger movement, "cannot hold aloof from the things that are of vital interest to her pupils and her pupils' parents."[85]

Teachers Unionist's activism was predicated on the belief that teachers' inability to create this political alliance in the past had created a sense of professional failure. Alice Citron, founding member of the Harlem Committee, argued this was the case. Once the "Negro people of New York City see teachers preaching democracy," she attested, "it will inspire a trust in our children that we do not have."[86] Such trust was required for teachers to be seen as advocates rather than adversaries of black students and for them to be able to teach most effectively. To remediate the situation, the Teachers Union, especially the Harlem Committee, worked with important, newly formed Harlem activist organizations, including the Committee for Better Schools in Harlem and the United Parents Association, to push for changes large and small. With the Committee for Better Schools, an organization of approximately four hundred religious, social, and political Harlem activists, Unionists fought for changes that would make teaching in Harlem schools more successful, including constructing more school buildings, reducing class sizes to no more than thirty-eight students, increasing the teaching staff, and appointing a black member to the Board of Education. The two groups also worked together to push for larger neighborhood reforms that would come to affect schools, including the establishment of more dental and health clinics in Harlem, the collection of winter clothing for children of the unemployed, and the transformation of the armory into a children's after-school center.[87] In addition, Teachers Unionists supported parents and teachers in individual schools, including a group of parents from P.S. 90, Harlem's largest elementary school. After the school's white principal hand-selected a new president for the parents association, a group of forty parents left to charter their own organization. Principal Mabel Tucker refused to allow the "rowdy" parents to meet on school premises, and the Union supported the parents. The following year, Tucker was charged with discriminating against black teachers' advancement in the school and with condoning corporal punishment.[88] To Teachers Unionists, principals such as Tucker and Schoenchen exhibited undemocratic behavior and, in the process, threatened the welfare of students and teachers alike.

The Union's vision was not without its problems, though, most especially for teachers in Harlem. Unionist Anna Kross argued that for a teacher to "really participate as a citizen in a democracy to the fullest extent" required her time and commitment outside of school as much as inside the classroom. Yet even the Teachers Unionist who chose to teach in Harlem worked "in the city but live[d] in some place on Long Island or in Brooklyn," Kross concluded. There, "her knowledge of the [Harlem] community is very meager," and "her interest [in the community] ends."[89] Critiques like Kross's challenged teachers to think about their social and professional obligations in an ever more expansive way. Without calling for Teachers Unionists to reside in Harlem, she encouraged them to think about how they might work to become a part of the community rather than just servants of it. This was a challenge that went beyond the scope of even many Teachers Unionists, who saw themselves as already doing much by willingly teaching in Harlem schools. "Of course, we realize the fact that the teachers do not live in the community," countered one such member. "But maybe the function of the teacher should not be to give up a great deal of after-school time, for it is the people of the community who will have to carry on the work of the community."[90] Partnering with the community and working for the community, then, took on a number of different shapes and levels of commitment for Teachers Unionists who, like any teachers, differed in where they wanted to draw the line between their professional and personal lives.

The Teachers Guild identified far larger problems in the Teachers Union's vision, both in terms of its emphasis on social politics outside of school and in its methods in achieving its gains. The key difference between the two unions' approaches to creating a new social order could be found in the differences of philosophy between their respective Teachers College mentors. While Unionists embraced Counts's view that teachers could be leaders in a new social order, Guild members tended to see things as Dewey did, that schools could not "in any literal sense be the builders of a new social order" but rather participants in a much larger movement of social change. This ideal participation was not to be like the Unionists' partnership with Harlem grassroots movements, however; instead, Dewey argued in 1934, if a teacher chose to align himself with such forces he would have an opportunity to act on that choice each day, in the "details of school administration and discipline, of methods of teaching, of selection and emphasis in matter."[91] While Dewey did not prohibit teachers from making political commitments outside of the classroom, neither did he necessitate it. Social activism for teachers, in his view, was largely a school-bound process, a means of transforming the classroom rather than attempting to transform society as whole. The products of educators' efforts would resonate in the quality of their students' thought rather than in teachers' protests.

The Guild illustrated what this philosophy looked like when applied to the everyday lives of teachers. "To some the teacher is in the best strategic position to further movements for a new social order," Linville responded to Hendley and his unionists in 1935.[92] But Linville doubted that most teachers saw things that way, especially not in the terms by which the Teachers Union defined a new social order. To Linville, most teachers lacked experience in "thinking about the social and ethical factors that bear a relation to the security of the profession," and, as a result, Guild leaders were "obliged to await the development of an awakened social conscience among teacher leaders."[93] Linville was unclear on what might awaken teachers' social conscience, since it did not appear to be the terrain of the Guild to either create or deny such an awakening. Clearer, however, was the mission of the Guild to attend to those "factors that surround the teacher in his job" and that would create a sense of professional security. Such factors, according to a staff-written Guild editorial, "relate[d] primarily to his economic well-being" and included issues affecting "wages, his tenure, his right to protection for old age. They are also his working conditions; such as healthful surroundings, reasonable teaching load, fair teaching equipment, cooperative supervisions, and friendly relations with his community."[94] These objectives left the Guild particularly focused on its relationship with education administrators, not parents. Administrators, from principals to superintendents, often obstructed teachers' efforts to improve their work conditions, but they could also serve as their best allies.

These beliefs were reflected in the Guild's most important campaigns of the decade, some of which put them at odds with local administrators. Guild members dedicated themselves to securing the mechanisms or rights that they believed were most essential for enabling teachers to perform their jobs well. Their efforts to obtain tenure rights and their 1939 protest of another budget cut, after teachers had suffered $100,000,000 in salary reductions between 1932 and 1937, focused on teachers' security and on addressing the kinds of problems that could leave teachers feeling distracted. [95] Their protest of the 1936 Ives Law, a second state law requiring teachers to take a loyalty oath, furthered their work in advocating for teachers' academic freedom. The Guild also pushed against what it saw as unfair or unprofessional treatment, urging the Board to revise and standardize how it assessed licensing exams, and it protested questionnaires that asked teachers to report their marital status. Asking employees to provide information "in no way related to the services they perform, or as to their ability, competency, and efficiency," the Guild argued, constituted "unlawful and unjust" practices on the part of the Board.[96] The practice, the Guild argued, was implemented to help administrators assess how many women teachers were married; in the economic collapse, the *Guild Bulletin* warned its readers, "the movement to oust women workers is nationwide."[97] Finally, in one of the most salacious of the Guild's campaigns, members petitioned the Board to fire its medical examiner, Emil Altman, who diagnosed over fifteen hundred teachers as mentally unbalanced and half of those as legally insane. The Guild maintained its protest even after Altman whittled his original figure down to 250. Most of the teachers were over sixty-five years of age; although almost all had been rated well by their supervisors, they were also at the top of the salary hierarchy and invariably would have been replaced with younger and therefore less expensive teachers. The Guild charged Altman with abusing his medical license to fire the teachers and save the city money.[98] Even more, they accused him of the "insulting and inhuman treatment of teachers" and cited their long campaign against him as evidence that "the chance of obtaining just treatment in the case of a teacher is markedly less than it would be in the case of one who is a citizen, and not a teacher."[99]

Guild members believed all of their efforts to secure better rights for teachers were made more difficult by the public image the Teachers Union created of the profession. In 1937, Linville held the Teachers Union responsible for undermining "decent, professional standards as they might have been accepted by the young teachers, many of whom have joined the Union on the promise of some economic gain."[100] The professional standards that Guild members had in mind were not unlike the standards that many education experts and administrators advocated—a teacher who was congenial, organized, self-controlled, and effective—although not at the expense of a teacher's academic expertise. As with the Union, the Guild's image of the professional teacher was directly related to what it wanted to accomplish. Parents and the public should expect the 1930s teachers to demonstrate "higher qualifications of mind, character, personality, and general culture than in the past," the Guild explained, distinguishing its own members from the colorless schoolmarms of yesteryear. This image was as connected to the Guild's vision of social progress as the activist image was for the Teachers Union, for this professional teacher would in turn be equipped to fulfill "the social obligation [of raising] the younger generation to a somewhat higher level than the preceding ones."[101] In the Guild's view, then, teachers were important for the example of rational, democratic behavior they set for students rather than for any specific ideologies they held.

For many Guild members, the Union's commitment to race equity was nearly impossible to distinguish from a style of professional activism they found untenable. To the Guild, Teachers Unionists' actions in the Schoenchen case and in the course of their daily operations were neither rational nor democratic. The Union's actions against the Harlem principal turned an education issue into a "'class-war' [campaign] with picketing of the school, speechmaking in the streets, and mass delegations at the sessions of the Magistrate's Court where the principal was being tried." These actions were unprofessional for multiple reasons, Linville explained, not the least of which was that the evidence against Schoenchen "was a complete frame-up."[102] To the Guild, the questionable evidence against the principal pointed to the Union's easy exploitation of the case to fight a larger battle of its own. Just as problematic, however, was the Union's style of protest, and its proclivity to practice "mass action, picketing, [and] vociferous public pressures . . . on every possible occasion." This was exactly the kind of conduct, Guild members argued, that made "enemies of those formerly friends of public education" and left all teachers to "pay the price of the unprofessional tactics of the few."[103] In contrast, the Guild explained, the union held "no pet formulas" for its own means of activism. Individual problems the Guild sought to address might require "an intelligent appeal in the form of a brief, oral presentation, publicity through meetings, radio, press, or even all of these," all methods of action that carefully corresponded with the Guild's image of the professional teacher.[104] This image was one of teachers as bureaucratic rather than combative; indeed, the greatest war the Guild fought was the "fight to recover lost ground in the field of professional standards."[105]

Central to the individual actions of both unions, and to the debates between them, were questions about the role of democracy and democratic behavior in creating better schools and better professionals. Both unions saw the creation of a new social order as connected to improving their professional lives and the lives of students who attended the city's public schools. The essential questions, then, were whether this new social order and the improvement of minority schools were to be driven by community activists or by teachers, whether schools would be better places for teachers to work if students were treated more democratically and equitably, and whether students would benefit from the improved professional treatment of the adults who taught them. While, in fact, the welfare of both students and teachers in minority schools needed to be secured, by the end of the decade, competition between the two teacher unions had begun to dichotomize the two sets of rights. The pattern set in this early development would come to shape teacher unions' agendas, actions, and social visions for decades to come.

Creating a Culture of Rights

In the midst of the Great Depression, black New Yorkers forcefully argued that schools had to be reformed from both outside and inside the classroom. Their community schools needed the political, structural, and mechanical improvements that only the Board or mayor could provide, but they also needed better, more dedicated educators who could only come from the city's teaching corps. In the context of these arguments, teacher unionists began to consider important questions about the teacher's role in school improvement and reform: How might teachers best serve underprivileged students? Were they equally equipped to press for reform both in and outside of the classroom? Should teachers of black students conceptualize their work as fundamentally different than or similar to teaching socially privileged students? What role did teachers want to play in "a new social order" or, for that matter, the social order already in existence? Their answers to these questions both were shaped by teachers' differing views of what constituted professionalism and shaped discussions of school improvement in the 1930s, setting a course for school reform efforts for decades to follow.

Very few of the debates in which black education activists and city teachers participated were framed explicitly in terms of the rights rhetoric that eventually took shape in the postwar civil rights movement. Just as a civil rights rhetoric did not fully exist for black Americans, neither did a teachers' rights rhetoric exist for teachers, even as they, too, advocated for their own interests. Nevertheless, these debates played a seminal role in creating a culture of rights consciousness. The demographic changes of the urban North in the first three decades of the twentieth century, and all of the resulting transformations to public school design and management, pushed city residents and municipal governments alike to consider more fully what a public education system promised to its citizens. Previously, most American youth had opted out of the pursuit of a high school education. But as more took advantage of this opportunity, including those whom educators considered difficult to educate, the terms of what was guaranteed to them grew less clear. The period's developing sentiment that public education—and education equity—were not just theoretical concepts but actualities which all citizens were afforded was seminal to a larger, developing culture of rights. The period also sheds light on why civil rights movements and teacher unionism took significant shape in tandem and why both embraced and resisted a feeling of partnership with other interest groups. Examining black school reform efforts in the 1930s—from the perspective of both the communities that sent their children to minority schools and the teachers who taught in them—reveals that the goals of civil rights movements and teachers' rights movements grew in conjunction and, at times, in collusion. This was not a historical coincidence but rather the product of a belief that creating a new social order depended on collective effort and that collectivity was made possible by a shared sense of identity and interest.

The difficulty in building a sense of collectivity—within and between groups—is especially apparent in the case of unionized teachers. As they experimented with different philosophies of and strategies for advocating for professional advancement, their efforts at defining teachers' professional rights—from the right to be paid well to the right to work under conditions that would make a successful job performance possible—were viewed with disdain and dismissal. An apt example of this dismissal occurred when Teachers Union and Harlem activists petitioned the Board in 1936 for more schools to be built in Harlem. Board member Walter Carlin simply replied that he "d[id]n't like the use of the word 'demand.'"[106] For minorities and teachers alike, to "demand" better schools was to transgress their social standing in the education bureaucracy, a bureaucracy that was designed and managed by white administrators. Unionists, like civil rights activists, still had to prove in this early period that the very concept of rights was a legitimate entity to which they were entitled.

This sense of demand for themselves and for others is exactly what George Counts hoped teachers in New York City and elsewhere in the nation would cultivate and act upon. Most liberals, he argued, "favor in a mild sort of way fairly liberal programs of social reconstruction . . . [and] have vague aspirations for world peace and human brotherhood." Ultimately, Counts found, most liberals favored theory over action and possessed "no convictions for which they would sacrifice over-much." Instead, they preferred to play "the role of interested spectators in the drama of human history." Real creators of a new social order, teachers or otherwise, had to prepare for "the costs of leadership: to accept responsibility, to suffer calumny, to surrender security, to risk both reputation and fortune," for society, he maintained, "is never redeemed without effort, and sacrifice."[107] In his depiction of liberals versus real reformers, Counts may as well have created portraits of the Teachers Guild and the Teachers Union. But his dramatic description also points to a central problem in the relationship between teacher unionism and social justice movements from an early era. Most teachers did not want to take the kinds of risks that Counts suggested were necessary. That is, for most teachers, just as for most people, it made relatively little sense to make their own lives less secure for the sake of improving the lives of others. Teachers Guild members who tended to be more advanced in their careers only had more to lose. Understanding this central dilemma is critical to understanding the choices that liberal teachers made.

Nevertheless, members of both teacher unions faced adversity and the threat of isolation from other teachers in a political culture in which unions were considered marginal and unprofessional. City administrators' attitudes toward unions ran a wide swath of opinion, and their critiques reflected the changing mission of teacher unions throughout the 1930s. Some principals belonged to either of the two unions, usually having joined as classrooms teachers and then retaining their membership as they were promoted to administrators. Certainly not all principals or Board administrators were this amenable to unionism, however. Superintendent John Tildsley advised that a sense of professional dissatisfaction was bred in teacher unions because "discouragement is infectious." Poor teachers served as "a positive injury" to the faculty as a whole, Tildsley reminded the city's faculty, for "as in every calling with union rules . . . all alike must tend to be paid what the marginal worker, not the best worker, is worth."[108] In arguing that teacher unions equated all to the lowest common denominator and made teachers into workers rather than professionals, Tildsley suggested that unions promoted mediocrity. It was precisely this philosophy that kept many teachers from joining unions.

The city's two teacher unions offered two different models for responding to this philosophy toward teacher unions and for conceptualizing professionalism and professional rights at the time. Teachers Union members were, by all accounts, genuine in their dedication to civil rights issues, but they also found the organization and momentum of neighborhood activists in the decade to be exciting and inspiring. In many ways, they pinned their own success to the momentum of the early black civil rights movement. The 1939 handbook of the Teachers Union flagged what it saw as its greatest accomplishments in recent years, and many of these accomplishments were enacted in Harlem. By working with community groups, the Union recorded, teachers had helped to bring about the construction of two new elementary schools, a partial rezoning of the relatively new George Washington High School to include black students, the establishment of large Union chapters in most Harlem schools, and the establishment or increased activity of parents' associations in schools across the area.[109] These accomplishments required the successful persuasion of the mayor, the Board, nonunionist teachers, and parents. Being able to name these tangible signs of success only aided the Union in garnering authority and energy for other parts of its program for teachers.

The import and implications of these accomplishments can be read in administrators' responses to the Teachers Union. By the late 1930s, it was clear that the Teachers Union represented a menace to some administrators, in most cases precisely because of its dedication to building community alliances. When fourteen Harlem principals collaborated on their report to the Board in 1938, they focused on the Teachers Union as a pervasive annoyance in their schools. Organizations such as the "The Communist Teachers of Harlem," as the principals referred to Teachers Unionists, and the Committee for Better Schools did not represent a productive partnership of school reformers but "groups of officious citizens who pose as champions of the welfare of the children," who spread "malicious propaganda," and make "impertinent demands" that create "an important source of friction between the schools and the community."[110] Even more to the point, Harlem principals appeared anxious about the ways in which the Teachers Union might have created more friction or tension for them. Teachers Unionists described the fallout of administrators' fears and contended that "whenever the choice lies between timid and colorless candidates and others who show strong and positive qualities in any ways tinged with radicalism, superintendents and schools boards invariably choose the innocuous candidates." The Union found evidence for this point of view in the discriminatory treatment of its members, such as Ruth Cohen, a teacher who volunteered to teach in a Harlem elementary school. In 1936, Cohen's principal requested her reassignment to another school because she did not like Cohen's hairstyle or "the people with whom she associated."[111] But even more challenging than the cases of individual teachers like Cohen was the larger skepticism of social movements created by such antiunion sentiment. The fear of teachers who might be radical, the Union argued, supported a larger "paradox of the 'educator' who is supposedly an expert in the realm of ideas" but in actuality exhibited "a profound distrust and fear of new ideas."[112] Such teachers, the Union members argued, resisted joining the fight for a new social order yet occupied classrooms across the city. The Union rejected this paradox but offered little to teachers who were less radical than its members.

In this light, the Guild's dedication to a more conventional view of professionalism seemed both to fall into the trap of this paradox and to offer a different model by which teachers might readily achieve things for themselves. While the Guild did little to aid black parents and students in the 1930s, it is also clear that the Teachers Union's dedication to civil rights issues offended the Guild first and foremost in its style of activism, one that threatened to unravel all that Guild members saw themselves as having gained in the previous twenty years. These gains included salary advances, work rights for women, and the entry of unionized teachers into administrative positions. But the gains also included a less tangible, although equally important, self-conception of themselves as professionals. This was especially important for teachers who were often the first middle-class people in their families and who served as teachers because they wanted to be teachers rather than out of desperation or necessity. One of the greatest obstacles to the Guild's success and to the "development of professional self-respect among teachers," as they saw it, was "the attitude of trying to avoid identification as teachers."[113] Teachers who appeared to prefer to be activists were exemplary of this attempted avoidance. This sense of professional pride and self-dignity was shared by black and white Guild members alike. In fact, when the American Federation of Teachers expelled the Teachers Union in 1941 because of its communist leanings, it was Layle Lane, the Guild's highest ranking black member, who defended the American Federation of Teachers for its effort to protect "democratic education."[114]

Most importantly, the Guild believed first in the power of politically neutral, public institutions — from the courts to the schools — to create equity, justice, and social progress. Democratic institutions, the Guild maintained, should create democratic behavior. This belief was tested by the Teachers Union's everyday actions. "Intolerant unionists," one Harlem teacher lamented, "disturb[ed] teachers' lunch hours with constant bickering" and conducted "whispering campaigns against non-members."[115] Guild leadership summarized the complaints they heard from their union brethren and critiqued the "unscrupulous methods of the Union, the selfish attitude of their leaders, [and] their vindictiveness against their opponents," including other teachers.[116] At the same time, the Guild attributed the Union's significantly larger membership numbers to its propensity to "systematically na[g]" nonmembers until "out of sheer lack of resistance and a desire to secure relief from this pestiferous nagging, they join the Union only to find that the nagging process has only then begun." Once becoming Union members, according to the Guild, teachers found themselves "the target for solicitation for various communist 'welfare' causes" rather than educational or professional issues.[117] The Guild distinguished itself from the Union both in its recruitment methods and in its treatment of teachers once they joined the Guild. "We do not harass people to join with us," boasted a Guild publication.[118] Instead, the Guild often assumed that professional teachers would be drawn to their movement.

These complaints about the Teachers Union stemmed from more than just a difference in manners or sensibilities between the two organizations. Rather, Guild members saw the Teachers Union as deeply intolerant to difference and, in this way, as less democratic than themselves. This belief echoed that of Guild members' great hero, John Dewey, who, although part of the school of social reconstructionists, often disagreed with Counts on the role of the school in transforming society. For Dewey, as Herbert Kliebard has explained, the schools' role in creating social progress was not to be brought about by teachers enforcing a particular ideological point of view or enacting an "organized effort to redress specific social evils" but in "the ability of the schools to teach independent thinking and to the ability of students to analyze social problems."[119] The Guild would say the same distinction held true for teacher unions. Its own union, a *Guild Bulletin* article explained, saw "democracy as a way of life" and, in this light, called for its members to "respec[t] and tolerat[e] differences of opinion" and to allow "free speech and open discussion." It saw this approach as an embodiment of "the democratic ideal," an ideal that was equally suited to politics and professionalism.[120] Far from seeing itself as a less committed version of the Union, then, the Guild saw itself as proactively embracing and enacting different principles. While the Teachers Union fought for greater democracy, the Guild actually was democratic, members argued, and they believed that this difference held the potential to appeal to a broader swath of teachers, even if 1930s membership numbers offered them little evidence for this conviction.

The two unions' distinctive views on democracy, professional activism, and social activism were important both in their ideological content and in the ways in which they were constructed in purposeful opposition to the other. Together, teachers' views of their role in the social order set out two different courses for their thinking about the relationship between professionalism and social politics as well as their relationship with other education stakeholders. These two courses set by New York City teachers would come to shape school reform movements throughout the century in their own city and nationwide. How the unions defined themselves in contrast to each other illustrates that, no matter how much each disavowed the politics and strategies of the other, early efforts at professional reform and school reform were always dependent on other movements for their very self-conceptualization.

CHAPTER 2

Muscular Democracy
Teachers and the War on Prejudice, 1940–1950

In 1949, Rebecca Simonson, in her ninth year as president of the Teachers Guild, wrote a call to arms to her fellow unionists. The war had ended, she argued, but "the difficulties and complexities which still face us are overwhelming and call for uncommon flexibility in our relations with our fellow-men." Like many liberals, Simonson took away from the war a conviction that better relationships needed to be built between black and white Americans and that teachers stood on the frontline of a domestic battle against intolerance. She called on Guild members to enact a "demonstration of active participation" to improve race relations, as teachers, unionists, and citizens.[1] In her address, Simonson, the city's first female teacher union president, termed such political participation "muscular democracy." The metaphor suggested that democracy was hard-won yet robust and powerful in the face of resistance. Teachers, she maintained, could not focus simply on their own rights and welfare but needed to be activists for the liberal political beliefs that she was sure they held. Yet too few seemed to be doing so. "We must admit" she urged her members, that "many of us could be making better contributions against prejudice and intolerance." In response, she asked Guild members to remain committed to fighting social problems even as the union remained "fully aware of the physical difficulties inherent in oversized classes, uncovered classes, and broken-up classes" and teachers' own professional challenges remained unsolved.[2]

Simonson's call for muscular democracy—and its significant contrast in content and tone from her predecessor Henry Linville—is indicative of the way in which World War II compelled teachers to examine the connections between their work and civil rights. As historians have shown, the religious and racial intolerance at the forefront of World War II profoundly shifted American political culture, bringing global attention to the nation's problems with racial discrimination.[3] This, in turn, enabled a more organized and visible postwar civil rights culture. In what Thomas Sugrue has characterized as a "newfound political assertiveness," black Americans fought for the double V: victory against intolerance abroad and at home.[4] White liberals also shifted away from the New Dealers' emphasis on economic inequity and began to respond more earnestly to political inequities resulting from racial and religious discrimination; by the war's end, a concern with racial civil rights played a central role in American liberalism.[5] Together, these developments came to influence city public schools, which adopted new policies for combating racial discrimination. In 1938, for example, the New York City Board of Education ordered all city schools to teach tolerance and to offer two assemblies focused on the theme per month.[6] This formal mandate echoed something that was enacted more broadly and informally as well: educators' increased recognition of and attention to racial minorities in their teaching.

While the Board mandated tolerance education, however, it did little to improve the condition of black schools or the racial segregation that guaranteed some schools would receive less funding and services than others. The effect of the Board's continued "color-blind" policy toward school districting constituted a lack of policy. By mid decade, Wadleigh High School's student population had dropped from twenty-three hundred to seven hundred. Once one of Harlem's few integrated schools, Wadleigh, black community leaders argued, had been turned into a "dumping ground" for black students by Board policies that allowed white students to transfer to other schools.[7] To neighborhood activists, Wadleigh proved that the Board's policies not only contradicted its rhetoric toward tolerance education but minimized what could be accomplished in schools to promote a more equitable society. Wadleigh was just one example in a pattern of events that suggested the Board did more than look askance at the ways in which housing discrimination shaped the public schools; rather, its policies openly reflected the racist sentiments of many white New Yorkers. Just as important, the bold discrepancies between sentiment and action at the heart of the Board's policies did little to guide teachers in how they should address civil rights issues—and violations thereof—in their schools.

For this reason and others that this chapter will detail, despite a political culture that in many ways supported teachers in advancing race reform ideas, the 1940s proved to be one of the most complicated and conflicted decades in teachers' understanding of the relationship between civil rights and their own professional rights. Enacting muscular democracy, Rebecca Simonson indicated, depended on a strong sense of conviction that students' civil rights were equally important as teachers' professional rights. Many teachers, including Guild members, willingly embraced a new attention to fighting prejudice. In and outside of the classroom, teachers worked to diversify their curricula, to integrate tolerance training into their lesson plans, to open the higher skilled vocational school tracks to black students, and to fight for the appointment of a black school board member. Their accounts of their work transmitted a sense of conviction and socially conscious thinking that focused explicitly on race and stood in marked contrast to many teachers' views in the previous decade. But, as Simonson's appeal itself suggests, adapting to a political culture that was more conscious of race rights was not always a natural or easy one for teachers, particularly when doing so appeared to conflict with their own interests. Instead, a more rights-centered political culture challenged and at times changed teachers' conceptions of who they were expected to be in the classroom and what their professional responsibilities entailed. Whereas teachers in previous decades were expected to exemplify democracy and patriotism, now teachers were told more explicitly to stand as models of liberalism. This more specific political stance, and the progressive beliefs about racial equity that accompanied it, were new to the professional qualities expected of a teacher and not something that all members of the city's corps possessed.

More interesting than the resistance of openly conservative or racist teachers was the struggle of liberal teachers to define what constituted race liberalism and meaningful race equity projects. At the heart of this struggle existed a frequent difference of opinion in how black and white liberals conceptualized the pathway to race reform. As Risa Goluboff has argued, in the 1940s, and up to the *Brown* decision in 1954, "the world of civil rights was conceptually, doctrinally, and constitutionally up for grabs . . . the boundaries of the bureaucratic state, the form of individual rights, and the relationship between them were still unclear."[8] For blacks in the 1940s, school reform was one piece of a broader agenda for legal reforms that would regulate equal access and treatment in the military, employment, and housing. For white liberals, however, including Simonson, race reform depended first and foremost on improving individual and communal relationships between blacks and whites. A focus on changing attitudes about race did not necessarily obstruct more pragmatic civil rights reforms, but it failed to address the issue of opportunity and the role of institutions, including schools, in upholding discrimination. Consequently, it enabled teachers to continue to separate the inferior conditions of the city's black schools from the acts of racial prejudice they taught students to avoid. While individual wartime teachers fought for improved race relations in their classrooms, they, like the Board, at times obstructed reforms that would have made minority schools more equitable institutions, including the recruitment of more teachers to black schools.

In addition, while a new attention to human rights led some teachers to embrace social justice activism as part of their professional responsibilities, it led others to become more conscious of and vocal about what they viewed as systematic professional inequities. Not surprisingly, these critiques were sounded most frequently by teachers in minority schools, where teachers' beliefs about civil rights and professionalism were put to the test. To be sure, many teachers, like many white New Yorkers, were not race liberals, even if they might have identified as liberal or progressive in other ways. A 1948 *Time* magazine article reported that "most teachers resented appointments to Harlem, [and] hated their Negro, Spanish, and Italian pupils," an assessment that bore out in teachers' testimonies.[9] Studies performed in minority schools revealed teachers' frequent perception of a "'Siberia' feeling of exile" in black schools and a conviction that they "would prefer teaching anywhere but in Harlem."[10] Guild member and Harlem teacher Lillian Leon echoed these beliefs when she lamented to Simonson that while teachers in minority schools such as herself "suffer[ed] trying to teach," colleagues in "easy," white schools were "privileged."[11] Adding to their sense of dissatisfaction was the fact that while many teachers worked overtime developing programs to verse children in new attitudes toward other races, the political structures that surrounded minority-school teachers' classrooms largely went unchanged. Across the board, black schools in the 1940s remained underresourced, served a higher number of students per teacher, and were located in antiquated buildings insufficient in their size and repair. Many Harlem teachers feared that they, like their students, were cast off by a Board of Education that showed little concern for the schools in which they worked and little promise that conditions would change. All of these factors contributed to teachers' resistance to spending their careers in minority schools.

The actions of teachers and teacher unionists during the 1940s illustrate that their more expansive participation in race reform projects shaped their beliefs about the relationship between teachers' rights, teacher professionalism, and civil rights. The wartime era challenged teachers both to advance race relations and to quell racial tensions, as well as to exhibit the skills to change the social status quo. But muscular democracy, even among self-professed liberals like Simonson, was more difficult to enact than to tacitly support. Race equity projects initiated during the war, including reforming vocational education and developing intercultural relations in the schools, did not survive the war's end. Yet the questions that the period raised on a wider scale about teachers' political and professional responsibilities had in many ways just begun a broad conversation about teachers, schools, and race equity that would remain fundamental for the remainder of the century.

A Special Problem: Civil Rights and the Board of Education

The same concerns about American democracy that contributed to the war period's attention to the status of racial minorities also supported the production of an abundance of literature on promoting more democratic work conditions for teachers. A democratic school, the U.S. Department of Education explained in 1949, was one in which teachers were not at the bottom of a decision-making hierarchy but were an essential part of it. "Do you have the opportunity to express your opinion in the formulation of school politics?" one Department of Education brochure asked teachers.[12] Even New York City's Board of Education had to admit that most teachers might have responded to that question in the negative. A lack of interest on the part of most teachers in faculty meetings, a Board committee reported, was "generally due to the absence of teacher participation in planning for them." But the issue was not one of simple professional oppression. Rather, the committee concluded, "some teachers do not press for greater democratization of the school system because they escape responsibilities which in an autocratically run school are delegated to the few who are 'in charge.'"[13] Such critiques suggested that teachers should assume greater control of and responsibility for what took place not just in their classrooms but in their schools. And yet teachers' experiences reveal the way in which the Board reified autocratic schools more than it allowed for them to be challenged. This was especially the case when teachers attempted to create more racially equitable schools. As teachers' work on behalf of civil rights grew more visible, it also confronted a Board that was rigid in the actual political changes it was willing to enact in the schools.

To black New Yorkers and black Americans more largely, the problem of segregated schools was not just one of treatment but of opportunity. The issue of opportunity was not unique to school equity but was at the heart of a range of issues, including the most important civil rights campaign in the 1940s, employment discrimination. As the war transformed the nation's economy from one with a surplus of workers to one that faced a shortage, a booming economy and union growth bolstered the black working class and established the groundwork for a civil rights movement focused on employment equity.[14] Black labor campaigns often highlighted job discrimination in weapons plants—some of the highest paid manual labor jobs available—as exemplary of the problem of black employment more largely. The results of these campaigns were positive in many ways. By 1945, the number of black workers in weapons-manufacturing plants had risen from 1.6 to 6.6 percent in three years.[15] Black unemployment dropped from 937,652 in 1940 to 151,000 in 1944.[16] These figures do not reflect the kind of work blacks found, or the ways in which many lost their jobs after the war as the economy stabilized, but the rapid employment of black Americans as a result of action on the part of the National Association for the Advancement of Colored People (NAACP), in particular, suggested that their lives could change in material ways with or without a change in white attitudes.

The labor orientation of 1940s civil rights campaigns shaped some civil rights efforts in New York City schools in the early decade. Statistical studies and the experiences of individual teachers proved that while the majority of black high school students attended vocational high schools, the majority of employers in the city would hire a white worker over a black one when given a choice. Vocational guidance counselor Estella Unna wondered, as a result, if she was "helping or hurting" her black students when she sent them to a clerical firm to find work upon graduation. "In the past, the only jobs open to them were light housework and factory work," Unna explained to her fellow educators. "They are simply thrilled when I offer them clerical jobs and there-after nothing else will do." For Unna, securing better jobs for her students in white-owned and -operated companies produced not just a challenge but a problem because she sensed that with the return of a more familiar, postwar economy her students would only be able to find factory work again. "Per-haps I have done the wrong thing in giving them a taste of heaven," she won-dered. Educators like Unna responded to the failure of war-era school reform to acknowledge or address systematic discrimination in employment. But her attempt to negotiate between her desire to give her minority students "a per-manent lift"—economically and emotionally—and her knowledge that she was making them vulnerable to disappointment led to her own self-doubt, and she worried that she may have "done the wrong thing" in encouraging her students to seek better job prospects.[17]

More than mere impressions, the doubts teachers held about their students' lack of opportunity—in vocational schools and beyond—were grounded in policy. Since the 1930s, social scientists had documented that two tracks of vocational education existed: one for white students and one for black. During and after the war, as black activists grew more focused on job discrimination, vocational schools also came under greater scrutiny. Teachers were informed by Board officials that it would be impossible to place their female students at high-end department stores like Lord & Taylor's and Altman's that refused to hire blacks. Instead, schools were advised to send their white students to such businesses or to risk losing the cooperative relationships that the city's vocational schools had developed with its industries for job placement.[18] Such discrimination was further endorsed in the Board's recommendations for students' placement in the vocational curriculum. Counselors were urged to assign students to tracks where they would graduate as "employable" or "acceptable to organized labor bodies and employers."[19] For black students, this meant being tracked in courses for the unskilled trades: janitorial or service-based jobs for boys and domestic work for girls. As a result, black enrollment in the Brooklyn Technical School and the Manhattan High School for Aviation Trades, two of the city's most elite trade schools, was extremely low.[20] This marginalization of black students was further echoed in the makeup of vocational school teachers themselves. In 1941, only six of the city's twelve hundred trade teachers were black.[21] Like many city businesses, the Board appeared uninterested in hiring its black graduates.

While all of this spoke to an uneasy collusion between discrimination outside of school walls and discrimination within, it also produced a significant challenge to well-meaning educators like Unna, whose professionalism was undermined by their inability to serve a growing percentage of their students. This threat to professionalism made the issue of black vocational students an ideal occasion for teacher unionists to practice muscular democracy. In 1942, Layle Lane, the Guild's highest ranking black officer, founded the union's Committee on Problem Areas. A devoted socialist and vice president of the American Federation of Teachers (AFT), as well as a leading Guild member, Lane was particularly committed to economic security as the most important means to racial uplift, professing that "[n]either education nor race equality butter any bread or pay rent. Only an opportunity to work at decent wages will do that."[22] A good friend of A. Philip Randolph, Lane also played a critical role in planning the 1941 march on Washington, an event designed to pressure the federal government to open more defense-plant jobs to blacks and to desegregate the military. The plan was partially successful, and the march was forestalled by President Roosevelt's issuance of Executive Order 8802 in June 1941, which prohibited discriminatory hiring practices by defense contractors. Lane's work earned her a meeting with Roosevelt, nonetheless, and a public profile that rivaled that of any teacher union leader, in New York City or nationally.[23] Lane, along with Jennie Sokoloff, Esther Cahan, and the other teachers who founded the Guild's Committee on Problem Areas, focused on three issues in their work on bettering minority schools: reducing class sizes; improving the quality of teachers in elementary schools, where the achievement gap between white and black students began; and securing jobs for black vocational students.[24]

Given the Guild's focus on professionalism and its previous hesitancy to pair with grassroots civil rights efforts, the attention to vocational education and the employment of black students once they graduated from the city's schools marked an unusual campaign for the union. It was an effort aided by Lane's personal interests and influence, both of which were substantial forces that grew all the more in the wartime political culture. The Guild brought its own methodological approach to improving vocational education, one that focused especially on working with the Board to address the problem. In the winter and spring of 1942, the Committee on Problem Areas members interviewed Board members, both to investigate black student placement in classes for low-skilled trades and to initiate a changed policy. In these interviews, committee members unearthed clear inequities between what took place in the city's vocational schools—which served a high percentage of minority students—and what took place in its academic high schools. Of the city's eighty-nine vocational schools, over half had no school counselors on faculty. The remaining thirty-nine schools shared a total of seventeen counselors among them. Committee members also discovered further evidence of the unequal treatment of black students by local businesses. In 1940, for example, a project had been developed at Wadleigh High School to focus on placing equal numbers of white and black students in jobs. While all of the students were given jobs upon graduation, all of the black students were dropped from their positions soon after they were hired.[25]

As disturbing as these facts were, the Board's acquiescence was all the more troubling. Several Board members reported viewing Harlem activists and black business owners as nuisances. "Negroes had approached the advisory board and asked to be represented," Board member Betty Hawley Donnelly explained, referring to a committee created by the Board to advise vocational school administrators, "but this was impossible, as the members of the board are not chosen because of race, but because of their preeminence in industry and labor."[26] This kind of response was typical of Board members and echoed its "color-blind" policy toward teacher licensing and hiring. Board member Charles Smith maintained that "Negroes . . . object to being considered a special problem." For this reason, he encouraged vocational school faculty to ignore issues of color at the same time that they acknowledged that "until the trade unions change their policy colored workers cannot be placed on an equal basis." Because blacks refused to have their differences garner special attention, Smith continued, black counselors usually proved to be the most adept at serving black students. He referred to one such counselor as an example of someone "who was not over-conscious of the colored problem" and who served her students well. In contrast, white counselors like Estella Unna who were "especially sensitive to the problem" were considerably "less effective."[27] The message that educators received from the Board, then, was to maintain the status quo, in terms of the discrimination black students faced both in the workforce and in the schools. The professional teacher, Board members indicated, ignored the "special problems" that black students presented to educators and administrators in their unequal treatment in and by schools.

The work the committee conducted—and the facts that its research revealed—were some of the most important in the Guild's history and in the history of wartime vocational school reform. Yet by 1948, the Committee on Problem Areas was noticeably absent from a list of the Guild's special committees. Federal law had helped to open jobs in the government and war manufacturing to black Americans, potentially altering the prospects for black youth in vocational schools as well. But the committee's work was also made difficult both by the Board's intransigence and by the Guild's commitment to partnering with the Board as a means to improving schools. In this way, the Guild's beliefs about and images of professionalism set it on a course of action that might be better characterized as accommodating than muscular. At a 1942 meeting of the Citizens' Committee on Harlem, following the Guild's interviews of the Board members, Guild member Inez Pollak assured Harlem residents that the recent opening of the defense industry would address many of their concerns about the issue of vocational education. She "pleaded for patience" from the Citizens' Committee members in addressing the discrimination that plagued vocational education "lest too much antagonism be aroused."[28] Such a plea was indicative of the Guild's sensibilities, but it also highlighted the ways in which the committee had worked on behalf of black New Yorkers more than it had worked with them. Interviews and reports had produced more information for the Guild than they had political partnerships or strategies for action.

This central distinction made the Committee on Problem Areas difficult to sustain once Lane left the Guild in the late 1940s to focus on her leadership opportunities in the AFT. Just as important, the effort to appease the Board at the same time Guild members critiqued its racist policies proved equally unsustainable. As studies produced in the following decades would indicate, black students continued to occupy the lowest tracks in the city's public schools, beginning in the elementary grades. While the Guild continued to protest the size of classes in Harlem schools, it entered the postwar era without a committee dedicated to improving the quality of teaching and of students' treatment within black schools in general. Even more important, the Guild was left to confront the challenge of wanting to collaborate with the very entity that made race-based school reform so difficult.

While the Board contributed to the derailment of the Guild's work on vocational school reform, it presented an even greater obstruction to Teachers Unionists who worked with black city residents to gain greater political participation in their schools. The relationship among Teachers Unionists, black New Yorkers, and the Board of Education in the war period was indelibly shaped by the Union's connections to the Communist Party. Many of the most important political figures in black Harlem in the 1930s and early 1940s, including Benjamin Davis and Paul Robeson, had held communist affiliations and remained influential and popular during the war. However, these allegiances between civil rights and communism ended after the war, as radicals black and white, including Davis, were fired and purged from the labor and political organizations to which they belonged. For black Americans in the late 1940s, Andrea Friedman has argued, "the meshing of racial reform with Cold War concerns had, in large part, turned the American debate about race into a debate about Negro loyalty."[29]

Like black Americans, teachers, who were always in the vanguard of any concerns about patriotism or loyalty, also represented a special problem and felt the effects of a growing anxiety about communism sooner than most. Notably, many of the earliest sources of anticommunist action for teachers came not from rightwing groups, as they would later in the decade, but from potential allies. In 1941, the AFT expelled the Teachers Union and two other communist-affiliated locals in order to attract more teachers to the national union, an effort that was orchestrated by Henry Linville and George Counts.[30] The Teachers Guild, which immediately signed a charter to become Local 2 in the Union's stead, predicted that its membership of 1,500 would see "an upward spurt."[31] Indeed, the Teachers Union remained the larger of the city's two unions but quickly lost several hundred members, many of whom joined the Guild.[32] Just as important, some black school reform activists rejected Teachers Unionists as quickly as they had their civil rights brethren. In 1943, for example, NAACP President Walter White accused communists of "making an unashamed appeal to the Negro vote" and using schools, including one in Harlem, "to present their doctrines."[33]

Left adrift by the AFT and with prospects of trouble from national civil rights organizations, by the early 1940s, the fate of the Teachers Union appeared increasingly bound to the support of black parents. To the Board, both groups, teachers and parents, constituted a nuisance, although teachers were easier to quell in some ways. In 1947, for example, Norman London, a Harlem junior high school teacher, supported a group of black parents in forming a parent-teacher association in his school. The principal denied the parents' request, claiming that "no one or two teachers, or any small group of teachers, shall use the parents as a sounding board for the Teachers' Union, Teachers' Alliance, Teachers' Guild, or any other group."[34] When London and the parents took their protest to the district superintendent, Clare Baldwin, she charged

London with insubordination, transferred him to a school outside of Harlem, and recommended that the parents at the school instead work with two black teachers who held "distinguished records of service in the school" but were not members of the Teachers Union.[35] Together, Teachers Unionists, the parents of the junior high school students, and eighteen other parent groups at the Harlem YWCA protested Baldwin's decision; other teachers in the school created a petition to reinstate London, arguing that he was needed "to help cope with the many problems of our school," but he was not reinstated.[36] While transfers historically had been used to rescue teachers and administrators from school situations where they were not desired—like Principal Schoenchen in 1936—the Board now proved that it was willing to use transfers as a punishment for teachers who sided with parents in wanting to improve and expose the inequities of their children's schools. London was transferred to a white school, parent Sallie Custus claimed, "because the principal and superintendent disapproved of a white teacher collaborating with black parents."[37] While the Board encouraged teachers to assume greater ownership in their schools, organizing critical parents was clearly not on their list of expected responsibilities.

Baldwin's charge of insubordination was as much a response to the growing activism of black parents as it was a referral on one teacher, and it was one of the many events in the public schools—including the Board's quiet endorsement of school segregation—that suggested black parents needed to gain greater influence not just within individual schools but over the administration of schools more generally. One of the most important ways in which black parents and activists sought to do this in the 1940s was in their campaigns for a black official to be elected to the Board. Because the superintendent's claims that teachers should work with parents for better schools appeared to "apply everywhere in the city except Harlem," the Harlem Council on Education explained, black representation on the Board was essential "for the good of our community . . . and for democracy itself."[38] No black member had been appointed to the Board since 1917, and even then, the appointment lasted only a year. When the Board was reduced from forty-six members to seven in 1918, Dr. Eugene Roberts lost his seat. In 1946, when a position opened for a Manhattan appointment, Teachers Unionists joined black community organizations, including the City-Wide Citizens Committee on Harlem as well as the United Parents Association, to push for a black resident to be chosen. Instead, Mayor O'Dwyer appointed George Timone, a conservative Catholic who in 1950 would draft and secure passage of a resolution that would forever deny the Teachers Union recognition with the Board. In 1948, Unionists and race activists convinced the mayor to appoint the black Brooklyn clergyman

Reverend John Coleman to the Board, but Timone, despite the calls for his resignation by both teacher unions and a range of race-reform organizations, would prove to be a more influential and decisive appointment than that of Coleman.[39]

Together, these programs of the Teachers Guild and Teachers Union illustrate the Board's desire to excuse itself from dealing with any kind of special problems. But they also reveal that some of the strongest civil rights work completed by teacher unions in the 1940s centered on the issue of political representation for black city residents, whether that representation be in the schools or on the Board. Although the Guild's Committee on Problem Areas was small in number of participants and limited in its ability to challenge the administrative status quo, its efforts represented a real advance in the union's ability to locate acts of racial discrimination and connect them to issues of professionalism. Similarly, the Teachers Union proved that teacher professionalism could be most powerful when it was supported by parents and activists. In their works, the Guild and the Union illuminated the possibilities and limitations for enhancing multiple sets of rights—those of black residents and those of teachers—based on their ability to collaborate and to see their concerns as mutually dependent, if not shared. Importantly, this was activism that took place outside of the classroom. As teachers would soon discover, enacting reform within the classroom was a different task and, for many reasons, was just as difficult to perform.

Shine Up Your Sensitivity

On a June morning in 1943, elementary school teacher Rose Nurnberg brought thirteen of her best students from James Madison High School in Brooklyn to P.S. 113 in Harlem. Nurnberg reported that her students delivered speeches at the black elementary school on "various aspects of Negro life," including art, education, poetry, jazz, and civil rights. Each speech, she noted, had been "carefully prepared to avoid being offensive or condescending, [and] ended on as hopeful a note as possible." Afterward, Nurnberg knew that her group had reached the audience by their warm applause and by the number of black students who volunteered to respond to her own. One such student, she described, "nine years old, looking like any pretty white child, with blue eyes and brown curls, spoke with great poise. 'My people, the Negro people, are all working together in war as well as in peace for a better world.'" An eleven-year-old Harlem student explained, "We are not doing so good now, but when the world goes better, we will do better too." After responding to their guests' speeches, the P.S. 113 students sang several spirituals for them. When it was over, Nurnberg found the experience to be a "thrilling and exciting adventure." Her students' visit to Harlem, she announced, allowed them to "ma[ke] contact with real life."⁴⁰

Nurnberg's report is just one in a copious body of professional writing produced by teachers in New York City and across the nation during World War II, writing that reflects the ways in which a shifting attention to race altered basic concepts of teacher professionalism. The intercultural movement to which she belonged began during World War I as a "cultural gifts" movement and first focused on ethnic tolerance and cultural exchange between immigrant and religious groups.⁴¹ By the 1940s, however, interculturalism had been adopted by school districts across the nation and shifted its focus on the more pressing "test of democracy in America," as one city teacher explained it, "the test of color."⁴² To prepare teachers to transform classrooms into bastions of racial empathy, textbooks, curricula design, and teacher-education programs underwent significant reforms. Much of the most important academic work in interculturalism took place in New York City institutions, including Teachers College and New York University. As a result, novice teachers entered the city schools in the 1940s versed in techniques for "changing race attitudes," developing intergroup relations, and planning activities that would provide students with a "common emotional core."⁴³ The majority of teachers in the city schools were already in the system, however, and these teachers were introduced to the methods and ideas of interculturalism through in-service workshops they attended for their required political alertness credits. Such workshops were offered by a number of organizations accredited by the Board, including the Teachers Union and the Guild.

Interculturalism's new dedication to improving black and white relations was produced by a greater recognition of the kinds of systematic discrimination that blacks faced as well as a fundamentally changed conception of race itself. No longer were Italians, Irish, and other ethnic groups considered "races" as they would have been when interculturalism began; instead, by World War II, race was conceptualized in terms of skin color.⁴⁴ This political transformation had a powerful effect on teacher professionalism and on teachers' professional writing, where black students, who infrequently captured the interest of white teachers in the 1930s, now served a new role in educators' assessment of their work. Nurnberg's account of the black students who were "pretty" and well-mannered like any white child is one such example. So too was the description of an intercultural concert by guidance counselor Mary Riley. The concert itself was a vision of harmony, Riley described, one in which "a tall well-built Negro" student "stood beside an equally blond girl." Most "outstanding" to her was the black timpani player. "Every fiber of his being," Riley wrote, "his delicate wrists, graceful hands, and his entire body accentuated the rhythm and brought perfection to the performance." The students' performance, she concluded, pointed to one fact: "no racism here."[45] As both teachers' reports reflect, the pageantry aspect of interculturalism, and its focus on exhibiting successful interracial encounters, often led to strained, uncomfortable moments, as teachers sought to be color-blind, or tolerant, and yet were very much focused on race as a phenotypical concept. Just as important are the reports' illustration that whether or not city teachers actually had black students of their own, they now sought to serve them in a limited capacity, both to fulfill the basic tenet of interracial relations central to interculturalism and to position themselves as modern professionals.

In addition to changing concepts of race, a new, wartime therapeutic culture dramatically altered interculturalism. As with any tolerance education, interculturalism emphasized psychological over political reform. Armed with new theories of the psyche of the battlefield, wartime psychologists came to influence many of the most important issues of the day, from war policy to parenting techniques. In contrast to the "authoritarian personality" that had created havoc abroad, they argued, a democratic morale was defined by optimism, reasonableness, and tolerance. Happiness, which they defined as the goal of psychotherapy, depended first on feelings of security, self-awareness, and reduced tension.[46] Influenced by the work of white and black social scientists who argued that black Americans faced systematic social, political, and economic duress, 1940s psychologists expanded theories about the mind-set of individuals to explain the psychology of communities. In a wartime culture in which all Americans were feeling stressed, they argued, some were more stressed than others. "Community disorders," they contended, heightened the psychological disorders of the people within them. This was especially the case for black Americans, whom psychologists and social scientists depicted as suffering from damaged egos and psychological repression caused by racism. In so doing, social scientists and psychologists across the political spectrum diagnosed a "pathological black lower-class culture" that had embraced a collective of inferior values—from loose sexual mores to a lack of motivation in work and school—all of which they believed could be changed through expanded economic opportunity and progress.[47]

Psychologists and educators understood childhood as the time when many of the most important psychological patterns were set; as a result, they considered schools and teachers uniquely important to remedying America's race problem and to providing "first aid [for] the wounded [black] personality."[48] Interculturalists, building from the belief that prejudice impaired white and black children alike, fervently argued that "prejudice is a psychological disease" and that "the price of psychological illiteracy is disaster."[49] Rooted in a commitment to psychological improvement for all, intercultural teachers hoped to make their students more psychologically and socially literate by changing the relationships between black and white youth and the terms upon which they met. In New York City, like many Northern school systems, these encounters were unlikely to occur within the racially segregated classes and schools students attended. Instead, intercultural teachers like Rose Nurnberg often artificially created interracial encounters—or, if needed, simply taught their students about racial others. Plays and assemblies, cross-cultural visits to private homes and schools, educational films, and extracurricular activities such as UNESCO and the Junior Red Cross—clubs that stressed the importance of international and interracial relations—served as important vehicles for the transmission of new cultural values. In the classroom, educators diversified their curricula to include literary and musical works, scientific achievements, and the historical accomplishments of black Americans.

In-service workshops offered by the Teachers Union and Teachers Guild taught teachers how to adapt their classrooms to an intercultural outlook and strove to connect race reform and teacher professionalism. Beyond these similarities, however, the two unions' programs also reflected their unique philosophies about civil rights and professionalism. The Teachers Union's in-service courses in the fall of 1945 offered presentations by Harlem Committee members and a range of radical academics, including Howard University professor and communist Doxey Wilkerson. Their sessions focused on black history and diversifying the texts teachers included in their classrooms to reflect black achievements and to highlight "outstanding minorities of the United States." They also included a course on propaganda analysis that focused on the construction and dissemination of racial stereotypes and on what agencies outside of the schools—including labor unions and the government—were doing to fight racism and anti-Semitism.[50] For the Teachers Union, an intention to improve interracial relationships in the classroom had to be based upon an investigation into the social and political mechanics of racial discrimination, a concept that was implicit to the task of interculturalism but rarely examined.

This investigation pushed Teachers Unionists to think more critically about the ways in which black students were also marginalized by biased classroom materials. As Diana Selig has shown, many radical black educators put forth provocative theories about race and education but did not actually create curricula or classroom materials themselves. As a result, Selig argues, "teachers who embraced [Doxey] Wilkerson's idea that education should prepare students to struggle for social justice may have wondered how to structure their lesson plans."[51] The Teachers Union's relationship with radical educators through its in-service workshops propelled its members to begin to fill the gap between intercultural philosophies and the classroom resources available to teachers. In a call for teachers to "shine up [their] sensitivity," Unionists implored their members to examine their classroom texts and to ask themselves to take note of the "distortion of the role of [their] Negro brothers" and the "great emptiness from the Reconstruction period" to the present. The "obliteration" of blacks from classroom texts, members argued, conflicted with tolerance training and called for a more expansive program of black history in the schools.[52] In February 1949, the Union announced the creation of its Committee for the Integration of Negro History in the School Curriculum; in fighting for the inclusion of blacks in the curriculum, Teachers Unionists argued, "we can participate in the making of Negro history right now."[53]

While the Guild might have agreed with the call for teachers to shine up their sensitivity, the ways in which they went about creating a stronger appreciation between the races were notably different and more truly focused on tolerance education and student relationships. The goals of its in-service programs, the Guild explained, were to outline "the basic principles of democratic human relations," to share lesson plans its members had designed to enact these principles, and to show "types of work actually carried on in the classrooms which may be an example and stimulus to large numbers of teachers." Together, the Guild argued, the workshops would provide examples of the "changes needed to do a better educational job."[54] These workshops, which were more often led by teachers than by academics, began in both the spring and fall 1949 series with a workshop entitled "Policies and Practices of the Board of Education." This beginning to their program suggested that the Guild saw their work as a part of a larger administrative, and therefore professional, effort to reform classrooms and race relations at once. Moderate and pragmatic in tone, the Guild workshops focused mostly on applying the theory of human relations to all subjects areas, offering workshops on topics from "Teaching Human Relations in the Elementary School" to "A Demonstration Lesson in Social Studies."[55] In their workshops, Guild members focused on diversifying the curriculum and creating the kinds of interracial encounters found in reports such as Nurnberg's and Riley's. But the Guild was decidedly less interested in conducting a critical examination of discrimination than was the Teachers Union; rather than focusing on all of the ways in which discriminatory beliefs were created and perpetuated, the Guild focused on developing in teachers the skills to repair relations between blacks and whites and to create in each a greater appreciation for the other.

How the Guild interpreted what constituted stronger human relations can be seen both in the typical intercultural teacher's account of her work and in the Guild's partnership with Rachel Davis DuBois, an expert in interculturalism and the first person to teach a college-level course in its methodologies.[56] When working with teachers, DuBois frequently framed interculturalism in terms of professional improvement as much as race improvement. To DuBois, who offered a seminar called "Do We Know Ourselves?" as part of the Guild's in-service course, most teachers appeared "conscious enough of the problems of prejudice" but remained unpracticed in "thinking about the cultural richness which could evolve from our heterogeneity." As a result, she charged, most teachers were not "'gripped by a goal'" but instead were interested "only in the immediate object of preventing street riots."[57] In recentering the work of improving race relations from the street to the classroom, and from an event that provoked anxiety to one that drew on determination, DuBois hoped that teachers would work to transform a potential fear of the racial other into a political and professional objective. Claiming that "no outside help can fight our own battles," DuBois promised that when educators overcame their own intolerance they would become "new persons" and "better teachers."[58] Her philosophies shaped the basic tenets of the cultural gifts movement, including a genuine desire to see a more racially harmonious society that coexisted with an equally strong belief that this society could be brought about through a healthy attitude. In other words, DuBois may not have been interested in preventing street riots, but neither was she particularly concerned with their causes. Adopting these beliefs for their own classrooms allowed Guild members and other teachers to hold broad liberal objectives for racial equality without having to commit to any particular form of social activism — or sacrifice — outside of their classrooms or schools.

DuBois and the Guild's approaches to interculturalism seem to have appealed to many of the teachers who wrote about their own intercultural experiments in the city's professional journal for high school teachers. Teachers experimenting with intercultural methods in their classroom recommended "stress[ing] the common rather than the different traits of each race" and "conduct[ing] lessons that point out the type of humor developed by various groups so that pupils may laugh with each other."[59] Even families were brought into educators' investigations. When a father of a white student made a derisive comment about his daughter riding the bus with black children, he was brought on a tour of his daughter's elementary school to observe black and white students working cooperatively. In the end, the father was reported to have seen the error of his ways and to have "promised to change his views and make them conform to the American spirit."[60] Students' assessments of what they learned in the course of their interracial encounters frequently sounded much the same note, largely because it was encouraged. In fact, Guild member Blanche Schwartz explained, "satisfying responses" to students' interracial encounters might include comments such as "We see that all people do the same things but in a different way, and the differences are nice."[61] Many accounts of interculturalism followed a pattern of stressing the sameness and compatibility of black and white children, even as the theories behind it were built on the basic assumption that the life experiences of the two were fundamentally different.

The union-led workshops were important to the Board and teacher unions alike. In its unusual endorsement for the courses, especially in its inclusion of the Teachers Union, the Board may have hoped to breathe life into tolerance education, something that reports had shown from its beginnings had been taught only in "superficial, abstract terms." "Thoughtful educators [had] questioned the value of this approach" to combating discrimination, the *New York Times* had reported in 1939 and in so doing suggested that the Board clearly needed a more grassroots involvement on the part of teachers.[62] Also important, despite their differences in political orientation, both unions found a great sense of advancement in the ways in which interculturalism allowed for teachers to serve as leaders and educators of other teachers. Teachers had been asked to play a role in wide-scale political and social projects as part of their work before. In the Progressive Era, when schools faced financially healthier times than they did in the 1930s, teachers were charged to visit immigrant students in their homes and to write reports and case studies of what they discovered about students' families, home conditions, and diets as part of a strategy to Americanize them. But even as these kinds of responsibilities uniquely linked teacher professionalism to larger social and political projects, they were tasks assigned and designed by experts and administrators. Interculturalism offered teachers a different relationship between a political project and their work, one that gave them decidedly more control over their own professional development. The "teacher-organized courses" at the center of intercultural training in the schools were something that unionists "fe[lt] mostly strongly about" in terms of interculturalism's success, Rebecca Simonson explained to the Board in 1949.[63] Similarly, the Teachers Union expressed excitement that two of its members' work on revising curricula to become more racially inclusive promised to "become the model for city-wide curriculum changes."[64] In their intercultural efforts, teachers made an important statement about the centrality of teachers and teacher unionists in leading curricular and professional reform.

Teachers on the whole may have been less impressed by the unions' workshops and the opportunities they developed for teacher leadership, in large part because they were skeptical of the movement itself. Even in the movement's moderate message of reform, some teachers expressed unease over its attention to race and, even more, over the implication that adopting interculturalism was no longer a freely chosen political position but an indicator of professional ability. In 1944, teacher Charles Slatkin confessed his fear that "the young people coming out of college into the teaching profession . . . will regard me as a fogey. . . . I have a feeling they will want to know how my classes study literature," he continued, "Have we a course on intercultural understanding? Do we have a Hall of All Nations? Posters on Interracial Unity?"[65] Slatkin feared that the new teachers entering the profession would evaluate him based on the degree to which the physical space of his classroom exhibited a commitment to interculturalism; interracial posters and other displays of tolerance had become a quick way to assess a teacher's talents and beliefs. If he was not intercultural enough, Slatkin feared, he would feel ostracized rather than expert. Slatkin's fears were representative of those who felt themselves at the center of a change not only in thinking about race but also in thinking about the practice of teaching. As the Teachers Union had argued during the Depression, civil rights could no longer be considered as an issue completely distinct from teacher professionalism.

Furthermore, teachers of various political persuasions critiqued interculturalism as "weird dogma" that was "geared toward the mediocre mind" and was "neither very demanding nor very rewarding."[66] In addition to questioning interculturalism's underestimation of their intellect and, thereby, their professionalism, many teachers also challenged the ways in which tolerance was "forced down the throats of the recalcitrant young . . . like castor oil" and "love-your-neighbor pills" were to be "swallowed three times a week for credit."[67] Both white and black teachers expressed an interest in learning Negro history, intercultural expert E. Harold Mason reported to DuBois after a meeting at one school, but instead they found the in-service courses "ineffective" and "a lot of spouting off."[68] Such critiques came not just from teachers skeptical of interculturalism but also from those deeply committed to it. Among his own misgivings about the intercultural curricula he had helped to develop, Guild member Michael Glassman explained in 1949, was the suspicion that he and others were "merely 'playing' with beautiful generalities and high sounding platitudes like 'Love your neighbor' and 'All men are brothers,' and only occasionally coming to grips with realities in our social relations." Rather than teach students to view the world through rose-colored glasses, Glassman urged, "Our constant problem has been to devise approaches which will answer the question 'What can I do?'"[69] Glassman, like other teachers seeking to enact muscular democracy, found that interculturalism by itself did not provide the answers.

The union-led workshops seem to have done little to change these opinions. Rather, the fate of the workshops illuminated the Board's consistent reluctance to go much beyond "weird dogma," particularly when unions threatened to make the movement too much their own. Even before the unions offered intercultural workshops for credit, both offered workshops on their achievements in interculturalism, and from the beginning, the Teachers Union's workshops attracted attention from political conservatives. In response to charges in 1947, a group of thirty-four teachers at the Central High School of Needle Trades wrote to Superintendent Jacob Greenberg, the member of the Board most interested in interculturalism, to testify that in their sessions they had "seen and heard nothing to date which remotely resemble[d] subversive or un-American teachings."[70] In 1948, however, the Board began an investigation into the Teachers Union's courses after articles in two conservative newspapers, the World Telegram and the Catholic Brooklyn Tablet, accused the courses and interculturalism, more largely, of being associated with communist propaganda, despite the public popularity of the psychological theories at the heart of the movement. To make its argument, the Tablet questioned the fact that six of out of the Teachers Union's twenty courses were specifically devoted to prejudice and claimed that an "overemphasis on prejudice is part of the party which seeks to divide and conquer by stirring up hate amongst minority groups by making them feel more discriminated against than they already are. . . . One lecture on the means of combating prejudice might be expected in such a course," the Tablet contended, "but six?"[71] The Tablet failed to identify what should constitute a course on antiprejudice education if not prejudice, but its critique was taken seriously by the Board.

In these particular criticisms, the Teachers Union would face the beginnings of a true anticommunist threat from outside the field of education.[72] "Teaching school kids not to hate each other because of race or religion is now communistic and must be done away with!" chided one Union newspaper editorial. But the Board's consideration of the accusations was only one of several recent events that had proved it was sensitive to the powerful interests of the Catholic Church; after it was announced that Superintendent Jansen had appointed a committee to review both unions' programs, Teachers Union leaders' comments suggested they foresaw the outcome.[73] "When does one ever hear of The Tablet engaging in a campaign to build more public schools?" the Union asked pointedly in response. The Teachers Union saw the Board, like the Catholic Church, as limited in its willingness to expand civil rights. The Board's claims that it offered a too "extensive program of intercultural education," was a farce, Union legislative representative Rose Russell argued. "There are at present only 2 courses in this field offered to 35,000 teachers," Russell contended. "No publication, statement of policy, or orientation programs have been offered by the Board in recent years."[74] In exposing the Board as less committed to interculturalism than it had previously proclaimed to be, the Union also exposed the Board's discrepancy between rhetoric and action.

At the heart of the Board's concern was the issue of communist teachers in the Teachers Union, an issue that was taking on greater import as the nation moved from a wartime culture to a postwar political culture, a period of hard-won advancement for black civil rights but retrenchment for communists. But equally important to this specific political anxiety was a broader concern over the Teachers Union's examination of systems of prejudice and discrimination. As Superintendent Jansen explained the situation to Rebecca Simonson, the in-service program had "gotten out of control" and therefore, the Board was forced to cancel the courses entirely.[75] In its fear that the workshops were un-containable in content, the Board highlighted its limited civil rights program, one that saw black students as a "special problem" in terms of their maladjust-ment and psychological damage but not one that required remedial policies that might have been unpopular to city residents. The Teachers Union chal-lenged this incomplete approach to civil rights.

Rather than uniting the two unions, the cancellation of the courses restoked fires between them. "In making no distinction between the Guild and the Union," Layle Lane argued, "the Board makes it easy for totalitarians to pose as the sole defenders of democracy."[76] Rebecca Simonson agreed but encour-aged her members not to lose hope. Leftists who "count themselves as liberals and who play with communism," she warned, overlooked the "basic test of justice to the individual." Harkening back to Depression-era Guild critiques of Teachers Union methods, Simonson explained that Unionists "tolerate injustice on one hand because at some point, justice will be meted out with the other." But the "scales of justice," she warned, "are not balanced in this way."[77] In their responses to the end of the in-service courses, both Lane and Simonson illustrated the ways in which liberals, black and white, struggled in the period to define civil rights work and, in fact, to define liberalism. In many ways, the two unions' shared, if separate, attention to interculturalism had marked a break from the open antagonisms between the Teachers Union and the Guild in the mid-1930s and early 1940s. While they may have interpreted interculturalism differently, their mutual dedication to the movement marked a significant change over their treatment of race issues in the previous decade. One of the challenges that became all the more clear to the Guild in the im-mediate postwar years, and that was exemplified in the case of the in-service cancellation, is that the success of its civil rights efforts would depend on its ability to distinguish its brand of activism from that of the Teachers Union.

Even as interculturalism afforded teachers new avenues by which to shape their professional images and agendas, it revealed the possibilities and limitations in what they could and would do to support civil rights. Historians have debated the merits of intercultural education, but many have agreed that the movement contributed significantly to the inclusion of racial toler- ance and racial diversity as an indelible, if not always satisfactorily initiated, part of the American curricula. Yet far more traceable than the changes inter- culturalism brought to students' lives were the questions it posed to teachers about how they wanted to participate in a relationship between two enter- prises that were becoming increasingly intertwined: civil rights and teacher professionalism. Could pathways to racial equity be taught as easily as racial empathy? What were the intended goals of tolerance education, especially as classrooms remained racially segregated? What were teachers' professional responsibilities to and possibilities in making schools more equitable insti- tutions? And what did it mean for teachers to be continuously committed to improving the lives and school experiences of black students, especially when those lives challenged the very platitudes upon which intercultural rhetoric depended? These questions, frequently posited by interculturalism, far outlasted the movement itself and became all the more significant as the systematic racial problems central to the city's schools grew more difficult to ignore.

A Chip on Their Shoulder

One of the central assumptions of intercultural theories was that white teach- ers, many of whom had few opportunities to develop relationships with black Americans because of the segregated pattern of many Northern cities, could serve as experts in race relations in their classrooms. For teachers whose first significant encounters with blacks were those with their students and their students' parents, this easy assumption was often put to the test. Con- sciously or not, liberal educators often demonstrated the ways in which they were both unpracticed at and uncomfortable with thinking about racial dif- ference. This discomfort often surfaced around a discourse about black stu- dents and in a pattern of equating black juvenile political protest with juvenile delinquency.

An example of such can be found in the case of a 1945 violent confrontation that broke out between black and white students in a gym class at Harlem's Benjamin Franklin High School. The fight eventually involved five hundred students and community members and required eighty police officers to quell. Five black students were arrested, sparking sympathy demonstrations at high schools in the Bronx and Brooklyn.[78] After the riots had ended, Mayor LaGuardia blamed angry athletic coaches for inciting students to fight and claimed that their lack of professionalism and expressed dissatisfactions with their salaries "[encouraged] the children to defy government." Benjamin Franklin principal Leonard Covello asserted that the battle was "merely a boy's fight and not a real race issue" and was an act of delinquency rather than a political act.[79] Both LaGuardia and Covello failed to address the ways in which the event echoed other demonstrations of black frustration during the decade. Both, purposefully or not, also failed to address the political issues that sparked them, including a second Harlem riot in August 1943, which left six dead and hundreds injured. The riot was sparked off by the police shooting of a black soldier, an event that garnered national attention. As with the incident at Benjamin Franklin, black New Yorkers understood the riot as a response to police brutality, while white officials, including Mayor LaGuardia, characterized the incident as a product of hoodlums and delinquents rather than discrimination.[80] Just as this characterization allowed LaGuardia to sidestep the issues at hand, Covello, who had developed a national reputation for his work in interculturalism and education, avoided examining the state of race relations in one of the city's most integrated schools.

Like many liberals then, even teachers who publically and purposely dedicated their professional lives to political work found race relations a difficult topic to explore or discuss, perhaps because it too readily challenged the state of governance in the city, its schools, and their classrooms. Instead, they focused on the more comfortable territory of pathological individuals. White teachers allowed psychological theories to stand in for a myriad of potentially politically nuanced situations that they witnessed in their classes and schools. Guild member and high school teacher Henry Hillson provides an example of how and why this occurred. Devising a Negro History and Culture Club at his Brooklyn school, Hillson explained to his colleagues, provided an opportunity for black students to "speak out" and "acted like a safety valve . . . [in] dealing with a group of pupils long subjected to prejudice and discrimination." If the safety valve the club offered promised to prevent the kind of violence seen at Benjamin Franklin High School, however, it also addressed a broader agenda, that of assuaging the damaged black psyche. "Many of [his] Negro pupils," Hillson contended, exhibited "hyper-sensitivity and a 'chip on the shoulder' attitude." Hillson himself provided some context for why black students might feel sensitive toward white students and teachers, if they truly did. When new district lines increased the number of black students at his school by 250 in 1943, he reported, they only accounted for 8 percent of the student body, but "their presence was felt [by white students and teachers] out of proportion to their number."[81] Like the incident at Benjamin Franklin High School, Hillson's account suggests that the rare cases in which black and white students encountered each other in the city schools did not always go smoothly, despite intercultural efforts. Yet, even as educators were willing to see white responses to black students as part of the problem, they were all the more willing to attribute the results to black students' pathology or, otherwise stated, their "chip on the shoulder attitude."

Hillson's writing unconsciously reveals the struggles white educators faced in reconciling racist occurrences (such as the anxiety provoked by the addition of black students to the school) with a rhetoric of good intentions. Following a familiar pattern of confusing political protest with bad attitudes and behavior, teachers' claims that black students were hypersensitive allowed them to explain racist incidents they witnessed in their schools while contending that, in fact, their classrooms were racially tolerant spaces. It also served to frame educators' inability to improve black students' experiences and performance in school as a psychological problem rather than a professional failing. Each of these factors can be seen in Hillson's own account. When the Negro History and Culture Club was first begun, Hillson reported, "members frequently brought up grievances which they felt existed in the school." But after these members discussed their problems with a faculty advisor, "It was found in practically every instance that the grievances were more imaginary than real."[82] In the end, Hillson's report and the club were oriented toward disavowing black students' accounts about racism in the school largely because teachers like Hillson saw something fundamentally amiss in black students' beliefs in the first place.

To address black students' feelings and the cycle of failure those feelings created, Guild member Mildred Englander contended, good teachers should shape their curricula to provide black students with "a feeling of confidence in meeting situations" both in and outside of school.[83] The Harlem Project, a study commissioned in 1943 by the Board and a private foundation to examine the ways in which minority schools could be improved through public-private partnerships, came to the same conclusion. For children who faced the kinds of odds Harlem children were understood to face, the Harlem Project report seconded, the schools "must be enlarged to assume new responsibilities," including "provid[ing] wholesome, warm, and supporting adult relationships where families fail to do so."[84] The report's assumption that black students did not possess the kinds of family relationships that children needed to feel secure and confident echoed theories that explained damaged communities and damaged psyches. The recommendation that the best teaching was performed by warm and supportive adults echoed larger philosophies about pedagogy dating back to the 1930s that emphasized the import of teacher personality. In this sense, making such recommendations for working with black students was no different from what administrators and experts expected of teachers of white students, even if their rationale was distinct.

But little in the Harlem Project's report indicated that teachers were ready to take on these roles in black schools. Instead, the facts surfacing from the report suggested that many teachers who deplored their assignments might be ill equipped to offer their students much comfort. The Harlem Project documented that teachers in black schools used corporal punishment with great frequency and otherwise conveyed the message that they either feared or did not like their black students. In one trial school, the report indicated, 47 percent of the participating teachers exhibited indifference or negative attitudes toward their black students. At the same time that the report urged teachers to "reveal the unhappiness and emotional burdens of children that lie behind misbehaviors and failures in school" and practice a more psychologically based teaching, it indicated that teachers in these schools also appeared unhappy and emotionally burdened.[85]

Not surprisingly, teachers often located black students' problems or behavior in sources outside of the classroom rather than in their treatment within it. Rather, the "misbehaviors" to which the Harlem Project alluded understated what many teachers, and the Guild as an organization, viewed as a major problem with juvenile delinquency among black youth. A 1943 article in the *Nation* claimed that black juveniles were five times more likely than whites to be delinquent, although this statistic reflected more accurately the difference in percentages of students who were referred to the Children's Court than actual behavior in the classroom.[86] Stories of juvenile crime, the Guild contended, "revealed what teachers in Harlem had known for years—that slum dwellings, lack of wholesome recreation, low wages, and severely limited vocational opportunities breed delinquency."[87] Following the 1943 riot, the conservative newspaper the *World Telegram* reported that Harlem teachers were "sitting on a keg of dynamite" and that most teachers were "reluctant to talk" about the issues of black students' discipline, and lack thereof, in school.[88] The Teachers Union frequently protested that reports on juvenile delinquency were exaggerated and reflected "a great deal of maligning of the poor."[89] But the Guild saw things differently. In the fall of 1942, a teacher in a Brooklyn junior high school was fatally shot by two students he had reprimanded. Weeks later, after an elementary teacher was assaulted by a student and his mother, the Guild appealed directly to the city's police commissioner to protect teachers and quell "the wave of terrorism in schools," particularly in poor neighborhoods.[90] The Teachers Union disagreed, and Bella Dodd, the Union's legislative representative at the time, protested the appeal publically, claiming that American soldiers had not gone to war so that American children could be "beaten and brutalized [and for teachers] to hand them over to the police." Rather, Dodd claimed, soldiers fought the war for much the same reasons that teachers should "fight for [black students'] rights."[91]

Central to Dodd's interpretation of events was that black students were driven to violence by corporal punishment. The day after the Guild appealed to Commissioner Valentine, yet another teacher was involved in a physical confrontation with a parent, in a case that served to highlight all of the complications to which Dodd alluded. This time the teacher was a sixteen-year elementary school veteran, Harlem teacher, and Guild member. Zelda Meisels was struck on the head in front of her class by Alice Thompson, the stepmother of one of Meisels's students. Thompson testified that her stepson had been kicked by Meisels after he dropped a box of chalk; when she came to school to confront the teacher, Meisels laughed and dismissed her. Meisels, who was reported to have suffered a concussion, claimed that she reprimanded the student but did not kick or otherwise physically attack him. The Meisels case was important in the attention it brought to the issue of corporal punishment, which, whether or not it was true in this particular case, occurred with enough frequency to convince Thompson it had happened to her stepson. While the sensationalism and seriousness of the Meisels case and of the other cases drew media attention to the Guild and several other teacher organizations, the case signified all the ways in which many teachers frequently experienced less dramatic encounters, such as having their inkwells thrown at them and other eventsthat made teaching a "'hazardous' profession."[92]

Yet, as much as teachers tried to explain away black students' behavior, they were confronted continually during the wartime era with the question of what role they thought they should play in improving the situation. In 1942, the Citizen's Committee on Harlem met with a group of Guild teachers and brought to the fore "the question of a more intelligent selection of teachers for the problem areas."[93] While the neighborhood activists hoped the Guild would help them, they also suggested that the Guild teachers already teaching in Harlem were not always the kind of teachers they were looking for. In response to these kinds of suggestions, the Harlem Project charted that many of the teachers in Harlem schools were fearful of being criticized by parents. Even more, the Project reported, teachers feared that "the only support or strength they had relied on, primitive discipline," was, as it was increasingly exposed, "being undermined and even frowned on."[94] Also frowned on, however, were teachers who objected to what they saw happening in minority schools and tried to do something about it. Rose Russell of the Teachers Union contended that there existed "a great deal of intimidation among teachers when conditions in [minority] schools are made public."[95]

As these kinds of pedagogical practices and beliefs became more publicly visible, teachers responded defensively. In 1950, Rachel Davis DuBois described a meeting held at a city school to allow white teachers to air their complaints. The teachers' complaints revolved not around black children but around black adults, including "extreme inferiority feelings on the part of some Negro parents and extreme bitterness on the part of others," the absence of black mothers from Parent Teacher Association meetings, and "the problem of the Negro teacher in the Negro districts who feels that if she understands Negro children that is all that can be asked of her."[96] White teachers, the report suggested, had a chip on their shoulders, as well. DuBois referred to the meeting not to challenge the veracity of the teachers' claims but to argue for a theory of "personal relations," in which white teachers could be leaders of intergroup discussions rather than feel themselves on the outside. But white teachers' concerns with black teachers and their characterization of them as anti-intellectual and unprofessional were more complicated than just a feeling of being ostracized. Rather, the teachers in this meeting registered, consciously or not, a crisis of expertise: they did not understand the behavior of their black students, black parents, or their black colleagues.

While DuBois wanted to explain this lack of understanding as a product of nonexistent relations, teachers implied that it might be something more. The characterization of the "Negro teacher" who "understands Negro children" suggests that white teachers realized their black colleagues and students were approaching the classroom with a different kind of knowledge than their own. This knowledge was experiential and instructive—unique from the child psychology and educational sociology training white teachers held and, at the same time, unavailable to them. Black teachers appear to have agreed with this assessment at least some of the time. E. Harold Mason reported that his conversations with black New York City teachers revealed that they "felt that their attitudes were more nearly correct toward the Negro pupils and intercultural education was not necessary for them."[97] Throughout the war and postwar eras, white teachers struggled with the dilemma of how to credit a certain knowledge to black students and teachers without diminishing their academic expertise in race relations. DuBois advised the teachers in her training to "[lean] backwards to refrain from any action that might be wrongly construed" as a means of response to the knowledge they did not possess.[98] She attempted to aid white teachers by assembling scripts and other materials for them to use in their classrooms and to refer to much like a book of etiquette. In a list of "dos and don'ts," for example, she warned against using terms such as "your people" and advised teachers to instead say "those of us of Negro background." Such a simple shift, she explained, could prevent "a patronizing air [that] can so easily slip into a phrase or the bearing of a white leader."[99] But as white educators were being asked to reconsider themselves as professionals, to investigate and overcome their feelings, many also sensed that what they were supposed to feel, like DuBois's "dos and don'ts," was scripted. Keeping black students grievance-free was hardly a position of agency for teachers not used to having their authority challenged by their most marginalized students, nor did it speak to white teachers'—and Guild members'—fear that they were physical targets for black students' hypersensitivity, however sensationalized the sources of those fears were.

To improve white teachers' confidence in teaching black children might have called for a stronger sense of human relations between white and black teachers. But little in school life suggested that this would easily occur. In 1947, the director of foreign languages in the city's high schools, Theodore Huebner, implored teachers to remember that "[m]ore important than elaborate assembly programs, native dances and folk songs, picturesque displays and interesting books [was] the daily conduct and attitude of the teacher." The teacher, Huebner urged, "must be on the constant alert to combat prejudice, not only among the pupils but also among her colleagues" and could participate in the fight by not "form[ing] a clique" or "keep[ing] painfully aloof from the one colored member of the faculty."[100] In addition to this social segregation was the segregation of faculty created by the Board and school administrators. In 1949, the Teachers Union revealed that black substitute teachers were systematically denied teaching examinations, despite their principals' endorsements, while white substitutes were invited to take the exams.[101] This was just one sign that whites were finding it easier to achieve appointments in the city schools than were blacks. A series of postwar surveys conducted by the Teachers Union in 1951 and 1952 revealed that while black teachers comprised less than 3 percent of the city's teaching staff, over 92 percent of black teachers were assigned to black schools. The Jim Crowing of black teachers to black schools was not just detrimental to the teachers' professional rights, the Teachers Union contended, but also to white students, who were likely to complete their education without ever having had a black teacher. This problem directly contradicted the Board's call for tolerance training, the Union argued, for a white child's instruction by a black teacher "would be extremely valuable in achieving an important aim . . . the inculcation of respect for the worth and dignity of all people, regardless of race, color, or creed."[102] The Union's assessment that segregation posed damage to the white child—radical for its time—could just as easily apply to white teachers. Because white teachers were unlikely to meet black teachers in their education experience or in their professional lives, they were unlikely to grow more comfortable in or practiced at teaching black children.

Much of the discourse about making schools into more racially tolerant institutions during the war period focused on students as learners of racial tolerance. But the era also proved that much of this reform, however ideologically simplistic, was to be carried out by people whose views about race were far more complicated. White teachers' expressed beliefs about black students often highlighted the degree to which important civil rights work was led by liberal teachers for whom black youth and black Americans were often an abstract idea. Such teachers included Rose Nurnberg, for whom Harlem was a field trip rather than real life. In contrast, teachers in minority schools often reflected, purposefully and not, the limits of tolerance and of openness to diversity, particularly when questions of prejudice conflicted with issues of professionalism. The problems of the white professional's psyche, like other social issues of the period, would soon become enmeshed in policy, as unionized teachers continued to debate what it meant to be a good teacher of black students.

Stepping into the Den

By the war's end, and as Rebecca Simonson's call for muscular democracy reflects, it was clearer to liberal teachers that they were supposed to support civil rights than how they should plan to transform that support into pedagogy. Not surprisingly, the distinction was most complex for those who taught black youth, students for whom teachers could either enable or deny their rights. Teachers' writing from the period and union activity reflect the ways in which educators' concerns about teaching black students grew increasingly public with the advance of a black civil rights movement. To be certain, for teachers who spent little if any time in black communities otherwise, being appointed to schools with a significant black student population forced them to confront their own feelings about race, a potentially challenging and uncomfortable prospect. Eugene Maleska described for his colleagues the moment of being assigned to teach in a junior high school in Harlem as such a confrontation. In the beginning, he described, "I was afraid. My previous contacts with the Negro race were few. I had nothing to guide me but word-of-mouth knowledge and stories from the newspapers. . . . Both sources," he confessed, "made me feel like a Daniel stepping into the lion's den." While interculturalists aimed for white students to overcome their fear of black children whom they did not know, Maleska admitted that teachers also often shared those fears. Seven years after he began teaching in Harlem, he understood his appointment as a critical opportunity for expanding his own social and political views. After a "first year of adjustment," he had found that he "liked just as many Negroes as whites among the faculty."[103] Only with a commitment to democracy in deed as well as word, Maleska argued, was he able to build more authentic and meaningful relationships with his black students and colleagues.

But statistics proved that teachers like Maleska were well within the minority. The 1940 census had drawn a bleak portrait of life in Harlem, where 83 percent of residents were black. Overwhelmingly, children in Harlem lived in families that were poor, and frequently these families were headed by a single mother and transient. Up to 90 percent of apartments in some areas of Harlem lacked private bathrooms; 67 percent of the families at one elementary school received government assistance.[104] Black New Yorkers protested the causes of this kind of cyclical, systematic poverty and the social neglect that created it. Schools, which had frequently stood as institutions of opportunity for immigrants thirty years before, clearly were not intervening in a cycle of poverty for black Americans in the same way as they had for white ethnics. The Harlem Project revealed that the schools children attended mimicked their living conditions. At P.S. 10, bathrooms were located outside of the building, where they first had been placed when the school was built in 1895. Almost a third of the classes at the school contained more than thirty students. Most importantly, teachers at P.S. 10 proved to be even more transient than students. In the first year of the study, twenty-two of the school's sixty-four teachers were new to the school.[105] The "constantly shifting teacher and student body" served as an impediment to any kind of sustained improvements in P.S. 10 and other schools like it, the study reported, and to altering the treatment of the black students who attended them.

In an effort to enact greater political change, teachers like Maleska hoped to convince colleagues that black schools were less different from other assignments than teachers feared. But in addition to all of the anxieties white teachers brought with them, little about teaching in minority schools was enticing. With the exception of two new school buildings, virtually nothing had changed in Harlem schools since the Depression; teachers were guaranteed to have larger classes, longer work hours, and fewer resources. In response to the assault on Zelda Meisels, the Guild filed a petition with the Board that made several demands for improvements in minority schools, most of which focused on the issue of reducing class sizes by appointing more teachers to them. Operating on the assumption that smaller classes would leave students feeling less hostile and teachers more equipped to respond to their problems, the Guild argued that "permanent substitutes" should be added to the regular teaching staff because they chose to remain teaching in Harlem when they might have been able to substitute elsewhere. Noticeably absent from the Guild's plan was an effort on the part of its own members to bolster the faculty rosters. To the Guild, sending qualified teachers to work in black schools—something that might have effected the most change for black youth—diminished teacher professionalism because work there was defined by greater demands and fewer rewards. "The whole situation in Harlem," a Guild document proclaimed, "was an abnormal one;" as a result, it was "futile to expect the schools in these problem areas to function adequately by normal standards."[106] In contrast to a possible enactment of muscular democracy, the Guild maintained, at the same time it embraced interculturalism, that "no teacher can be expected to work under the conditions that prevail in some of our schools."[107] The Board's search for teachers to work in minority schools, one Guild recruitment flyer stated, was like making "a call for volunteer summer work."[108]

Adding to the problems of professionalism in black schools was the question of what teachers who worked there should strive for. More specifically, many teachers feared that if they proved successful at their jobs, they would be "frozen . . . in their positions for life."[109] Guild member Lillian Leon saw herself as representative of this dilemma. She reported that teachers such as herself, after requesting transfers out of Harlem, found themselves confronting administrators who asked, "Whom can we send to take the place of you experts? If you can last three years you can last." For administrators who would certainly face resistant faculty, new or experienced, it was likely easier to hold onto those they had. Leon, who likened her Harlem school to an "unholy place" that made teachers "premature[ly] aged and . . . neurotic" was one example of the increasingly common type of Harlem teacher, a newer teacher who replaced the veteran time servers as they retired.[110]

But even teachers who had spent much of their careers in Harlem at times publically protested their placements there, in part because they were supported by the news stories of assaults on teachers and all the stereotypes about racial minorities that those stories perpetuated, from delinquent, uncontrollable youth to angry, uncontrollable mothers. A twenty-year Harlem veteran teacher who wrote to the *New York Post*, for example, lamented that she had seen "the situation get worse and worse each year without anything being done about it." The neighborhood's problems with juvenile delinquency, she testified, had led to "a fine state of affairs" in which "teachers have to be escorted to the subway by policemen."[111] Teachers who needed police escorts spoke to a long-lived problem with Harlem schools: the fact that unlike schools in select neighborhoods of the city, most Harlem teachers lived elsewhere. Most city teachers "[sought] appointments nearer to home," a Board of Education report explained. "Home" for most city teachers was a white neighborhood "where problems of behavior are less trying and where immediate scholarship returns from pupils are more satisfying."[112] The problem with subway-bound teachers, then, was not just one of their own physical safety but of their frequent resentment of teaching in Harlem in the first place.

The economy of wartime America had an important influence on Harlem teachers' complaints. While teachers during the Depression were often fortunate to have any job, New York City schools in 1945 reported a serious teacher shortage for the first time since the early 1920s. Substitutes who had waited for appointments for fifteen years, the *New York Times* reported, were now declining jobs offered to them. So too did 450 of 915 prospective teachers who were offered positions by the Board that year. At the top of the candidates' list of explanations as to why they were no longer interested in teaching was the issue of class size, a problem that was not unique to black schools but certainly characterized them in greater proportion than white schools.[113] As a result, the Guild noted, the Board "now face[d] a crisis in Harlem and the 'little Harlems' throughout the city."[114] By January 1944, the Board was stated to be considering a rotation plan as a means of sending more teachers to schools in Harlem and areas of Brooklyn.

The Guild's immediate response was one that it would maintain for more than a decade. Claiming its sympathies "to teachers and supervisors who have served long and well and to the limit of their physical and mental resources in these areas, and to whom relief [was] terribly overdue," the Guild forthrightly and unambiguously challenged the plan. Arguing that "the solution to the problem of underprivileged areas lies not in the mechanical rotation of teachers in these areas, nor in arbitrary assignment of teachers to these schools, nor in freezing teachers now on the job in their positions for life"; the Guild contended that the real solution lay in "making conditions of work in these areas favorable."[115] To do so would entail a platform of reforms, including changes in building construction, curriculum, teacher training, and teacher and supervisor testing that would require the Board to address the large-scale problems that made minority schools unfavorable places to teach.[116] Just as important to the Guild, however, it would ensure that the Board did not simply "cur[e] one evil by substituting it for another and opposite evil."[117] In posing the involuntary transfer of teachers to black schools as an "opposite evil" to that of students' unequal education, the Guild suggested that, contrary to Simonson's definition of muscular democracy, students' civil rights and teachers' rights were not simply distinct, parallel movements, but, in fact, had the potential to intersect and to conflict. This tension was furthered as the Guild, inspired by the greater discourse around civil or human rights in the years immediately following the war, constructed its response as one of teachers' rights. The union opposed the Board's suggestion to transfer more teachers to black schools, read one statement, because doing so would "unduly and unnecessarily limit the freedom of teachers to select the schools in which they can do their best work."[118]

In its claim for teachers' rights to work in schools where they could be most professionally productive, the Guild reflected the limits of its liberalism and drew on a conceptual limitation of wartime liberalism more generally: the consistent provision that racism was a psychological problem as much as a political one. To be sure, the Guild's policy was a response to teachers like Lillian Leon, although not the one for which she had hoped. Leon wanted the Guild to support a rotation policy so that teachers such as her were not "frozen" in black schools for doing passable work. Specifically, she endorsed a rotation system that would assign teachers to five years in "the ever-so-difficult place" followed by "the reward of a simpler solution," a transfer to a white school. Any "martyr" who "wishes to remain in the problem school," she suggested, could be considered "a waiver" rather than a committed professional, as the teacher might otherwise have been understood to be. As the efforts of the Board in the war period reflect, attitudes such as Leon's were supported and enabled by a school system that treated black students as racially inferior and by larger theories that black students presented unique challenges to teach. The Guild argued that black schools should not be staffed by martyrs but by "able teachers, teachers especially trained to meet the special problems which they will encounter, teachers willing to serve in these areas."[119] Teaching psychologically damaged students, pedagogical theories reinforced, required distinct skills from teaching psychologically whole ones. As a result of this construction of teaching in cultural and psychological terms, it was easy for teachers to believe — or at least claim to believe — that they lacked the skills to teach black students effectively without undermining their professional skills as a whole.

Leon must have been disappointed in her union's unwillingness to consider a rotation plan and thereby potentially commit a greater number of its teachers to teach in black schools. But even with its limitations, the Guild remained important for teachers like Leon, who were otherwise rendered invisible by the Board. Harlem schools, Assistant Superintendent Clare Baldwin contended, were "smeared with tales of horror" and were "much better than people generally know."[120] The Guild took these tales seriously and responded accordingly; notably, Simonson's call for teachers to enact muscular democracy and to initiate better human relations did not ask of or require them to enter the lion's den. In her call for her union to perform as an activist association rather than a social organization, Simonson suggested that civil rights and teachers' rights might both be considered the terrain of teacher unionists. Yet, in the tradition of the Teachers Guild, Simonson framed improving work conditions and addressing racial discrimination as independent, if noncompetitive, objectives rather than two pieces of the same problem of the status of minority schools. That is, instead of viewing teachers' and civil rights as dependent on each other, she and many teachers continued to separate the two sets of concerns.

Like the Guild, the Teachers Union resisted Superintendent Baldwin's sunny discrediting of the problems that continued to plague black schools, even as it also celebrated the achievements and unique work that its partnership with black parents had created in them. In a 1949 booklet created especially for such parents, the Union reminded its readers that to "equalize education opportunities of . . . deprived communities" required teachers and communities alike to "give them extra care."[121] In contrast to the Board, the Teachers Union called for attention to black schools as unique cases that required different treatment to improve. On the Teachers Union's list at the end of the decade remained the familiar issues of better buildings, more medical services, more guidance counselors, and "more teachers, remedial teachers, sympathetic teachers."[122]

This call for more sympathetic teachers was appreciated by minority parents, who came out in greater numbers than any other group to support the Teachers Union during the 1950 Board hearings over the Timone Resolution, the municipal legislative act that, once passed, would deny the Union any recognition with the Board of Education. For teachers to be able to protest their work conditions was essential, Harlem mother Wilhelmina Bustamante testified. "You know what happens when teachers leave because of overcrowded conditions in the schools such as ours. You know what happens when the teachers voice their protest and don't just stay for two terms," she argued forcefully before the Board. "We mothers can't go. We have to stay where we live and we have to see to it that our children, when they grow up, can take their places in the world of work." Mothers like Martha Knight spoke of appreciating all of the ways in which Teachers Union members helped parents when they asked for it and expressed interest in their children that extended far beyond their work in the classroom. Teachers Unionists, Knight declared, were "on twenty-four-hour duty." At the trial, black women also came face to face with critics of the Union, who included leaders of several prominent Catholic organizations, white parents, and other conservatives. These critics, Enid Tyler, mother of three, contended, accused the Union of creating "a phony angle on the Negro-white relations in order to stir up hatred among people and tension." But the causes of such tension were there for "the perusal of every parent concerned and interested in what her child learned," Tyler argued. "When I look into textbooks, the manner in which the Negro has been portrayed is that of an inferior personality." Because of the Union's willingness to take a stand against these representations, and because of its other campaigns during the decade, Tyler claimed, "I am very happy when I have an organization as strong as the Teachers Union to speak on our behalf—so that I might be heard when I get up to raise my voice."[123]

The 1940s marked a period of increased activity and visibility on the part of both New York City's black residents and its teachers in raising their voices to secure their own rights and, at times, the rights of the other. As both groups strove for a more equal, more democratic experience in the public schools, both came up against a basic truth: equality could not be created by appeasement but was something to fight for. What each union was willing to fight for would become all the more specific and tense in the following decades. In the war period's best moments, teachers realized that thinking about their work in a larger political context, and thinking of the inequalities black students faced as something that called for remediation, did not have to represent an additional task but could be an indelible part of their work. Teachers Union member Eugene Jackson, for example, explained that he was proud to belong to a union that stood "in the forefront of the battle of the teachers and the children in our schools and in the battle against bigotry, racism, and thought control." Serving as a soldier in this battle, Jackson testified, kept him true to the "ideals of our country." Reflecting on his accomplishments, he concluded, "I know the union ha[s] made me a better teacher."[124] Regardless of how teachers fought to make education more equal for black students, what was clear by the war's end, and all of the tensions it brought, was that teachers would need to believe that doing so was not just a political or psychological project but a professional one, and one in which they gained as much as they gave. Their ability to see civil rights work and professional rights work as mutually effective rather than competitive was possible yet.

Organizing the Oppressed Teacher

Teachers' Rights in the Cold War

The tensions between feeling good and doing right that surfaced for white teachers during the war heightened in the 1950s as the city's black civil rights movement gained momentum and grew even more focused on school reform as a site of larger political reform. This strategy mirrored that of the *Brown v. Board of Education* case. The 1954 *Brown* decision was bittersweet to black New Yorkers; while it clearly attacked the issue of Southern de jure segregation, it left Northern de facto segregation untouched. While black parents and residents fought for integration for reasons of ethical principle, many also believed that integration might be the most expedient and certain solution to the problems that defined black schools. For every dollar the Board spent on a black student, it spent over seven dollars on a white student; this difference in spending was evident in the physical state of the school buildings, classroom resources, and the number of experienced teachers on staff.[1] Despite activists' efforts, however, New York City schools would only grow more segregated in the years following the *Brown* decision. By the end of the decade, more than a fifth of the city's public schools would serve a student population that was over 90 percent black and Puerto Rican. For elementary schools, the fraction was one-quarter.[2]

Harlem activists had tracked these unequal conditions since the 1930s, but the issue of who was and was not teaching in minority schools garnered new attention as a series of reports on the schools further substantiated their concerns. Teachers in minority schools in the 1950s were guaranteed to experience longer work days, fewer resources and staff support, and larger classes composed of students that many teachers seemed to dislike or fear. Such realities inspired relatively few teachers to volunteer to teach in impoverished schools, leaving novice teachers who had the least control over their teaching assignments to dominate faculty rosters. This cycle lead to further inequities. In one Harlem junior high school, nine of the school's eleven math teachers were not licensed to teach math; the head of the school's Science Department was not licensed to teach science. Several Harlem schools were reduced to half-day schedules, serving one group of students in the morning and another in the afternoon. While white children safely attended city schools, one Harlem community group noted, black children "were locked up in their apartments . . . [or left] wandering the streets."[3] The situation, Brooklyn National Association for the Advancement of Colored People (NAACP) president Milton Galamison pronounced, begged a fundamental question of "whether the New York City School System exists for the benefit of the children of New York City or whether it exists for the benefit of the professional staff."[4]

Galamison's question revealed a line of thinking that would come to characterize debates around minority schools in the decade: that public schools must necessarily exist to benefit one group or the other, students or teachers. This chapter explains why and focuses on the issue of teacher assignments to minority schools to show how city teachers both troubled and sanctioned a developing dichotomy between white teachers and black students. The cold war put pressure on the federal government to do more about race equity and civil rights, both because of concerns over national security and to ensure that American policy reflected the democratic message it projected internationally.[5] This pressure resulted in a number of seminal legislative verdicts in the 1950s, the most symbolic of which was the *Brown* case. But bridging legislation and individual attitudes was not an easy process. White parents in the urban North fervently protested school integration, even as many Northerners considered segregation a Southern problem. Less known than the resistance of Northern white parents to school integration, however, is the complex and multitudinous roles white teachers played in civil rights efforts to improve minority schools during the 1950s. While many white teachers resisted working in black schools because of workplace quality issues and their own prejudice, those who worked to advance minority-school reform often paid a high price. The increasingly tense relationship between civil rights and teachers' rights in the 1950s came to test existing partnerships between the two and to undermine the efforts of both.

As it had been twenty years earlier, the Board's and teachers' neglect of minority schools was documented in a series of scathing reports. In 1950, the Harlem Council on Education found that 76 percent of Harlem students tested two years behind their grade level in reading; 83 percent were two years behind in math. Not only was this double the rate of failing students citywide, it also reflected a nearly 20 percent decline in Harlem students' test scores from five years earlier. Warning that "the children of Harlem are faced with mass illiteracy unless drastic action is taken," the council focused on the physical limitations of the neighborhood's schools. Harlem schools served 6,374 more students than they were built to serve, with each school averaging 277 more students than it should have. In addition, nearly half of the schools in Harlem were constructed at or before the turn of the century, and their poor repair often made some of their space unusable. The long-standing problem of overcrowding produced classes in which students received too little attention, a situation that itself created "retardation, maladjustment, and juvenile delinquency."[6] Other studies would support the Harlem Council's findings. Harlem's thirty-five schools offered 103 classes for children with "retarded mental ability" but only six classes for gifted children.[7]

The decade's most important and influential investigation, however, came with the Public Education Association (PEA) of the City of New York's 1955 report, *The Status of the Public Education of Negro and Puerto Rican Children in the City*. While the study was commissioned by the Board to placate black activists who charged the city with creating Jim Crow schools, it empowered them by offering statistical evidence for their claims. Studying two kinds of schools, "X" schools, whose student population was at least 85 percent black or Puerto Rican, and "Y" schools, whose population was at least 90 percent white, the PEA sought to document the causes of the gap in white and black student achievement. Finding "no great discrepancy between the per pupil instructional and administrative costs" in the two kinds of schools, it concluded that the more significant inequity was that of teacher quality. While nearly 80 percent of teachers were tenured in white schools, only 50 percent were tenured in minority schools. The other 50 percent was largely made up of novice and substitute teachers. At the root of the problem, the PEA concluded, was "an unfortunate condition [that] persist[ed]" in teachers' preference to teach in white schools over black ones. The reasons found for this were various, from the fact that black schools were labeled as "difficult" by teachers and administrators, to white teachers' desire to work in their own neighborhood schools, to a fundamental difference in prestige that teaching assignments at white schools held over those in black and Puerto Rican schools. But the PEA stopped short of recommending that more experienced and talented teachers be required to teach in or be "transferred" to minority schools, realizing that incentives would draw more satisfied and willing faculty than would mandates. Instead, it recommended that "everything . . . be tried to encourage experienced teachers to remain in Group X schools," including reducing class sizes, improving facilities, and providing salary increases.[8]

The PEA study indicated that while black New Yorkers pressed for more integrated and equitable schools in the future, white teachers had more influence over education quality at the time. Teachers who had professed intercultural understanding a few years before were now pressed by a range of interest groups—including civil rights organizations and the Board of Education—to actively contribute to improving minority schools by electing to teach in them. The growing pressure for teachers to act on their beliefs brought sharp focus to how relatively few teachers had propelled the earlier civil rights advances in the schools. Brown, the American Federation of Teachers (AFT) charged, would change that. The AFT's Human Relations Committee, led by the Teachers Guild's highest ranking black officer, Richard Parrish, stated in 1954 that teachers in a democracy could no longer "regard themselves as passive instruments of the law, but must take an active part in assuring that the decision will continue to be upheld and not subverted in any way."[9] In focusing on schools as the most effective and expedient means to challenge prejudice, the case imbued them with a special responsibility to transform race relations by developing more democratic citizens. In so doing, the AFT argued, Brown made teachers into upholders of democracy and civil rights activists, whether they liked it or not.

But these sweeping statements put forth a different vision of the profession than many embraced in their ordinary work lives. In postwar New York City, where 97 percent of the teaching faculty was white, their commitment to civil rights was tested especially through debates over teaching assignments. The Teachers Union, the Teachers Guild, and civil rights activists, including parents, agreed on the problems that defined minority schools and concurred on the need to integrate schools, secure more supplies and equipment, reduce class sizes, provide more health and social services, and improve the physical space of the schools, including restrooms, lunchrooms, and teacher lounges. Rather, the disagreements that surfaced between the groups centered on the responsibility of teachers in improving the schools. The Teachers Union supported the assignment of experienced teachers to minority schools and saw this platform as an enhancement of other civil rights projects in which they were invested. Understanding and serving minority children, the Union argued, could be an indicator of greater professional skills. The Guild, on the other hand, focused largely on what they saw as inherently unequal work environments between minority and white schools and viewed transfers to schools in the city's growing number of "Little Harlems" as symbolic of teachers' lack of agency in their professional lives.

The two unions' policies on teacher assignments irrevocably shaped their future development and existence, including their relationship with civil rights groups, the Board, and nonunionized teachers. The unions' ideological disagreements over the issue of teacher assignments to minority schools, and the definitions of professionalism that accompanied those disagreements, served as an important means by which they could distinguish themselves from each other all the more, especially for the teachers they both needed to recruit to their respective organizations. Of the city's forty thousand teachers, neither union had managed to attract more than a relative handful by the mid-1950s. The Teachers Union boasted seven thousand members at the beginning of the decade, but that number dropped steadily and rapidly in the cold war political climate.[10] Although the Guild disavowed communism, the cold war did little to help it either. While the Guild reported nearly twenty-nine hundred members in 1950, its rolls had dropped to 2,239 members by September 1955.[11] Both unions were losing favor with teachers rather than gaining, and this could only mean limited power for either. The unions' stance on assignments to black schools represented a critical opportunity for both to appeal to city teachers' ideals and anxieties about black students, civil rights, and the future of the profession at a time in which all were commanding greater attention.

Race Ideology and Professionalism

The PEA study changed the terms of the debate about minority schools by identifying teacher quality as a source of inequity as great as any between white and minority schools. At times, teachers agreed with the assessment that black children were being offered an inferior education. In a few cases, they even agreed with the causes. Teachers described the ways in which insufficient physical conditions and resources subtracted from students' learning and re-directed the ways in which teachers ideally would have liked to teach. "Modern education methods presuppose a small class with space to move around," one such Harlem teacher explained, but "that's impossible here." Instead, the overcrowded classrooms meant that teachers had to "go back to the old style of teaching; discipline comes first, learning second." Other teachers spoke of the ways in which the inferior educational environment and, even more, the city's lack of regard for black students attracted teachers dedicated to civil rights as well as those who were apathetic. In Harlem, a teacher explained, "teachers and principals, too, can get away with 'lapses' in teaching and administering that would not be tolerated in other communities."[12] Such assessments proved that teacher quality was not just an issue of training or commitment but was tied to all of the other inequities between white and minority schools, from the condition of the physical plant to the quality of administration and leadership in black schools.

The Board of Education's Commission on Integration, founded in 1954 in the wake of the *Brown* decision, was left to develop solutions to these systematic, coordinated problems. The commission was composed of members of the Board, including President Charles Silver and Superintendent William

Jansen; the NAACP; the United Parents Association; and various civic activists, including Kenneth Clark, but neither teacher union nor any other teacher organization was represented. Of the commission's five subcommittees, the Subcommittee on Zoning and the Subcommittee on Teacher Assignments would produce the most controversial and important recommendations. To promote integration, the Subcommittee on Zoning recommended that new lines be drawn in "fringe" areas—areas where black and white neighborhoods bordered each other—to produce racially balanced neighborhood schools. It also advised that busing and permissive zoning plans—allowances for parents in segregated areas to send their children to integrated schools—be put into place for students who lived in neighborhoods too far from racial boundary lines to be helped by redistricting.

Most of the city's teacher organizations, including the High School Teachers Association and the Bronx Boro-Wide Association of Teachers, rejected the recommendations, some arguing that they would create "an obvious race-consciousness that does not exist."[13] Only the Teachers Union and Teachers Guild supported plans to better integrate the schools. But more problematic to the Board of Education and the superintendent of schools were parents' reactions; neither was willing to confront the organized response of the city's working-class white parents who were dependent on its public schools. In effect, the zoning plans and the ensuing public discussions of minority-school performance echoed the same shortcomings as the *Brown* case in their failure to offer incentives to white parents to support integration. The extent of white resistance was made especially public and clear in the case of Junior High School (J.H.S.) 258, a school in Bedford Stuyvesant whose student body was almost exclusively black and Puerto Rican. In 1956, the NAACP protested the school's total segregation and pointed to it as a "'test of the [city's] integration process." The Board, however, refused the case, and several members confided their fear that if white children were bused to J.H.S. 258 and forced to attend, white parents might respond with violence.[14]

In contrast, the Board was more willing to confront white teachers and to ask them to cross the city's race lines. The Commission's Subcommittee on Teacher Assignments made several specific recommendations, including that teachers with less than three and more than twenty years of experience not be assigned to minority schools. Instead, the committee argued, teachers with midlevel experience should be required to teach in the schools for at least three years, and regular and substitute teachers should be assigned in equal numbers.[15] The recommendations were intended to prevent the problem of inexperienced teachers being systematically placed in minority schools, while at the same time appeasing teachers who were long established in schools they liked. To Sophia Yarnell Jacobs, president of the Urban League, the suggested plans were "responsible" and "realizable," largely because they were "really quite moderate."[16] But like white parents, white teachers found the plans less than moderate. When School Superintendent Jansen asked for one thousand teachers to volunteer to work in minority schools in the fall of 1957, only twenty-five responded. As a result, the Board of Education reported that it was considering a formal procedure for the reassignment of teachers to minority schools in the upcoming year.[17]

In the coming months, the Teachers Union proved the only teacher organization or association to profess support for the transfer of experienced teachers to minority schools. It did so while demanding that the other significant issues of class size, the physical conditions of the schools, and insufficient administrative staff also be addressed and while calling for rezoning plans. The union had rarely proved itself an ally of the Board of Education, and its support of the position was a rare break in antagonisms, one made possible by the Union's track record on civil rights. Transferring experienced teachers to minority schools both aligned with the Union's political sympathies and promised the Union the possibility that more teachers would find more in common with Teachers Union members. But even within the Union, support for teacher transfers was complicated. While the Union had long been committed to civil rights, it had also always stood for teachers' and workplace rights, and in the teacher assignment debate, the two often conflicted. Teaching classes with more students for longer hours was harder work, argued the James Madison High School chapter to the Union's leadership, and support of the transfer policy would erroneously "isolate the Union from the large mass of teachers."[18] For an organization that was facing membership decline, some argued, supporting transfers would be self-defeating. But Teachers Union leadership, and much of its membership who had been involved in civil rights efforts, disagreed. The final vote among the leadership "was so overwhelmingly in favor of approving the plan" to support teacher assignments to black schools, they explained, "that an actual count did not have to be made nor was one called for."[19]

This disagreement within the Union showed to its leaders how delicately the issue of teacher transfers would need to be handled by the Board of Education; closely tied to leaders' support of the policy was a set of demands that they saw as benefiting teachers as well as students. They called for a budget that would support "basic improvements" for minority schools, including smaller classes, more planning time for teachers, and better facilities, both to improve the schools and to dispel "some of the jitters teachers feel about being sent to schools all-too-casually described as 'difficult.'" They also implored

Jansen to clarify the policy the Board was putting forth and to emphasize that black schools would not be staffed by a "rotation" plan that would leave them with "a permanently insecure staff playing a sort of game of musical chairs . . . made up of presumably unwilling teachers constantly being rotated in to 'serve time' until they can be rotated out again." Instead, the Union envisioned a set of professional incentives for teaching in minority schools that would quell teachers' desires to be reassigned to white schools at the end of their term. Such incentives included "alertness credits"—credits that teachers normally accumulated by attending in-service sessions and that contributed toward salary increases—and partially and fully paid sabbatical leaves after five and seven years, respectively.[20] In its platform, the Union argued that working in minority schools required special professional skills that could be learned on the job and that teachers should be commended and rewarded for doing so. Rather than seeing teaching minority students as a liability, it argued, teachers in black schools should be encouraged to think of themselves as leaders in a movement toward the ultimate objective, more racially balanced schools.

As with its previous activism around Harlem schools, the Union's commitment to staffing black schools tied its fate to black public support. Yet the Union's actions were not just political but professional in spirit. Unlike black civil rights activists, who based their arguments for school reform on philosophies of intrinsic human equity, Teachers Unionists based their arguments on their professional expertise. Unionists, not board members, they argued, knew best how to resolve their shared problem of staffing black schools. Despite the political challenges it faced, the Union put forth a civil rights agenda that in many ways was more visible and successful in the 1950s than ever before. Consistently in these efforts, Unionists proved that they, not the Board, had the experience and knowledge needed to resolve the grievances of a growing black population.

In fact, the Union argued, the Board was frequently at the heart of the problem. In 1950, the Union embarked on a campaign to remove biased texts from the city's public schools. Members found that their long-standing efforts to build a more racially inclusive curriculum had been consistently undermined by the Board of Education's adoption of texts that presented "offensive, unscientific, and misleading" information about black Americans.[21] In response, the Union conducted extensive surveys of books across the curriculum. Its findings were published in the 1951 booklet *Bias and Prejudice in Textbooks in the New York City Schools: An Indictment*. Included in the report was a critique of a widely used series of geography textbooks written by Superintendent Jansen himself. The Union took Jansen to task for repeated characterizations of Africans as "very backward" and indolent and for simplistic, sunny portraits of colonization. The report quoted passages from Jansen's *Distant Lands* such as, "Most people predict a bright future for Sudan. The climate here is more healthful and less unpleasant for Europeans than the land further south, and the British and French are helping to develop the region," as an example of text's endorsement of colonialism and "the ways of white people" as a civilizing force.[22] The Union's critiques motivated black parents, as well, who in May 1952 formed the Committee for the Improvement of Textbooks to further pressure the Board to remove racist texts from classrooms.[23] As with its campaign for teacher assignments to minority schools, in its critiques of textbooks, the Teachers Union examined the ways in which racism was perpetuated and institutionalized within schools. To Teachers Unionists, systems of prejudice were inherently linked, and the problematic claims in textbooks and the shortage of teachers in minority schools were two expressions of the same racist beliefs, both sanctioned by the Board of Education.

The Union also brought the Board to task in its push for more black teachers. In 1951, the Union undertook a survey of the number of black teachers in the city schools. While blacks made up 10 percent of the city's population, less than 2 percent of the city's licensed teachers were black. "School after school with nearly 200 people on the faculty has no Negroes," the survey asserted. Half of the city's high schools had no black teacher on staff. A major cause of the lack of black teachers was discrimination on the part of the Board of Education, especially through its conduct of teacher exams, a practice that had been charted since the 1930s. Black teachers testified to being ordered by the Board of Examiners to wait to take their exam for several days, all the while "watch[ing] them examine white applicants." Others were told they failed without being allowed to see their exam results. If black candidates were performing poorly on their exams, the Union suggested, it might be because of the inadequate education being offered in black schools. Whether they were "'shunted' into vocational schools" or simply offered poor academic curricula and guidance, most black students in the city were not prepared for nor encouraged to consider a college education, making them ineligible to pursue a career in teaching.[24]

Four years later, a follow-up survey showed virtually no change in the percentage of black teachers, even though the city's black population had grown. In this post-*Brown* study, however, the Teachers Union also noted that 87 percent of the black teachers who entered the city's system were assigned to black schools and that consequently "the majority of white children go through their entire school career without ever having had a Negro teacher, or perhaps never even having seen one."[25] The problem surpassed the Jim Crow segregation of black teachers, the union argued, but included the schools' facilitation of a cycle of prejudice. As with its stand on teacher assignments, the Union saw changes to the current program to offer something to gain for whites as well as blacks. Just as white teachers could become more professionally adept by teaching in black schools, the Union argued, white students could benefit from working with black teachers. For Teachers Unionists, then, beliefs about race and beliefs about professionalism supported each other.

The Guild's thinking about race and professionalism in the 1950s led it to create radically different policies. In contrast to the Teachers Union, the Guild argued that any Board policy on transfers was insupportable and, in fact, begged for opposition. President Charles Cogen encouraged his members to fully support the integration committee's rezoning and integration plans and to fight the tendency of many Northern liberals to see both sides of the integration debate. Instead, he argued, liberal teachers should "stand by a forthright and consistent decision" to push for integrated schools.[26] Publicly and privately, Cogen and his unionists backed policies that pushed for integrated schools, smaller class sizes, and better facilities and resources in minority schools. But Guild members were unwilling to consider assignments to difficult schools until they were made less so. Arguing for "a constructive program of action to alleviate or remove the conditions" that made teaching "well nigh impossible," the Guild argued against what it called "the forced transfer of teachers" to black schools. Assigning experienced teachers to black schools, in the Guild's eye, would not "remedy the basic difficulty" and, in fact, would only deflect attention away from all of the other inequities between white and black schools.[27] Quoting Thurgood Marshall, the Guild claimed that "integration in the public schools could not be fully achieved until there was an end to housing segregation" and that the "forced transfer" of teachers "was no solution" to the segregated neighborhoods that produced segregated schools.[28] If Guild teachers refused to tolerate these inequities, they promised they would be "happy to apply themselves to those challenging positions" once these conditions were corrected and the schools were made "better places to work."[29]

While the Guild's advance of integration plans echoed its belief that segregated schools were created by segregated housing, the Union consistently argued that its policy toward transfers was color-blind, shaped by problematic discrepancies in work environments rather than teachers' attitudes about black students. The conflicts present in this position mirrored a sense of political conflict held by the middle-class whites whose support the Guild sought. A 1959 Gallup Poll study revealed that 75 percent of Northern white parents approved of the Court's decision in *Brown* and that 92 percent would have no objection to sending their children to a school with a few black students. But 58 percent reported they would object to sending their children to school where half of the student population was black, and only 17 percent said that they would select integrated schools over all-white schools if they had a choice.[30] In other words, most Northern whites supported integration so long as it applied to other people's children. Likewise, the Guild stood by improving minority schools so long as its members were not asked to sacrifice their own professional well-being for the cause. Because they understood black schools to be inherently more difficult places to work, Guild members were also bound to see race rights as in tension with professional rights.

Both unions correctly foresaw many of the problems that would result from the teacher transfer issue. By the spring of 1957, the Teachers Union found evidence for its insistence that how the policy was explained would have great bearing on its success. In the Board's failure to speak forthrightly to white parents and teachers on what integration would require from both, the Union documented, the following spring, that "misinformation ha[d] flourished and fear inflamed." Seeking to avoid teacher resistance, the Board had talked about teacher assignments without delivering a clear policy, enabling some teacher organizations, including the Guild, to define faculty rotations as "forced transfers" to black schools. This alone, the Union asserted, led some principals to "mobiliz[e] their faculties and parent-teacher associations in a frantic letter-writing campaign" and "whipped [teachers] into a panic" when local newspapers reported that teachers would be "drafted" to work in black neighborhoods.[31]

The protests of unionized and nonunionized teachers took their toll; by January 1958, no funding existed in the Board's budget to support extra pay for teachers who were assigned to minority schools, even as school segregation and the issues of teacher quality that led to the consideration of the policy worsened. Black parents and civil rights activists protested and condemned the Board's inaction. Part of the cause of teachers' resistance, the Urban League charged, was that the "plans" for teacher transfers, left as talk rather than actual policy, had offered "no incentive . . . beyond the moral challenge to teach in a run-down, overcrowded school" and, as a result, had "not made any real efforts to secure volunteers among the experienced teachers." The incentives that Jansen might have been able to offer—including additional pay or hiring more faculty so teachers could be given extra planning periods—contended the Urban League, "were deliberately played down or withheld."[32] In essence, the Urban League recognized the reality that working in minority schools was more demanding and that the Board of Education failed to make concessions for that fact.

But multiple civil rights groups also registered complaints that the Guild actively worked against the staffing of minority schools and that its argument about unequal teaching situations was an attempt to camouflage its members' racist views. Paul Zuber, attorney for the Harlem nine—nine parents who withdrew their children from a neighborhood junior high school in 1958 because of the inadequate education offered to their children—threatened to protest with seventy-five other community leaders against salary raises for teachers at the Board of Estimates hearings if the Guild did not change its position. "We are tired of hearing the phony reasons teachers give as to why they don't want to teach in Harlem," Zuber charged. "If the teachers want our tax money, teach our children. It is that simple." While Guild members fashioned themselves as innocent bystanders, their passivity appeared to black activists to be a purposeful strategy to prevent school equity and improvement. Such teachers, Zuber argued, underestimated the dedication of black parents and their willingness to "also use pressure to get what they are entitled to."[33]

In responding to the criticisms of local civil rights leaders, Cogen again retreated into a color-neutral argument, claiming that nothing would be solved "by calling the teachers bad names and attributing to them bias and hostility."[34] Instead, he maintained, the issue was one simply of workplace quality and a fight for professionalism. At the same time, the union sought to defend its own position by differentiating itself from the larger, more radical Teachers Union, whose members often voluntarily taught in black schools. In a letter to Edward Lewis, executive director of the Urban League, the Guild's largest and most influential civil rights ally, Cogen implored Lewis to understand that because of their different constituencies, it was impossible for Guild and League policies to always be aligned, even as the Guild considered itself a partner in the battle for equal schools. "At least you knew where we stood" on the issue of teacher rotation, Cogen argued to Lewis, "and you could count on us to speak out honestly and forthrightly on the real issues of integration." This partnership was important for civil rights groups, he further argued, for in contrast to the Teachers Union, when the Guild spoke out in favor of integration, their word was "respected in the responsible community."[35] Cogen defined the "responsible community" much as he defined his union's policy on civil rights: as moderate, race-blind, and professional. This community was also implicitly white, since whites could more easily claim that race might be made invisible.

This truth highlighted a central irony in the Guild's position in the teacher assignment debates. Even in its opposition to the Board's considerations of involuntary teacher transfers, the Guild was clearly the more conventional of the two teacher unions and the more compatible with the education bureaucracy. Its "respectability" came from its moderate political views rather than its size, but these views earned it a unique position among civil rights groups, nevertheless, particularly in a cold war climate that made relationships with the communist Teachers Union riskier than before. In 1954, the Guild was awarded a position on the Intergroup Committee of New York City's Public Schools, an association formed by approximately thirty political organizations, including the Urban League, the NAACP, and a number of neighborhood-based welfare and civil rights groups. It was an appointment that the Guild would often site as a sign of its commitment and role in bridging teachers' rights and civil rights. So too would it cite its participation in a national civil rights movement. In 1953, the Guild's highest ranking black officer, Richard Parrish, filed a brief in the *Brown* case, signaling "the active participation of the Guild in the fight to destroy racial segregation in public schools." The Guild also supported the AFT's movement against segregated locals in the national union and held informational meetings on the New York City teachers' exam for Southern black teachers who lost their teaching positions after Southern schools desegregated.[36] These important endeavors, however, presented much less of a threat to the Board than had the Teachers Union's grassroots efforts to mobilize parents. Finally, even though Cogen was disappointed that several op-eds that he wrote to the *New York Times* went unpublished, the Guild's opposition to teacher transfers had garnered significant press coverage, especially in the *Times*, helping to transform the union from a marginal organization in the media to one that was consulted and reported on. Even as it remained smaller than the Teachers Union, the Guild altered the magnitude of its role in the city's civic culture over the decade.

To Rose Russell, a former high school teacher and now the full-time legislative representative for the Teachers Union, the Guild's ability to generate more attention than her union's own was deeply problematic, both because it overshadowed the Teachers Union's more significant efforts and because all teachers became represented in the media in the Guild's image. The Guild position toward transfers, she argued, cloaked disingenuousness in the form of naiveté. In refusing the assignment of experienced teachers to minority schools "unless and until all the bad conditions that make certain schools 'difficult' are wiped out," Russell contended, the Guild promised that when school conditions changed, so would teachers' attitudes toward working in them. "In that sweet by and by the problem will disappear and there will be no need for 'forced transfers,'" she chided, but "in the meanwhile, it's right and proper to staff these schools with substitutes and newly-appointed teachers, who are presumed to be happy." The Guild, she pointed out, "has never explained why *they* should be there." Even more unsettling than the union's conflicted view of professionalism, however, was the way in which the Guild's stance "provided an alibi for those who never lifted a finger or voice against the second class education of the children in Harlem and Bedford Stuyvesant to pose as crusaders against substandard education." In its "compromise with conscience," the Guild had gone beyond prioritizing the needs of teachers over those of students, and, in fact, had "pandered to prejudices—real and latent among teachers" toward difficult schools and the children who attended them.[37]

Teachers Unionists were particularly sensitive to the Guild's compromise with conscience because by the time of the teacher assignment debates in the mid decade, hundreds of individual Unionists had suffered for their political beliefs. The Board responded to the Teachers Union's claims of bias against black teachers with a race-blind argument that echoed that of the Guild. Superintendent Jacob Greenberg, who replaced Jansen in 1958, contended that the Board had "no knowledge of race, color, or religion of [teacher] candidates" and that "anyone who charges discrimination where none exists is equally guilty of racial discrimination."[38] But behind the equanimity and gentility of this public response lay the Board's active effort to remove the Teachers Union leadership from their teaching positions. In 1950, eight Unionist teachers were dismissed on charges of membership in the Communist Party. The group of eight included Abraham Lederman, who would remain president of the Union, and Celia Zitron, who had made her career in Harlem schools and had led the Union's Harlem Committee since the 1930s. The number of suspensions, dismissals, and forced resignations grew exponentially in the next three years, however, and by 1954, Rose Russell reported to Jansen that over two hundred of the Union's members had been ousted.[39]

The loss of these teachers' jobs was devastating to the Union, even if many of them remained on as members. But as troublesome as they were to the Union's membership and ability to recruit further teachers to its organization, the firings again signaled to the Union that the Board was out to do more than quell teachers' civil rights efforts; it wanted to actively dismantle them. Individual teachers who were summoned to appear before Board and its hired investigator, usually with several days' notice or less, were advised by the Union not to address accusations of communist affiliations but instead to document their distinguished teaching records. Transcripts of the hearings, however, indicate that these records were almost never taken into account. Purged teachers included Dorothy Goldman, who taught English in the Southeast Bronx for seventeen years and belonged to a neighborhood organization to improve its schools, and Dorothy Rand, who taught at a Harlem elementary school for fifteen years and was a twenty-two-year teaching veteran. She had also been active in the Union's biased textbook project. Cyril Graze, a math teacher of nineteen years, was convinced that he and others were suspended because they "believed that the deplorable conditions in the neighborhoods in which [they] taught constituted a great wrong done to the children, particularly the Negro children" and they "opposed that wrong."[40] Graze had claimed at a Board of Education meeting in March 1950 that "there was a 'cesspool of bigotry' at the Board of Education" and that much of the racism that existed in the schools flourished "with the knowledge of Dr. Jansen himself."[41] He contended that his suspension was retribution for these public critiques. "Those of us who will not keep quiet," Unionist Stella Eliashaw concluded, "are hounded by these investigations."[42]

Union leadership also argued that the Board focused on teachers concentrated in Harlem, Bedford Stuyvesant, and the southeast Bronx, areas of the city where most residents were poor blacks or Puerto Ricans and where Union teachers' "special training and experience won for them the love and affection of the Negro children and their mothers."[43] In contrast to the Teachers Guild's participation in civic committees and its cordial, if also at times strained, relationship with civil rights leadership, the Teachers Union's efforts won the greatest recognition with the ordinary parents who saw Union members teaching their children and who worked with them in grassroots neighborhood organizations.[44] The Union threatened the Board of Education, then, both in its stronger, leftist critique of institutionalized racism in the schools and its perceived ability to partner with, if not mobilize, black parents, an interest group that gained increasing influence and power throughout the decade. In dismantling the Teachers Union, the Board of Education worked to destroy this partnership as well.

In the end, the suspension and firing of so many communist teachers, Rose Russell argued, only exacerbated the issue of teacher assignments in minority schools. When school opened in September 1954, Russell wrote to Jansen, two hundred new teachers failed to appear at their posting. Russell argued that one reason why was "the assignment of these inexperienced young teachers to the very 'problem' areas from which superlative teachers had just been fired."[45] More than refusing to act on the issue of staffing minority schools, then, the Board of Education had actively contributed to the problem. The failure of the education bureaucracy to address the disparities and inequalities of minority schools put all the more pressure on individuals to do so, and it highlighted further causes of white teachers' resistance to working in black schools.

Damaged Psyches

Teachers' views of working in black schools, and their views of the relationship between professionalism and social activism, were closely tied to their views of the black Americans the city's public schools served. In fact, the larger ideologies about race with which teachers aligned themselves were tied to a growing popularity of urban schools as a site of larger cultural fascination. In one of its several exposes on New York City's public schools, for example, a 1953 *Time* magazine article centered on one of the city's many novice white teachers. "Nobody warned me about a thing before I went to a near slum district in Brooklyn," she lamented. Although she entered the profession "full of ideals," she quit after four years, convinced that "none of these children want to be in school. They do not want to learn. They already belong to the streets."[46] This teacher's description of "slum children" aligned with a wider public fear that teens who "belonged to the street" were instead attending school for longer than before and there threatened violence and disorder. Such an anxiety was echoed in the 1954 best-selling novel and 1957 film *Blackboard Jungle*. The novel begins as Rick Dadier, its protagonist and an English teacher at one of the city's vocational schools, interrupts an attempted rape of a teacher by a student. More violence follows, including a brutal attack one night on Rick and his colleague. One of the most important messages of the novel was that for teachers "surrounded by kids who were acknowledged problem kids" it was easy "to feel bad yourself."[47] Like the teacher from *Time* magazine, *Blackboard Jungle* suggested that teaching impoverished, minority children could only lead teachers to feel dejected, insecure, and unprofessional.

Such portraits of the New York City schools had a cost, educators contended. The Teachers Union criticized *Time* for its article and the "inexcusable disservice" it provided in its "false and slanderous" view of the typical city teacher.[48] When principals such as himself attended conventions in other cities, Jon Leder held, they met other administrators who "simply refuse[d] to believe that conditions in New York City high schools [we]re not as portrayed in *Blackboard Jungle*." These perceptions came not just from the novel and film but from the fact that "every bit of bad news [was] played up by the metropolitan newspapers and television and radio stations. . . . Let a gang member commit a felony at midnight, miles from his home or school," Leder argued, "and the press will invariably tag him as 'a student at Blank High School.'" Leder's complaint that juvenile delinquency in the city was misrepresented was right. While referrals to the city's Juvenile Aid Bureau had increased from 16,500 in 1948 to 23,304 in 1954, the student population had grown as well, and the overall delinquency rate remained at 1 to 2 percent.[49] But the close connection between delinquency and the public schools in many people's minds had its price, educators like Leder contended. A generation before, "a middle class parent would have felt mildly apologetic about sending his child to a private school" but now such a parent felt "ashamed to tell his neighbors that his child attends a public high school."[50]

Alongside these protests, however, lay the fact that city teachers' professional writing often echoed many of the same big themes found in journalistic exposes and fiction, as they contended with what a "desperado instinct" prevalent in youth indicated for the profession of teaching.[51] An example of this kind of concern is the story of Irma Gelber Rhodes, a Queens high school teacher who left the profession before World War I to raise her own children and returned thirty years later. "The ethical and moral tone" of what she found when she returned, Rhodes lamented, "was more relaxed" than she was prepared for. In her article in the city's journal for high school teachers, High Points, Rhodes recalled an incident of a male student who purposefully overturned a stool in the hallway and then ordered Rhodes to pick it up. When the student began to approach her, screaming, Rhodes wondered "what I'd do if he treated me as he had the stool," but unlike the accounts of physical conflict in Blackboard Jungle, the situation ended as quickly as it began. Rhodes found such defiance to be common to school life in the 1950s. Just as disillusioning as the boy with the stool were the students who refused to erase her blackboard and a girl who told her "that she would not care to fill a vase with water for me (I had of course supplied the flowers) because she'd have to walk way over to the other side of the building."[52] While the occasional delinquent had always been part of school life, Rhodes suggested that something more fundamental had changed among students and that the social codes teachers previously had expected and lived by had come to an end. Whether these codes had ever truly existed, her essay argued that teachers' traditional sources of authority in the classroom were no longer effective and operational.

Other teachers echoed Rhodes's claims about student behavior. In fact, the New York Times reported, many teachers thought that violence in schools in 1955 was about as it was in 1935. Instead, the bigger distinction was a decline in the "general level of respect for authority" and the way in which it was "much harder 'to save face' in classroom incidents."[53] Evidence from the period shows that minority youth paid a greater price for teachers' fears and disillusionment than did white ones. Educators, social scientists, and psychologists argued that unruly and unsocial behavior was created by broken homes, mothers who worked outside the home, and poverty. Because each of these factors affected minority children more than white children, juvenile delinquency became an axis around which many larger anxieties about race revolved. Since the early-1940s, Judge Justine Wise Polier of the New York City Children's Court had documented the fact that a high number of the children who reached her court were black, while the majority of teachers who referred them there were white.[54] Educators often contended that compulsory laws kept resistant and disinterested students in school, leaving, as one principal described, "New York City Public High Schools, in the course of one generation . . . to adapt themselves to an entirely different caliber of student."[55] But the city law that required youth to attend school to age sixteen dated to 1936. Rather, the more significant, recent change was the growing ratio of minority to white students in the city's schools, which was reported to be 1:5.6 in 1950 and was predicted to rise to 1:2.3 by 1960.[56] While educators often talked about minority students as euphemistically as they discussed "difficult" schools, the black and Puerto Rican students who attended the city's schools in greater numbers and for longer than in the past were the "different caliber" of student that concerned teachers.

Defining black students as a different type of student than was served before and, ultimately, and inferior one, white teachers also described the distance they felt between them, academically and psychologically. The kinds of "language handicaps, cultural differences, and cultural deficiencies" found in black students, Guild president Charles Cogen explained, even if a product of segregation, nevertheless prevented an "interest in learning" and created "a resistance towards school" with which teachers could not identify. "To a greater extent than in other schools," Cogen asserted, youth in difficult schools came from one-parent homes or had mothers who worked, thereby making them "not available to exercise frequent supervision." The result was behavior that "[ran] the gamut from annoyances to serious crimes" and ranged from students "talking out whenever they please, refusing to stay in their seats, using obscene language towards the teachers and fellow pupils, [and] ringing false fire alarms" to "criminal behavior includ[ing] assault, robbery, extortion, destruction of property, [and] starting fires."[57]

High school teacher Carl Fichander documented some of the same observations from his own experiences in the classroom. Because minority students were disproportionately tracked to vocational schools like the one where he taught, it was "not surprising to find a large number of children in vocational schools with a record of frustration in the lower schools, antagonism to authority, and maladjustment in various areas." Such "low-ability" students, he explained, drawing on a Board of Education report, came from "lower socioeconomic brackets, from poor family situations, and from broken homes."[58] Likewise, teacher William Isaacs reminded his colleagues that the minority students who "show little interest in school" often did so "because they feel there is no significant place for them in our society." This situation could not be blamed solely on white racism, Isaacs contended in the spring of 1954; for although the "minority situation [was] admittedly bad," advances like the *Brown* case showed it was improving. Yet black students' increasingly "uncalled for attitude . . . persiste[d]" nonetheless.[59] In their comments, Cogen, Fichander, and Isaacs echoed three versions of the predominant white liberal view of black youth: because their lives were more likely to be marked by poverty and racial segregation, they felt inferior and frustrated, and they acted out their frustrations in the one supposedly middle-class institution to which they were invited: schools.

Such sentiments more than aligned themselves with liberal arguments about race from the time; in fact, they were bolstered by the same psychological rhetoric of the period that made the *Brown* prosecution's defense and the Warren Court's decision possible. Perhaps the most famous aspect of the case was Kenneth Clark's study with black children and dolls, which was performed to prove that black children were psychologically damaged by the constant message of their own inferiority that resulted from segregation. As Christopher Schmidt has argued, however, complex psychological findings were often simplified in the case by "the psychologists who offered expert testimony, the lawyers who interpreted these findings in their arguments, and the jurists who reinterpreted these findings in their opinion." This effort at simplification was made for different reasons by different participants in the case, but, Schmidt proves, it resulted in a shared emphasis on the damage of black children while virtually ignoring the damage segregation created for whites.[60] Consequently, the psychological argument may have appealed to moderate whites, but it did little to create a sense of investment or self-gain in desegregation for them. Instead, the damaged black psyche argument, and the psychological and postwar social science theories that had enabled its development, created a damaging effect of its own. Lani Guinier has succinctly summarized this effect as an "inadverten[t] reinforce[ment] of the identification of blackness with inferiority and stigma in the minds of whites" and a message that segregation led black children to become unwilling or unable to learn.[61] Thus, civil rights rhetoric may have inadvertently bolstered teachers' fears about black students as much as it challenged them.

The same psychological emphasis that shaped civil rights strategies and policy in the 1950s also came to influence teachers' professional development. As in the 1930s, teachers, like students, were made the focus of many psychological studies over the decade. One popular such study, *When Teachers Face Themselves*, laid out a basic premise that "a teacher's understanding of others can be only as deep as the wisdom he possesses when he looks inward upon himself."[62] Psychologists and education experts compelled teachers to get in touch with their inner selves as a means of creating an atmosphere in which students could develop secure, healthy personalities and in which they were psychologically prepared to learn. To some city teachers, this theory was appealing. High school teacher Ida Steinburg dreamed of a time "when psychoanalytic services will be a 'must' not only for analysts, as they are at present, but for parents, teachers, civic leaders, and all those whose behavior has a crucial influence on the lives of others."[63] Helen Hiller agreed and testified that, psychologically speaking, too many of her colleagues had "grown up not nearly as well as they should have and could have." To overcome the personal shortcomings that resulted, Hiller was pleased to see, many teachers "have not only started on the path of self-examination, but continued along it, painfully and gropingly, our destination not self-satisfaction but self-knowledge and understanding."[64] Such portraits of teachers in pursuit of self-knowledge presented them as ideal professionals in a culture shaped by the import of psychological well-being. They also suggested that teachers had the ability to transform students, even delinquent students, by having a stronger grasp on their own feelings and setting better examples for their students. But whether teachers adopted the dominant psychological rhetoric or questioned the way in which it seemed to be encouraging "soft" teaching, as some did, was in many ways beside the point for teachers of black students. The predominant theories on black youth argued that their egos were systematically damaged by events that occurred outside of the classroom. From broken homes to segregated neighborhoods, black children faced challenges that left them underprepared to succeed in school and that teachers, regardless of any degree of self-examination, were unable to change. The psychological theories about black children and white teachers alike gave teachers little by which to develop more successful teaching techniques or the confidence that such techniques could create a different outcome.

Psychologists may have recognized this shortcoming in their theories, but there was little they could do to address it so long as the theories themselves were foundational to civil rights advances. In a speech entitled "Segregated Schools in New York City" at a conference for the Intergroup Committee in the spring of 1954, Kenneth Clark attempted to dismantle the image of all black children as of one type. In the well-attended speech, he explained that while black children in the North felt the same sense of inferiority as in the South, not all black children acted on that sense of inferiority in the same way. The resulting behavior on the part of minority children, he argued, depended on "many interrelated factors, among which are: the stability and quality of his family relations; the social and economic class to which he belongs; the cultural and educational background of his parents; the particular minority group to which he belongs; his personal characteristics, intelligence, special talents, and personality pattern." In the speech, Clark revealed his trouble over three basic misunderstandings and assumptions on the part of white New Yorkers: first, that all black children were the same or responded similarly to racist acts; second, that because segregation was considered detrimental only to blacks, there was little incentive for whites to desegregate; and third, that the argument of black damage at times furthered a cycle of racism more than it remedied it. "Some children, usually of the lower socio-economic classes, may react by overt aggressions and hostility directed toward their own group or members of the dominant group," Clark explained, but "the larger society not only punishes those who commit them, but often interprets such aggressive and antisocial behavior as justification for continuing prejudice and segregation."[65]

Clark's argument that not all black children, not even all poor black children, were psychologically damaged conflicted both with popular representations of black children and, in fact, with much of the social science literature of the period. Neighborhood organizations documented the effects of what Clark described, including the ways in which teachers magnified black children's problems. In 1954, the Harlem Central Council investigated an elementary school where a large number of students had been sent to the principal's office, reportedly "because they were difficult to manage." The disagreements that had brought about these expulsions, the council found, "were due to a lack of understanding of [the students'] motivation by teachers."[66] Organizations such as the Harlem Central Council contended that white teachers' prejudiced views of black children caused them to find what they were looking for and that these incidents said as much about teachers as they did about the behavior of black children. The prejudice of individual teachers, however, was exacerbated by the unique problems of staffing minority schools that the council also found, including a high teacher turnover rate and a lack of supervision of or orientation for new teachers.[67] Together, these logistical challenges conveyed the message that black children were unruly and difficult to teach while doing little to prepare teachers to make different kinds of judgments and decisions.

Teachers' characterizations of black students had pointed political consequences beyond the treatment of individual students, especially in relation to the issue of staffing minority schools. "Wittingly or unwittingly," Edward Lewis wrote to Cogen, Guild members had "strengthened the stereotype prevalent about these schools that they represent a kind of 'Blackboard Jungle' of juvenile delinquents and mental deficients, in which teachers in these schools are under constant threat of physical harassment." Such characterizations, as well as the Guild's portrayal of Harlem schools as "all broken down to the extent that they are fire and health hazards," hindered "the recruiting of volunteer teachers for the deprived schools."[68] While Guild members and some other white teachers wanted to blame black students' economic and cultural impoverishment, Lewis argued, the decline in black students' test scores pointed to "the poverty of their educational environment."[69]

At the very least, white teachers' pathologizing of black students helped to take teachers out of the equation when explaining the systematic failure of minority students in the city's schools. Instead, white teachers often described the "anxiety, hostility, and deep rooted fears of failure" that black children brought to the classroom as impacting the profession and oppressing the teachers.[70] Rather than focusing on the academic disciplinary knowledge that drew them to the profession, high school teacher George Kaplan lamented, teachers in minority schools were "to devote themselves to social work, psychiatric ministrations, and educational nostrums" and "to make learning palatable for the non-intellectual, the indolent, and the obstreperous." Assignments in minority schools, teachers like Kaplan argued, were more work, not just because of the greater number of students per teacher, as the unions typically argued, but because of the greater number of problems and needs that poor, black students brought to the classroom. "High schools are not welfare-states," Kaplan argued, but teachers were being asked to take on the responsibilities of the larger social problems that some youth brought with them to school.[71]

Nationally, teachers responded to a growing sense that social and political responsibilities were becoming translated into classroom chores. A 1959 study by the National Education Association showed that some of the most common causes cited by teachers who left the profession included class size, a work week that exceeded forty hours, and too many clerical demands. More than salary, teachers' concerns in the 1950s were centered on work conditions.[72] A Teachers Union survey on noninstructional chores proved that these same concerns dominated teachers' professional lives in New York City. The report born out of the survey listed pages of responsibilities that teachers were required to fulfill on a daily or weekly basis including patrolling the halls, bathrooms, and schools buses; collecting students' lunch money; ordering weekly bus passes for students; mimeographing and ordering supplies for their classrooms; creating conduct reports for students on the principal's trouble list; filling out postcards for each student who was late to class; completing forms for the Department of Welfare; and writing referrals and reports to guidance counselors and school psychologists.[73] These activities, just some of many listed, indicated the increased clerical demands made on postwar teachers without any greater allotment of time in which they were expected to accomplish these tasks. They also suggested that delinquent students were more work for teachers, not just in personal interactions but in paperwork.

In addition to teachers' mounting concerns that poor or black children were more work to teach than middle-class white students, many expressed unease over their increasing perception that they were on the wrong side of a battle for administrative and public sympathy. The number of school integration and civil rights cases that black parents had brought before the city courts over the decade had created tension, in the eyes of some teachers, between civil rights and teachers' rights. Abraham Lefkowitz, longtime Teachers Guild member and high school principal, objected to the children who were sent to youth court for truancy and other offenses but were "seldom held to accountability by some judges."[74] Lefkowitz referred to judges like Justine Wise Polier whose decision in In re Skipworth supported the nine Harlem parents who had taken their children out of their neighborhood school because of its inferior conditions. In the 1958 case, Polier condoned the children's truancy in light of the deep inequities that all Harlem children faced, including the quality of their teachers.[75] To Lefkowitz, teachers were not only misunderstood by decisions like Polier's, their jobs were made more difficult. "The attitude evidenced by some judges who hold by their decision that a child must not be held responsible for his conduct, breeds not only disrespect but even contempt," he argued. Unlike teachers, Polier and others did not have to "fac[e] reality" because they did not have to work with delinquent youth on an extended basis.[76]

Teachers who did "face reality" often found that their relationships with black parents and activist groups were growing more strained as numerous teacher organizations resisted public efforts to improve minority schools. Guild chapter chairman Murray Hoffinger described feeling "caught in the middle" between fighting for his own professional reputation and protecting his students' rights to a quality education. Hoffinger taught at J.H.S. 136, one of the schools indicted in In re Skipworth for a "watered-down curriculum" and for steering students into vocational or trade schools rather than into academic high schools.[77] When testifying at trial, Principal Alfred Nussbaum admitted that in his three years at J.H.S. 136, not one of the school's sixteen hundred students had ever participated in the city's annual science fair, that only forty-three of the school's eighty-five teachers were licensed by the Board of Education, and that of those forty-three, only twenty-nine were teaching in the field in which they were licensed.[78] Teachers in the schools, parents found, lacked motivation and incentive and relied on stereotypes of black youth rather than cultivating an "aware[ness] of real problems and real living standards and [the] true background of Negro people in [the] Harlem community."[79] Administrative failures and charges of prejudice ignored the facts of teachers' daily work, Hoffinger contended, and both substitute and licensed teachers "performed far beyond the regular call of duty. . . . Nevertheless," he argued, "we have been subjected to a twisted series of attacks by local groups, and have had to withstand a drumfire of unwarranted abuse by the local press."[80] While the school's statistics about its faculty indicated that not all teachers could have been performing above and beyond what was expected of them, they also indicated that the serious problems that existed far surpassed the ability of any individual teacher—or even of an entire faculty—to repair. Rather, Hoffinger's union was in a better position to address and change the issues of faculty assignment that came to bear on individual teachers and unionists such as him.

Altogether, these tensions between supposedly damaged black students and teachers who frequently portrayed themselves as psychologically worn-out had results that were more than rhetorical. In 1954, 1,131 teachers retired, double the number from four years earlier. Many of those who retired upon reaching their mandatory thirty-five years of service, the *New York Times* reported, cited "changes in classroom conditions" as the cause.[81] In the years following, the Board of Education reported an increasingly difficult time recruiting new teachers to the profession as it publicly vacillated between various teacher assignment plans to minority schools.[82] Together, these factors marked unwelcome news for a school district already facing severe faculty shortages in many schools. But it stood as increasingly good news for teacher unionists who saw that they could capitalize on issues of teacher morale by developing agendas that might speak to it.

Organizing the Oppressed Teacher

For American culture at large, the postwar preoccupation with juvenile delinquency was a product of anxieties about many factors, including integration of the races, an increase in the number of white working mothers, and the middle-class exodus from American cities to suburbs. For teachers, delinquency and the corresponding issue of teaching black students served as a symbol of a larger professional concern: a growing sense that their expertise went unrecognized and that others had more control over the profession than they did. This concern, coupled with the shifting political terrain in the city in the 1950s, laid the groundwork for a radically changed teacher unionism by the end of the decade.

Just as the psychological development of the black child stood at the center of political arguments about school reform, so too did arguments about teacher morale come to frame larger conversations about school resources, increased administrative duties for teachers, and changing conceptions of the profession. Like the "damaged psyche," "morale" was an especially important concern within what historians have labeled the therapeutic culture of the 1950s. A preoccupation with morale, as Ellen Herman has shown, began with wartime psychologists, who found that positive morale served as the foundation for "determination, sense of purpose, superb leadership, and occupational competence in military and civilian populations."[83] Psychologists' focus on morale suggested that Americans could control their response to life events if not the events themselves. In this way, morale was even more than an attitude, which could come and go, but an indicator of one's personality and overall mental health, both of which were longer standing. For teachers, the focus on morale meant that professionalism was once again viewed in terms of attitude rather than skill by the administrators and experts who so frequently used the terminology. Good teachers, educators were told ubiquitously, "were never complacent about the present" and "never hopeless about the future."[84] For teachers to discuss the problems that challenged them in the profession, they had to address the issue of morale.

While the rhetoric of delinquent students located teachers' sinking morale in difficult students, teachers cited two other sources for their problems. The first of these was that school administrators made decisions about their professional lives without consulting them. "Our superiors at headquarters," teacher Ralph Heller explained to the city's high school teachers, "do not know what we are accomplishing, are not aware of the problems we face, and are too frequently unreceptive to suggestions and recommendations of those who are on the job." The result, he contended, was that an already "poor morale" among teachers was "deteriorating fast."[85] New teacher Dorothy Schwartz confessed to never "appreciat[ing] how much a teacher must do" because her professional training failed to correspond to the "day-by-day problems and tensions of teaching." But it was just as much the fault of the Board of Education, Schwartz contended. "I wish somebody had told me that there is no orientation to the school system in general—no communication of those basic facts that all employers manage, in one way or another, to tell their employees," she wrote in the city's journal for high school teachers.[86] This lack of communication between the Board and teachers amounted to a lack of professionalism, teachers like Schwartz maintained.

One of the reasons why Board members were out of touch with teachers' daily experiences, teachers argued, is because their opinions and ideas were rarely solicited, even by their own principals and within their own schools. Isador Millman estimated that he had attended over three hundred faculty meetings in his career, yet at no time had his principal ever asked him his opinion in them. Instead, faculty meetings served as "briefing sessions" in which "teachers take no part in preparing the agenda, nor are they asked to participate." Because teachers "are not stimulated at these meetings," Millman explained, they often remained silent, hiding their "boredom, resentment, and indignation."[87] Former PEA director Frederick Redefer found evidence for teachers' complaints while also arguing that claims suggesting teacher morale was lower than ever before were "nonsense and reflect[ed] headline publicity." After conducting a survey that showed teacher morale was not low in all of the city's schools, Redefer concluded that it was highest where teachers felt they were influential to the design and administration of the school. But giving teachers the kind of responsibility and authority that Millman and Redefer argued administrators should represented a paradigm shift, one that many principals saw as unfounded from their own observations. Teachers' problems were self-created, argued one principal, as "lowered teaching competence and sagging staff morale go hand in hand." The high number of teacher retirements had led to "the easing of licensing requirements and examination standards" and "'put[ting] bodies into the classroom,'" he continued; "deadwood" teachers threatened to "infect their colleagues with cynicism, mediocrity, and timidity."[88]

While teachers' feelings of alienation from education administrators was nothing new, they took on new relevance in a political climate of 1950s race politics. "The morale of the teacher is low," Guild member Clara Goldwater wrote in the union newspaper, "not only because of financial pressures, but because of the responsibilities spelled out for her by judges, psychologists, psychiatrists, social workers, business men, and religious leaders."[89] In fact, this collection of other professionals had always been part of the community that influenced public school design and teachers' work. But after the war, the psychologists, social workers, and religious leaders who sought to influence the public schools were frequently connected to a growing civil rights movement, one that had come to question and criticize city teachers. The 1950s teacher, Goldwater claimed, was "oppressed by continuous attacks upon her profession," the attacks themselves due to the public's proclivity to "project its anxieties and feelings of guilt on education."[90] Essential to the Guild's argument about professionalism and teacher assignments was a belief that city residents and the Board consistently asked teachers to do something that most white New Yorkers were not willing to do. In this respect, the union was right. More than changing the racial composition of the public schools or more equitably distributing resources between them, the *Brown* case and the movement for equal schools in New York City had produced a larger, more visible conversation about the problems that overwhelmed minority schools, including insufficient teachers.

Just as important as the changed influence of other professionals on school life, however, was the increased visibility and influence of black parents. A survey of Harlem teachers' attitudes conducted by the *New York Amsterdam News* in 1953 offered a more expansive view into white teachers' beliefs about black parents. Many teachers echoed the popular belief that Harlem children were limited in their attitudes about school because they "got it from home." While teachers named all of the well-known challenges to teaching in Harlem schools, they also consistently returned to the failures of black parents. Of the five or six parents who came to talk to her each month, one elementary school teacher lamented, none asked the right questions. "They only want to know 'does my child mind?'" the teacher explained, "They don't ask 'how is he doing?'"[91] Such anecdotes revealed a possible difference in expectation between black parents, who, with all of the discussion of minority youth and delinquency rightly may have been concerned about their children's respect and obedience for their teachers, and white teachers, who may have hoped to have their professional expertise consulted in conversations over academic performance. But the elementary school teacher's comment was also significant of a pattern in white teachers' responses that consistently undervalued and underestimated the efforts of black parents. Complaining that the Harlem parents lacked the savvy of the "clubwoman's outlook," many teachers surveyed commented on black parents' inability to advocate for their children. "They are not beggars," one teacher argued. "They can get almost anything they want if they organize and put pressure on the Board of Education."[92]

Such comments not only underestimated black parents; they misrepresented and misinterpreted the efforts and accomplishments of black parental activism in the decade. Black mothers, in particular, organized and grew militant in the 1950s, protesting school conditions through legal channels, as did the Harlem nine, through their work in community organizations, and through several strong, influential parent teacher associations to which the Board of Education was forced to respond.[93] In the course of these actions, what black mothers had to say at times echoed white teachers' comments. Black parents often agreed that their children "just don't seem to do anything in school or at home." "In Harlem . . . everyone strides along, no one cares," one parent explained, "and when the children go to high school and may be called upon to do a little work, they drop out of school or get dumped into vocational schools." But parents differed from teachers in their diagnosis of the problem. It was in school, from white teachers with low expectations, not at home, parents argued, that their children learned "defeatist attitudes."[94] Such arguments often struck a chord with teachers' own anxieties about their professional expertise. In response, teachers argued that they were not social workers and that the "relationship between the community and the school" needed to be defined as one that would leave teachers "free . . . to do the job they are trained to do."[95]

While no one disputed the conclusions of the PEA study itself, the public forums held in response to the integration committee's plans—and to black parents' protests—often consisted of debates between black parents and white teachers over minority parents' and students' rights to a high-quality education and teachers' professional rights. While parents and neighborhood activists argued that "if the police department could send a 'flood of cops' to Harlem, the Board of Education could send experienced teachers there as well," educators contended that assigning experienced teachers to minority schools would be "disruptive to morale" and would cause mass resignations. Teacher rotations, May Andres Healy, the chair of the Joint Committee of the Teachers Organization, argued, would ensure that "teacher morale," already low, "would hit rock bottom." Calling on a rights rhetoric of her own, Healy contended that the Board's plans "overr[o]de the rights of the many" for the "rights of a few."[96] Healy's argument signaled an important line of thinking that would grow increasingly popular among teachers in the late 1950s and the following decade: that teachers' identification as a group was based on more than their shared professional status: it was based on a common set of rights that accompanied their professional identity, including the right to work where they chose and without submitting to the pressures of lay individuals. That is, even as teachers wanted professional recognition from the black parents they served, they also wanted to operate free from their oversight or suggestion. The tensions inherent in this argument only heightened a growing sense of divide between teachers and the black public.

Although arguments about teacher morale were echoed by individual teachers like Healy, they were rightly interpreted by others to be the product of teacher groups' purposeful deployment of a rhetoric that held important cultural capital. Both unions' newspapers frequently referred to teacher morale throughout the decade, capturing headlines such as "High School Morale at 'All Time Low,' Conditions Unbearable," "The Low State of Teacher Morale," and "Low Teacher Morale Due to Many Factors."[97] While the two unions pinpointed different causes from which the loss in morale stemmed, the common use of the term in both presses indicates its importance to the unions in defining their purpose. To administrators and interested observers outside of education, the state of teacher morale itself was rarely questioned. Instead, many questioned the role of teacher unions in manipulating teachers' unhappiness. The debate over teacher assignments heightened this skepticism, even as the Guild made a politically conservative, rather than radical, argument. The Board of Education's plan for teacher assignments, the New York Times argued, would have been problematic in any form because "some teacher organizations fear . . . the loss of teacher morale" any time that "compulsive change is suggested."[98] More than disputing the reality of teachers' morale, the Times contended that union leadership resisted measures that threatened to ask teachers to look beyond the status quo. Administrators frequently agreed. To turn to a union, claimed one city principal, reflected a lack of self-discipline and a willingness to permit "their teacher organizations to set their standards for them . . . [and] 'protect' them against those who would endeavor to have them do their jobs properly."[99]

An even greater challenge to unions than public opinion, however, was the opinion of teachers. For decades, most city teachers had resisted becoming union members, although they had joined any one of over fifty various special interest organizations for teachers. At the same time, teachers in the 1950s appeared to need unions in a way that they had not in the past—to do more than address their bread-and-butter issues: but to address issues of professional agency that appeared to be growing all the more threatened. Even more, teachers needed unions to help create policy, rather than simply protest it. Frederick Redefer identified one of the teachers' problems in achieving this, asking how the Board could "listen to the voice of teachers if teachers' groups are as numerous as are the ways an individual can be sliced and classified?"[100] Neither union was likely to succeed so long as that union was considered just one in a crowd of teachers' associations.

At the same time, teachers' fears—both personal and professional—of being linked with certain forms of political activism impaired union membership and strategies in the early years of the cold war. Charles Cogen expressed particular frustration that "the hottest talkers are often those who won't even join the Guild or will fear to see their names in print." The militancy of the Guild and its ability to raise teacher morale, Cogen explained, was "tempered by all the circumstances that hem us in."[101] Not the least of these circumstances was the popular perception that unions were for laborers or political radicals and that collaborating made teachers less professional rather than more so. Even more, the Guild needed to counter images created by Teachers Unionists, who at the beginning of the decade surpassed the Guild in numbers but who were now fighting their own problems of morale in response to the witch hunt that "victimized teachers who . . . brought to public attention the problems of their Negro students and have tried to improve their conditions."[102] Teachers Union members were often branded by administrators and other teachers as "eccentric in their habits . . . not always well mannered, well dressed and well behaved," and "much less likable" than their colleagues.[103] In this sense, Unionists were portrayed by many other teachers as stereotypical communist organizers: overzealous, unsocialized, and out of the mainstream.

The Guild never fit this image, nor did it fit the way in which Unionists described themselves or their agenda. It was the attention to larger political issues, Teachers Unionists contended, more than the specific political parties to which they did or did not belong, that got them into trouble in the 1950s. "The person who stayed home at night and watched television and was indifferent to the social and political issues of the day was not faced with questioning," Teachers Unionist Charles Eckstadt explained to his colleagues at Bryant High School upon his forced resignation. Instead, the "teacher who is questioned is the one who . . . signs petitions of one kind or another, favors labor, opposes bigotry and Jim Crow, and works for peace."[104] Even if this description of political activism did not suit the Guild's political or social sensibilities, the union's leadership nevertheless wanted the same intensity of dedication and activism from its own members. "The morale of each of us is tied in with the morale of all of us," Cogen reminded his members and other readers of the union's newspaper, "Each one of us must make a choice, and inaction is also a choice."[105] Until more teachers made a different choice, the Guild would be hampered in its efforts to increase teacher morale.

Low union membership proved that many teachers believed in what Guild member Edward Siegel called the "responsibility to demean ourselves as to the professionals we purport to be" and to place a sense of public service above personal gain. But in nonunion publications, teachers had long critiqued their professional treatment, from salary to administrators' evaluations, indicating that the real challenge to unionization was teachers' associations with labor and political activism rather than their eagerness to subsume themselves under the mantle of public servant. Strikes and other typical union strategies, Siegel concluded, echoing the sentiments of other teachers, "are as unprofessional as you can get."[106] To Cogen and other Guild members seeking to become more influential in education politics, teachers like Siegel appeared to suffer from a "lack of confidence" in the union's "potential and ability," and from "a fear of attempting to lead any kind of militant action for themselves."[107] But in order for union militancy to effect any kind of change, Cogen and others saw, the Guild could not afford to alienate teachers like Siegel.

By the second half of the decade, with the hot-button issue of teaching assignments catching the attention of a wide swath of teachers and teacher organizations, Guild leadership saw that the union could profit from addressing more issues in its recruitment campaigns. Most important to union growth, Guild representative David Selden concluded in 1956, was "conducting a program of interest and service to the teachers." While to that point "the salary campaign has been the staple of our organizing appeal," he reflected, "it may now be more effective to emphasize and develop more activities of a service and welfare nature."[108] Selden's observations were also at the heart of the 1957 Annual Fall Conference for the Guild, the union's largest annual meeting of members. The theme for the three-day conference was "The Role of the Teacher in School and Community Today" and was broken into three subtopics: the amount of emphasis that should be placed on bread-and-butter issues, the union's role in political issues like integration, and the influence of collective bargaining rights on the union's mission and program.[109] The program reflected that the union's stance on teacher assignments might have been more complex than it seemed and that members really were interested in the larger social and political issues that undergirded the more specific problem of staffing black schools even if they did not want to work in them.

This tension between wanting to support student integration but not teacher transfers and being interested in civil rights in the South if fearing them at home was one that Guild leadership had to find a way to negotiate. Contrary to their liberal image, and even self-image, New York City teachers were of a diverse spectrum of political beliefs, and what appealed to one teacher as "service" might alienate another teacher. Longtime Guild member Tess Gloster remembered that the union leadership came to see that although existing Guild members were "strongly convinced that change was necessary not only in their own profession but everywhere else . . . great numbers of teachers were not concerned, and the issue had to be presented more in terms of the needs of teachers."[110] If salary was not enough then, some social programs risked being viewed as too controversial and too far from the field of professional concerns of teachers.

In this light, teachers' growing sense of their own injustices became an especially important rallying point for bringing new members to the Guild. More specifically, teachers began to frame the struggle they experienced in the schools in terms of human rights, something that they could draw on without striking a communist-sounding chord. Gloster would later reflect that the union's strategy in the 1950s "promoted a sense of involvement on the part of the teacher. . . . [to] use his experience of injustice or unfairness . . . to make him feel he needed to band with his fellows and bring change."[111] To do so, Guild leaders had to locate a specific source of oppression. While in the past teachers had often framed workplace issues as a series of individual, if pervasive, annoyances, unionists now more clearly articulated their dissatisfactions as a larger political problem in the schools, one in which principals and Board of Education administrators denied them a sense of professionalism, when all the while parents and community activists appeared to have a greater say than ever. They called on the language of injustice and oppression to make their point. Previously, Guild membership had always been open to administrators; in fact, principals such as Abraham Lefkowitz had served as leaders within the union. Now the Guild made use of a popular antagonism toward administrators in order to "swell the ranks and draw in people whose support was needed in order to accomplish things that the union wanted to accomplish."[112]

Yet even with this increased membership, by 1960, the Guild still reported six thousand members, more than the Teachers Union's reported four thousand and a marked improvement over its membership statistics from the mid-1950s but still a small percentage of the city's 43,500 teachers.[113] At the same time, Guild leaders saw that competing organizations could make the same appeal to teachers' sense of injustice and could just as easily increase their own membership. Out of this realization, Cogen and other leaders developed a plan to merge with the Committee for Action through Unity (CATU), a group of approximately one thousand teachers that broke off from the long-standing High School Teachers Association (HSTA) because they also sought to become a larger, more powerful organization. The HSTA and Guild had always been at odds over salary issues; the HSTA sought higher salaries for high school teachers, while the Guild, whose membership historically included a large number of elementary school teachers, opposed salary differentials. But the HSTA had also been vociferous in its protests against teacher assignments to minority schools and to the Board of Education's integration plans more generally. In March 1960, despite its previous disagreements with CATU, some of these HSTA teachers also joined the new union that developed out of the merger, the United Federation of Teachers (UFT). The UFT reported to have ten thousand members at its start, an increase of four thousand from the Guild's initial membership. Therefore, the merger brought an even more conservative group of teachers to unionism.[114]

This conservatism in social politics contrasted notably with teachers' growing acceptance of more radical action on the part of their own professional movement. With teachers' growing sense of injustice in the latter part of the decade came an equally powerful recognition that their former methods of complaint had not been effective. "I want to be treated with respect by everyone, including my superiors," wrote one such unionist to the UFT newspaper in November 1960, "How am I going to get this respect? By writing letters? Signing petitions? By other methods proven to have failed over the years? No."[115] That month, the UFT conducted a one-day strike for increased pay, more sick leave, free lunch periods for teachers, and collective bargaining rights. Although the Board of Education called the strike a "flop and a failure," it was less so in Harlem, where 35 percent of teachers honored it, as compared with the 15 percent citywide.[116] Leaving already understaffed Harlem schools to have to devise ways to serve their students, the strike signaled how teachers' rights and students' rights had grown at odds in the 1950s.

In December 1961, the UFT won the right to serve as the teachers' official collective bargaining agent, with 20,045 votes, versus the Teachers Union's

2,575.[117] The Guild's victory in the collective bargaining election marked a final challenge for the Teachers Union, one it could not overcome. In 1963, members of the Teachers Union's Executive Board adopted a resolution for its members to disband and join the UFT. In the resolution, the Union cited a history of what it called "increasingly severe handicaps" dating back to the 1950 Timone Resolution and the purging of much of its leadership. The result, the resolution stated, was that many of the city's newest teachers had never heard of the Teachers Union, "never receive[d] its material, kn[ew] little or nothing about [its] past struggles." As it had in the 1930s, the Teachers Union once again found itself in the midst of a generation gap. This time, however, it was the Union that had the older members and was less adept at speaking to the ideals of a younger, more conservative generation. Instead, new teachers who lacked historical perspective took the Union's "hard-won gains for granted" or, equally frustrating in the eyes of the Union's old guard, "attribute[d] them to the only union they [had] hear[d] about—the collective bargaining agent."[118]

Together, these dilemmas begged questions of how much influence the Teachers Union could hold and to what degree it could truly serve as a teachers' union rather than a social activism group. While the teaching staff benefited from being consolidated into one union, the Teachers Union lost any remaining authority it held in existing outside of the UFT. Refusing to merge with the UFT asked Teachers Union members to accept that they would have no say in the decisions of the UFT at a time when the union had an unprecedented ability to shape policy that would influence all teachers.[119] In November 1963, Teachers Unionists voted 301–40 to accept the resolution. In their letters to the Union's newspaper, members expressed a variety of viewpoints about the decision. While some expressed misgivings over UFT policy in "matters other than bread-and-butter interests," others claimed that the two unions' programs were essentially the same and that only "organizational lines" kept them "artificially separated."[120] To the Union's old guard and hundreds of former Teachers Unionists who fired or were forced to resign, the social and political commitments of the two unions were distinct. But in the political context that had developed since the war, the Union's existence increasingly asked teachers to put students' welfare before their own. The resolution itself gave some indication of the struggle of Teachers Unionists in determining what a professional and social movement for teachers needed to accomplish. After "countless hours of discussion and argument," the executive board decided that the "objectives of both unions [we]re similar, and many of the issues on which the Union pioneered or on which it often fought alone [we]re now accepted parts of the UFT program."[121] These program developments included the unions' creation of multicultural materials for the classroom and the support for structural changes to Harlem schools, minus the ever-important issue of who would teach in them.

The creation of the UFT and its victory in gaining collective bargaining rights supported unionists' contentions that new gains needed to come from new forms of protest. The result, Richard Parrish testified, was that New York teachers "dramatized the struggle for status and security for all teachers of the nation. . . . The ripples from New York City," he predicted correctly, would fan out nationwide.[122] In the next decade, the birth of the UFT, and the political grounds and compromises on which it was forged, would further entrench and intensify the dichotomies that developed over the 1950s. Milton Galamison's question of whether schools existed for the benefit of students or teachers would be all the more relevant, and the relationships between black students and white teachers even more central to public discussions of school reform and teacher unionism.

"An Educator's Commitment" Professionalism and Civil Rights in the 1960s

CHAPTER

In the fall of 1963, black parents in New York City decided that something more had to be done to push for integration in the city's schools. Despite their efforts over the past decade, black New Yorkers still had only been given "promises, pilot projects, [and] tokenism." Calling for "Jim Crow schools in New York City" to end, the newly formed Harlem Parents Committee pressed for improved, integrated schools. "We are sick and tired of promises which do our children no good today and tomorrow," the committee protested. "We mean for our children to have the best that this—the richest city in the world has to offer now!"[1] The following winter, joined by the Brooklyn-based Parents' Workshop for Equality and with the support of local chapters of the National Association for the Advancement of Colored People (NAACP) and the Congress of Racial Equality (CORE), the Harlem Parents Committee organized a boycott of the city schools. On February 3, 1964, over 460,000 students—a third of the total student population—and thirty-five hundred teachers observed the boycott, shutting down schools in Harlem and Brooklyn neighborhoods. The demonstration, local news reports stated, brought a "deep South flavor" to the Northern city.[2] United Federation of Teachers (UFT) president Charles Cogen did not call for his forty-three thousand members to boycott but promised to support those who did. Even this partial support became important when city officials created a blacklist of boycotting teachers to prevent any from being awarded administrative positions in the future. The UFT accused the city of "invad[ing] the civil rights of teachers" and organized its own demonstration in response; the Reverend Milton A. Galamison, who headed the Parents' Workshop for Equality, charged the Board of Education with an "act of tyranny" against teachers.[3] All in all, the boycott and its aftermath represented what UFT members and civil rights organizations had accomplished in New York City by 1964: a limited but at times supportive relationship based on their mutual dissatisfaction with the Board's treatment of black schools.

Four and a half years later, classrooms across New York City were once again empty, this time owing to three continuous teacher strikes. From September 9 to November 19, 1968, nearly fifty-four thousand of the city's fifty-seven thousand teachers struck in what began as a response to black parents' and community activists' attempts to have nineteen teachers and administrators transferred out of schools in the Brooklyn neighborhood of Ocean Hill-Brownsville. The nineteen—all union members—were accused of sabotaging the local community control board. The failure of the 1964 boycotts to improve the city's schools in any significant way had changed race activists, including black parents. While many still wanted to see integrated schools, they nevertheless refocused on gaining greater control over the quality of education offered in schools that they now assumed would remain segregated. They did so through community control boards, which were organizations of parents, community members, and teachers created by the Board of Education to give city residents a voice in improving their neighborhood schools through influencing teacher assignments, the curriculum, and the budget. The fight for community control of the schools, the New York Amsterdam News explained, was an expression of the collective "desires of parents and communities to determine the quality of education in their areas." To more radical black activists, community control was an effort to "employ dissent as an instrument to reshape the relationships between the have-nots and haves" by demanding "new roles from teachers," including "learning from the students how they learn most effectively."[4] In their organizational structure and the agendas that developed out of them, community control boards called for a paradigm shift in race relations through a changed relationship between teachers and minority students, parents, and communities. To the Ocean Hill-Brownsville board, the nineteen educators in question represented a danger to the schools, not because of their performance in the classroom but because of their open hostility to its decisions and beliefs on behalf of the district's black students and parents. To many unionists, community control boards represented the sanctioned power of noneducators over educational matters, including some that teachers themselves had only recently gained the power to influence.

More specifically, the demands of the Ocean Hill-Brownsville board threatened the UFT's hard-won battles with the Board for a greater control over their professional lives. In sharp contrast to the previous decade, teachers now petitioned for their right to teach in minority schools. The issue was not just one of protecting a group of teachers in one neighborhood but of what the teachers represented and the threat of community groups "tak[ing] over teacher appointments." "If one parent group sets a precedent . . . others will surely follow," warned member Naomi Salz, and teachers would be assessed by parents' political agendas rather than by their professional aptitude.[5] Calling themselves "militant integrationists," UFT members equated the transfer of its union members with being fired for being white and saw all teachers as embroiled in a "life-and-death struggle" for the "right to due process" before being reassigned.[6] This right, they contended, stemmed from the Fourteenth Amendment, which "[bound] together into one indivisible whole freedom, equality, and due process" and had been "paid for with blood and tears."[7] In a public advertisement, the union argued that the issue teachers were fighting for was "the right not to be fired arbitrarily by your employer because he doesn't like the color of your skin, or the way you wear your hair, or the political opinion you hold."[8] Unionists' conviction that their professional right to teach where they chose was one and the same with civil rights further angered many black education activists. "What 'right' of the teacher must be protected?" asked one neighborhood organization, in sharp contrast to the allegiances professed between teachers and parents several years earlier. "The 'right' of the teacher to teach issues repugnant to the children and the parents in the school district? The 'right' of a teacher, no matter how bigoted, to impose on children an attitude and outlook that would cripple them for life? Is this the sacred 'right' the power of a strong union . . . is used to defend?"[9] To community activists, teachers' fight for their rights appeared morally bankrupt, a cover for their racist viewpoints rather than an articulation of a professional cause.

The differences between teachers' relationships with civil rights activists in 1964 and those same relationships in 1968 illustrate a growing division between teachers' professional goals and civil rights objectives over the decade. This chapter traces teachers' greater commitment to unionization over the 1960s and the vital role that race politics played in creating that commitment. Historians have been drawn to the events in Ocean Hill-Brownsville because of what they tell us about race relations and political thought in the 1960s. As Jerald Podair has skillfully argued, the strikes marked a consolidation of white and black values in the period and illustrate how black activists' demands for "an expanded definition of equality that promised substantive equivalence of conditions" caused "self-professed racial liberals," including many New York City teachers, "to pull away."[10] Daniel Perlstein has shown that the battle over community control "exposed growing strains in the political coalition that promoted racial justice and decent working conditions since the New Deal" and "gave voice to ideologies that justified liberalism's eclipse."[11] Both of these valuable studies begin with a "liberal" New York, one in which blacks and liberal whites alike were influenced by social scientific definitions of racism that argued that law and public institutions held the power to regulate people's behavior and influence their beliefs.

While a liberal coalition between teachers and black civil rights activists had existed since the beginnings of the civil rights movement in the 1930s, understanding the events of the city's schools in the 1960s in terms of that coalition tells just part of the story. This chapter expands on and departs from the work of existing scholarship, including that of Podair and Perlstein, in two important ways. First, as the history of teacher unions in New York before the 1960s shows, teacher unionists' connections to race liberalism were complicated and questionable well before Ocean Hill-Brownsville. Indeed, teachers' resistance to assignments in black schools shows liberalism was a minority position within the Guild as early as the 1950s and that significant groups of nonunionized teachers were even more conservative on racial issues. Teachers' conservatism differed from the violent acts of race hatred committed by working-class white Northerners in the 1960s and 1970s.[12] Instead, teachers' conservatism was shaped by a new rights-conscious culture and was founded on a conviction that they were competing with black parents and city residents for the right to control the operation and policies of the city's schools. Second, this chapter reveals that as the UFT expanded and improved on Guild strategies to fight for teachers' rights, it drew on the rhetoric of civil rights, and it did so to protect teachers from the objectives and influence of black parents and education activists. The contextualization of school reform efforts by both unionists and black activists in terms of rights only deepened a growing opposition between the two, empowering conservatives, dividing liberals, and compelling teacher unionists to redefine the relationship between professionalism and social justice movements. Examining the rhetoric the UFT used to protest black school reform efforts begs new questions about the ways in which rights talk contributed to the decade's schisms.

More than at any time previous, the successful organization of teachers in the 1960s was indivisible from the changing activism of black city residents, including the adoption of new goals and approaches for improving their neighborhood schools. Black parents, like race activists more largely in the 1960s, became increasingly radicalized as the promises offered by federal legislation and their municipal governments failed to change the actual circumstances of their lives. Northern black mothers, the Commission on School Integration reported in 1963, were at "the center of the struggle" over education equity, "lobbying, organizing, demonstrating, getting arrested, and pressing their associates toward ever more militant action."[13] Just as court cases such as *Brown* had little impact on school integration in New York City, so too had parents' efforts to change Board of Education policies. At the same time, a growing black power movement offered a new way of thinking about restructuring educational institutions, from the relationships between the people within them to the curriculum, as an essential tool for building community and race consciousness.[14] A stasis in policy outcomes combined with a changing race rights movement that critiqued individuals' participation in maintaining racial inequities brought new attention to teachers and their work in the classrooms of minority schools. In the high-water decade of civil rights, a number of commissioned studies served to confirm what many black residents said they knew from experience, that "far too many teachers lack[ed] the insights, the skills, and sometimes the motivations essential . . . to overcome the prejudices of the society of which they [were] a part."[15]

This sharper critique of teachers' beliefs and their work altered unionists' definition of teachers' rights and their relationship to the civil rights movement. In the previous decade, teachers' battle for their rights was largely a struggle for control over whom they wanted to teach. Now teachers were being told how and what to teach, and this concern served to energize and unite them. "Life in the classroom should be guided by people who are responsibly concerned with education," the UFT insisted, and "educational policy and practice [should not] be dictated by an assortment of miscellaneous 'militants.'"[16] But the UFT's assertions that only they had the expertise to evaluate the quality of education minority students were receiving, and the union's dismissal of activists' efforts as the work of random "militants," failed to address both the powerful criticisms and the successful organization of black city residents. Widening public accusations that white teachers did not know how to teach black students, coupled with a rapidly growing number of black and Puerto Rican schools in the city, put unprecedented pressure on teachers to explain the causes of minority student failure, even if they were given few options to discuss openly and honestly their experiences in the classroom. This climate of accusation, coupled with many teachers' belief that their professionalism was violated by the intrusion of noneducators, pushed teachers to be "driven by a sense of desperation," one in which "the desire for unity" had "become an overriding force" among them.[17]

Like other social groups, including Chicanos, white ethnics, feminists, and the New Left, teachers borrowed from the black civil rights movement to shape their own sense of identity and to organize.[18] The credibility the 1950s and 1960s civil right movement brought to public protest and calls for human rights made the kinds of public demands and demonstrations teacher unions increasingly depended on more acceptable to a broader range of teachers, including political conservatives. A growing desire for unity and the import of professional freedom as a basic concept was evidenced in teachers' mounting demonstrations for their rights. In 1960, forty-six hundred of the city's thirty-nine thousand teachers struck for the right to collective bargaining. By comparison, in 1968, over fifty-four thousand of the city's fifty-seven thousand struck against black community members' attempts to assert control over their neighborhood schools. The wide statistical gap between these two strikes was in part a result of growing union membership, itself a product of moderate and conservative teachers' new attraction to unionism. After reaching an all-time high membership of thirty-one thousand in 1965, up from fifteen thousand in 1962, the UFT set out to grow its membership by another nine thousand in a single year.[19] By 1968, UFT membership had grown by 66 percent in just three years. This growth enabled the union to focus on altering its political influence in the education bureaucracy at large, and its campaigns reflected this confidence. But it also signaled a change in the political composition of union membership. While the Guild and Teachers Union had generally attracted the most liberal of teachers, the success of 1960s recruitment campaigns—made easier in the context of the larger racial and social politics in the city—meant that the UFT now included a broad swath of professionals, and not all of them shared these earlier unionists' political views. Unionists who had once enacted progressive social and political works through their unions now found themselves at odds with a growing number of new members who wanted little to do with civil rights projects. The result, unionist Sol Stern lamented, was "the degeneration of a once exciting union," one in which "the conservative and the mediocre have become the . . . majority."[20]

As late as 1969, more than three-quarters of black Americans still professed to support school integration.[21] At the same time, many unionists, black and white, saw something fundamentally wrong in the performance of minority schools, and some even saw teachers as central to the problem. But just as the visibility of black power activists came publicly to define the goals of black New Yorkers in the later part of the decade, so too did an insistence on teachers' rights—including freedom from the "pet projects" and "bizarre efforts" of black "vigilantes, racist extremists, and ordinary crackpots"—come to stand for all teachers' point of view.[22] Unionists saw teacher professionalism as pitted against parents' and activists' meddlings and unsocialized students' best attempts to wreak havoc in the classroom. As a result, by the late 1960s, teachers' rights and civil rights were both intertwined and at odds as never before. What had begun as a labor-based campaign for professional self-determination came to dissolve the solidarity that defined teacher unionists' relationship to the civil rights movement only a decade earlier, pitting teachers against parents, whites against blacks.

Black Students and White Teachers

In 1964, Harlem Youth Opportunities Unlimited (HARYOU), an organization directed by the Brown psychologist and New York State regent Kenneth Clark, drew a bleak portrait of the city's minority schools in its report *Youth in the Ghetto*. More than 75 percent of junior high students in Harlem performed below grade level in reading; 84 percent failed to test at their grade level in mathematics. Hundreds dropped out of high school each year. "The basic story of academic achievement in Central Harlem," the report stated, "is one of inefficiency, inferiority, and massive deterioration."[23] This story had been told before: since the 1930s, studies by the city and by parent groups showed that black students were failed by their public schools. But the failure of black students had an ever greater impact and became ever more representative of New York City schools as racial minority students made up a larger percentage of the city's students as a whole. Postwar white flight to the suburbs, combined with the further migration of blacks and Puerto Ricans to Northern urban areas, caused minority youth to become the numerical majority of public school students in the city. In 1964, 165 city schools had a minority student population of nearly 100 percent.[24] Three years later, 71 percent of students in Manhattan, 64 percent in the Bronx, and 52 percent in Brooklyn were black or Puerto Rican. Most of these students attended segregated neighborhood schools. Equally problematic was the concentration of black students in special service schools. While black and Puerto Rican students constituted 34 percent of the total student body in academic high schools in the city, they made up 58 percent of the student body in vocational high schools and 71 percent in special high schools like the "600 schools," which were designed for delinquent, behaviorally maladjusted, or otherwise at-risk students.[25] As they had been historically, black students were overrepresented in remedial, nonacademic programs, promising them a lifetime of low-wage work.

Pointing to the deep inequities in teaching assignments due to the Board of Education's neglect and white teachers' historic resistance to teaching in black schools, the Harlem Parents Committee concluded that the quality of their children' education was undermined by a "lack of experienced teachers and in all too many instances classes [not being] covered at all." Minority schools offered fewer courses and had larger class sizes than white schools, and teachers in minority schools were more frequently in the position of teaching subjects areas in which they were not trained to teach, leaving them to become "just . . . a warm body serving as a babysitter" rather than experts or professionals.[26] At one East Harlem high school in 1961, 60 percent of the faculty had begun teaching that year; the longest any teacher had taught was two and a half years.[27] Anecdotes and statistics such as these pointed to the resistance of experienced teachers to teach in minority schools. As a result, parent groups that had focused on Board of Education policies toward teacher assignments in previous decades became more openly critical of the ways in which teachers willfully contributed to such inequities. Fundamental to teachers' resistance to working in minority schools, from the point of view of black parents and activists, were their attitudes about black students. Responding to the popular argument in teachers' professional writing about "culturally damaged" black children, HARYOU contended that "the fact that 85 percent of the children in the public schools of Harlem are retarded in reading and arithmetic cannot be logically explained as being due to social and personal pathology. . . . Not all of these children are from poor or broken homes." Instead, "the tendency on the part of some educators to lump all children in a racial ghetto under one heading of 'culturally deprived,' and 'therefore uneducable,'" explained black students' academic failure.[28]

Reports like HARYOU's supported black parents' contentions more than they offered them new information. Rather, anecdotal evidence already proved to parents what HARYOU's statistical studies had shown about black student failure. The Harlem Neighborhood Association, an umbrella organization for a number of community groups focused on improving the quality of life in Harlem, concluded that "[s]ome of our white teachers feel we Negroes are not capable of learning too much, and they don't bother to teach the kids too much, you know just keep them quiet until the three o'clock gong."[29] The Harlem Parents Committee reached the same conclusion, arguing that "they do not expect our children to learn."[30] While community-based organizations focused on teachers' experience and skill in the 1950s, they now questioned teachers' commitment. The dual challenge of teachers' problematic attitudes and insufficient pedagogical training suggested that improving black schools required more than policy change but fundamental revisions of teachers' beliefs in black students' abilities. Reconceptualizing the relationship between white teachers and black students became one of the most important goals of education activists in the 1960s.

Teachers confessed that they too often felt like babysitters rather than professionals, both because of an increased number of bureaucratic chores that defined teachers' work since World War II and because of their students' lack of discipline and motivation. "Very often, I find myself standing in front of the class wordlessly speaking to nonattentive, tuned out faces. At other times the room seems a chaos of chatter and laughter and noise," described a teacher at one of the city's black high schools. "The situation is tricky because I don't want to be an authoritarian. I don't want to be the teacher I am 'supposed' to be but sometimes I am unable to be the teacher I want to be."[31] Teachers across the political spectrum complained of the impact of what they saw as "cultural differences" between themselves and their students on their abilities to fulfill their professional duties. "Teachers, white or Negro have, for the most part come from homes where learning is respected and encouraged," explained Goldie Curtain. "These teachers are at a loss, completely frustrated, when it comes to dealing with children from homes where learning is not eagerly sought and where reinforcement from environment is nonexistent."[32] Regardless of the causes for students' lack of interest, Jeanne Tenenbaum declared, "I'm not sure why I should feel guilty when some students will have nothing to do with school."[33]

In their professional writing, teachers often went to great lengths to explain the cultural or attitudinal problems that they saw as fundamental to their students' lack of success in the classroom. The average teacher in 1961 was born in 1917; teachers born around this time spent their formative years in the profession when interculturalism shaped how teachers thought about and designed work around race in the classroom.[34] Evidence of this kind of liberal sentimentalism could still be found in some teachers' writing about teaching, especially in the ways in which they adapted arguments about the psychology of minority groups to the 1960s classroom. Elsa Voss, for example, explained to her colleagues that she saw the role of teachers such as herself in minority schools as "set[ting] the standard of 'middle-class' values" and that "the teacher in a culturally deprived area should consciously demonstrate the customs and niceties of our particular culture."[35] In addition to shaping the ways in which sentimentalist teachers' viewed their role in the classroom, race also shaped how they developed their curricula. From the point of view of Virginia Anderson, many teachers "lacking the understanding of why Puerto Ricans react in certain ways to our culture" were "partially responsible for the development of hatred or inferiority complexes in their students." In contrast, she had come to learn that there were two obstacles in working with Puerto Rican students. To address what she called "the *aburrido* complex,'" Anderson encouraged her colleagues to create lesson plans "varied and lively with many changes of technique in order to make up for their short attention span." To quell the "*mañana* complex," she suggested teachers "make advance preparations for homework assignments" rather than "trying to force the artificial pressures of our society on a relaxed and happy people."[36] The writings of Voss and Anderson reflect the ways in which educators familiar with intercultural rhetoric adapted a pedagogical theory designed largely for white students to teaching minority youth. The outcome was that the kinds of cultural and racial stereotypes teachers had once used to teach white students about people from other racial and cultural groups now served as stereotypes teachers imposed on their own students, guiding their expectations of these students just as many black parents and activists feared.

Such efforts came under fire by blacks and white alike. Board member Charles Savitsky argued that often times, psychological theories about the damaged black psyche were taken too far and created artificial tensions between white teachers and their black and Puerto Rican students. According to such theories, Savitsky argued, "the school is a mock arena of vast conflict where middle class teachers proceed to impose middle class culture and standards on the poor, defenseless child or adolescent, shattering his self-esteem." In this scenario, the student is "pushed around, rejected, wounded; and, in bitterness, he fights back; he is never offered an opportunity to define himself or develop his individuality." Such theories, Savitsky and other skeptical educators argued, pandered to liberal arguments that "strain[ed] to explain away behavior and class patterns, [and] rush[ed] to defend, to protect, and to increase permissiveness."[37] The low expectations that resulted from such liberal attitudes, in the end, were not that different from the expectations of conservative teachers who believed that minority students were unfit for the academic classroom. "Sentimentalists who slobber[ed] over 'the poor Negroes'" a city principal concurred, were as damaging as teachers who were outright racist.[38]

These sentimental attitudes were also difficult to maintain in a political climate in which white teachers were seen to be lagging in race relations rather than leaders of a race rights movement as they were during the war. As teachers openly spoke and wrote about the ways in which parents and students were to blame for black students' failures, they frequently assumed a defensive posture. The argument that students lacked the kind of home lives that prepared them to acquire or value an education was long-standing; but by the mid-1960s white teachers' anxieties became intertwined with their fear that growing black militancy had also come to influence their students' views. "All a teacher has to do is stand up to a [black] pupil," Harlem teacher Jim Haskins contended, and "he is in a lot of trouble."[39] If students had gained political power in the education system, so too had parents and community members. White teachers, Marjorie Drabkin explained, were now vulnerable to criticism in and outside of the classroom, because they were "attacked by civil rights groups . . . attacked by the community . . . and called inferior by their fellow Negro teachers."[40] At least "white parents do not complain that their children receive an inferior education," echoed William Isaacs. "It is inferior, but again, for the same reason—their children do not come to school with a learning readiness for education." In fact, white parents did organize around education issues in the 1960s, but they did so to fight school integration rather than to critique white teachers.[41] White teachers' assertions that black parents were more difficult to respond to than white parents reflected the specific nature of black parents' critiques as well as their increased organization and influence. By the decade's end, the *New York Times* reported, the UFT was "full of members . . . eager to be protected against the increasingly insistent 'Black Power' activists" from telling them "how to run their classrooms."[42]

Union policies focused on addressing the issues that unequally affected minority schools without addressing the critique of teachers' capabilities and attitudes. This left the UFT limited in what it could accomplish. The most notable plan the union put forth for improving minority schools was the More Effective School (MES) campaign, a program that began in select elementary schools after the 1964 school boycotts and reduced the teacher-to-student ratio by creating smaller classes and pairing teachers in individual classrooms. In its focus on team teaching and smaller classes, the MES program held the potential to reconceive the teachers' role in a radical way. But in reality, such a shift did not take place, as unionists themselves admitted, even as they backed the MES program. Edward Gottlieb reported that the smaller class sizes made school "easier for everybody" and that "discipline was easier." But he also confessed that "nothing special was happening in the classrooms," even if the program made school a more "livable place for teachers [and] children."[43] Such objectives did not meet the aspirations of parents who strove to make school more than livable but an institution in which their children could succeed rather than survive. MES, parents charged, represented a UFT "power-play to obtain a greater voice in school policy" rather than a real effort to improve their children's education.[44] As the program came under criticism from black activists, including some teachers, for lacking evaluation procedures and serving as "a haven for incompetent teachers," MES became an example of the very kind of tokenism that served to organize black parents in the first place.[45]

The MES schools' attention to discipline touched on one of the most charged and divisive issues between parents and teachers in the late 1960s, one that again focused attention on white teachers' attitudes. In 1967, the UFT sought to renegotiate its contract with the Board of Education, and, in so doing, asked for more funding for MES schools and for the right for all teachers to expel delinquent students from their classrooms and reassign them to special service schools. Unionists' claims that teachers were facing unruly and disruptive students were supported by evidence and a wealth of news reports. By 1966, 213 teachers had reported being assaulted by students in just three years.[46] The new teachers most likely to be teaching in minority schools described feeling unprepared to deal with the kinds of discipline problems they encountered in the classroom, in part because while they "were wondering how to handle a kid who called us a 'motherfucker,'" the professors who had trained them "were discussing model lessons for the Scarsdale system."[47] A variety of factors—including white teachers' beliefs about black students, the overcrowded and otherwise insufficient conditions of minority schools that could drive students to act out, the lack of resources low-income children had to psychological help—contributed to a disproportionate number of suspensions for black and Puerto Rican students. Consequently, the disruptive-child issue became a contest between teachers' expressed desire to create a productive and professional work environment and parents' and community members' contentions that their children were being made into scapegoats.

In March 1967, the UFT supported the mass resignation of eighty-five teachers from a junior high school in the east Bronx. While the teachers complained that cases of verbal and physical abuse went undisciplined, they generated little sympathy, especially in light of the union's larger, racially charged campaign to remove disruptive children from city classrooms. The UFT's attempt to use the resignations as a challenge to the Board, a *Times* editorial declared, exacerbated tensions between the school and the community and reflected how the "militancy of labor negotiations" prevented "the flow of highly skilled, specially selected and relevantly schooled manpower to cope with the educational ills of deprived and often understandably hostile children."[48] When the Board refused to meet the UFT demands over MES and student discipline in the fall of 1967, forty-six thousand unionists struck for two weeks; to parents, activists, and sympathetic teachers, the UFT sought the "power to act as policeman, judge, and jury over [black] children."[49] The union's actions and the antipathy they created anticipated many of the dynamics that would resurface during the larger and more extensive strikes the following year. Groups of black educators dissented from the UFT opinion, as they claimed that the union's actions threatened students' rights and failed to address the ways in which teachers had contributed to the problems they faced. "It is the miseducation and ineffectiveness of education for black youth," not their home lives, assistant principal Albert Vann argued, "that have driven youth to the brink of social revolution."[50] The UFT lost in their efforts with the Board, but the strike had lasting effects, including the reinforcement of an existing image of white teachers as racist and uncommitted to black children.

Both MES and what came to be called the "disruptive-child issue" gave weight to parents' and activists' fears that white teachers were creating a cycle of black student failure; this belief led them to address the ways in which black teachers could play a unique role in breaking the cycle. "If our community is rife with problems," activist and Columbia University professor Preston Wilcox explained, "it is important to understand that it has largely occurred because our community has been controlled by people other than us." Such control was in the hands of "educators who have successfully failed to educate Blacks and Puerto Ricans in the past—and are afraid that Blacks and Puerto Ricans will do a better job."[51] HARYOU also highlighted the need for black teachers. Annual Negro History celebrations may have offered inspiring one-time assemblies or pageants, the organization contended, "but the child is shown little of his own image in superior or even equal positions of status during the school year." HARYOU's observations that black children lacked positive role models in school extended both to the everyday curriculum and to those who taught it. Because they better understood black students, HARYOU found, black teachers were often "better able to control their classes" and were ultimately better teachers.[52]

But across the city, still fewer than 10 percent of teachers were black or Puerto Rican. In 1964, not a single one of the city's eighty-two high school principals was black.[53] Three years later, only four of the city's nine hundred principals were black."[54] In many ways, the sidelining of black professionals paralleled the marginalization of black students in the city's schools. Black parents and activists protested the Board's systemic failure to license black teachers through the use of oral exams that penalized against "Southern" accents. In 1964, black teachers within the UFT organized to support these protests when a group of forty-nine hundred teachers formed the Negro Teachers Association (NTA), an organization dedicated to examining the political issues surrounding the employment of black teachers and administrators and the treatment of black students. In the spring of 1967, the NTA also petitioned for a parent assistant to be placed in every elementary and junior high school classroom in the city's minority schools. The role of the parent assistant, the NTA explained, would be to relate the needs of the children to the teachers, to educate white teachers on the students' home environments, and to "orientate teacher[s] with [the] neighborhood and style of living of its inhabitants."[55] Changing its name to the African-American Teachers Association (ATA) and breaking off from the UFT later that year, the organization created further plans for training teachers to work in minority schools that included attending twice weekly classes on black history and culture provided by the ATA. In addition, teachers would be required to attend monthly weekend "sensitivity training" sessions and monthly seminars for teachers to "share their experiences" with ATA coordinators and other teachers.[56] All professional training, the ATA argued, needed to include cultural training, whether it was to be gained through life experience (for black teachers) or in-service workshops (for whites).

The NTA proposal for parent assistants and the ATA plan for sensitivity training lacked appeal for most teachers for multiple reasons beyond the additional demands it made on their time and energy. The most important of these reasons was what the plans suggested about white teachers' inabilities to comprehend the lives of their students. In contrast to earlier multicultural initiatives such as interculturalism, which had been designed and implemented by white educators and experts, the NTA and ATA were now asking for black parents and teachers to train white teachers about minority students. This offended many white teachers who, if they expressed a sense of cultural division with their students, did not see themselves as deficient or race as relevant to professionalism.

The UFT also rejected the NTA's accusation that the union divided teachers along race lines by failing to investigate "the legitimate demands of black teachers."[57] But it did develop its own strategy for addressing the historic underrepresentation of black teachers, a problem that evoked a greater sense of tension than ever before. To do so, it focused on a program to recruit black teachers from across the country, as a means to both integrate "the teachers and supervisors that comprise the instructional staff" and to offer minority students more role models. The union favored this plan because it "permit[ted] the recruitment of teachers who are experienced and more mature," raising "teacher selection standards while promoting staff integration."[58] Given the academic statistics of minority students in New York City, turning to teachers from outside the city's school system promised to offer a necessary, higher quality pool of applicants. The program also allowed the UFT to argue for specific attention to be paid to hiring black teachers and improving race relations without sacrificing the union's commitment to merit-based professionalism.

But even this plan did not sit well with some members, and response to it reflected the more conservative membership that had come to join the union over the decade. The group Solidarity, calling itself the "only organized group of UFT members that believes in a school integration policy that do[es] not violate the professional rights of any teacher," feared that the call for more black teachers and principals threatened the Board's merit system and, more specifically, its members' own success in the system. Opposed to what it saw as the "slander [of] every teacher in a special service school," Solidarity also opposed "Board of Education coaching courses" designed to enable "Negro teachers [to] pass future tests for assistant principal and department chairman."[59] Solidarity members expressed an especially deep-seated commitment to a view most UFT members shared, that professionalism could not be divorced from issues of work climate and advancement, both of which were competitive ventures in the education bureaucracy.

Since World War II, the Guild and UFT had approached issues of race equity and education by walking a middle line of advocating for equal rights without making unpopular demands on their members. Hence, the unions had created proposals for integration without transferring white teachers to black schools, developed alternative school programs without radically revising the system, and focused on student discipline without confronting minority students' systematic failure in the schools. These efforts stood between conflicting political sentiments in the 1960s, neither of which would find the current program satisfactory. On one hand, black parents and education activists, and some teachers, pushed for more to be done and for changes that were not just superficial but addressed the fundamental belief systems that they saw harming minority children. Because of the disruptive-child issues and the UFT's lukewarm support of many of their goals, minority parents and community groups came to see the union as upholding these belief systems. On the other hand, conservative teachers were now coming to critique UFT policies as conflicting with teachers' interests. By the late 1960s, the union's hand was forced; rather than continuing to walk a middle line, the UFT would need to define its commitment to minority students and to teachers.

An Educator's Commitment

Despite what was taking place in city schools, in the years leading up to Ocean Hill-Brownsville, the UFT made some of its most important contributions to the civil rights movement. In the past, unions had served as places where teachers could involve themselves in local civil rights projects. In the 1960s, the UFT served as a vehicle for teachers to take a part in a national movement. These contributions took multiple forms, from financial aid to volunteerism. In 1963, the union sent four busloads of teachers to the march on Washington and staffed freedom schools in Prince Edward County, Maryland. Charles Cogen served on President Kennedy's advisory group on education and civil rights. Cogen and Albert Shanker both developed relationships with Martin Luther King, and the civil rights leader spoke at a UFT function in 1963. In 1965, the union raised enough funds to purchase two station wagons for King's voter registration drive.

But no project was more important, both in national eyes and in terms of its eventual consequence within the union, than the UFT's involvement in the Mississippi freedom schools in 1964. That spring Cogen and the union's highest ranking black officer, Richard Parrish, had recruited thirty-six New York City teachers to spend their summer working in the Mississippi freedom schools. Together, Cogen and Parrish had convinced the American Federation of Teachers to recruit teachers from across the country to work in the schools as well. The New York City contingent, comprising almost half of all unionized teachers participating in the freedom schools, was dispatched for its assignments in July 1964, just days after the well-publicized disappearance of James Cheney, Andrew Goodman, and Michael Schwerner in Philadelphia, Mississippi. Older, more professional, and less wealthy than the white college students who made up most of the Freedom Summer volunteer ranks, UFT members brought professional training and expertise to the schools that many other participants lacked.

As with interculturalism, the UFT involvement in the freedom schools was genuinely exciting to its participants. Both volunteers and teachers who donated funds to the cause argued that getting involved in social movements was not extrinsic to the job but a vital part of it because "teachers and their union, by virtue of their profession and educational backgrounds, have no other choice but to be social-minded" and "whether the human race will survive is surely as important as getting 'the best contract in the U.S.'"[60] Mississippi became symbolic of the union's potential to create social change because it represented an opportunity in which, in the words of Cogen and Parrish, the UFT could "provid[e] skilled personnel to function in an area of unparalleled need, and testif[y] to the devotion of American teachers to the cause of human rights."[61] Even if only a relative handful of educators participated in the freedom schools, their efforts allowed a select group of liberal city teachers to represent unionists' unique contribution to the 1960s civil rights movement.

The politics and expectations of student-teacher interactions in freedom school classrooms were far removed from New York City classrooms but nevertheless highlighted UFT members' special role in the project. The curriculum as handed down by the project organizers in Mississippi was part academics and part activism, with an emphasis on leadership development, organizational skills, and a complete knowledge of black history.[62] Although black history month celebrations came under criticism by HARYOU and others, Teachers Union members had developed a national reputation for their work on black history curricula in the 1950s, including writing and publishing lesson plans, protesting biased textbooks, and compiling lists of suggested readings for all teachers to use. Their progress in the field was affirmed by the hiring of former New York City teacher Noel Day to write the black history curricula for the freedom schools.[63]

But not all went smoothly in Mississippi, and the schisms that developed echoed divisions that were growing between the UFT and civil rights activists at home. UFT volunteer Deborah Flynn had loaned a car to another volunteer, who in turned loaned the car to an unlicensed local youth. The young driver crashed the car, killing one volunteer and seriously injuring another person—a chain of events that earned Flynn an indictment. That fall, Albert Shanker, still in his first months as president of the UFT, wanted to use funds the union raised for the Mississippi project to pay for Flynn's legal defense. This brought a quick response from Liz Fusco, the coordinator of the Council of Federated Organizations (COFO), which, along with the Student Nonviolent Coordinating Committee, organized Freedom Summer. In a pointed letter in February 1965, Fusco asked Shanker whether his commitment to the project "[went] beyond commitment to the subsistence of UFT teachers." In her eyes, in addition to the union's self-interest, Shanker's desire to redirect funds raised for Mississippi schools to insulate one New York City teacher indicated that teachers might not be positioned to assess what real civil rights activism entailed. To Fusco, COFO's responsibility was clearly to the poor blacks of rural Mississippi, not to middle-class white teachers in New York City, and the UFT's suggestion that it might redirect its contributions challenged both the organizational structure and the very spirit and culture of the freedom school project. The incident had revealed to Fusco "late . . . but perhaps not too late" that political movements "must arise from people and that people with only a summer's, only an educator's commitment tend to hinder that fact by the very fact of their coming to 'teach Freedom School.'"[64] Underneath Fusco's desire for Southern activists to retain control over the project then was a question of definition. UFT teachers, she charged, might play activists, but at the end of the day, they were driven by a professional culture that put their own needs before those they served.[65]

Fusco's claims that an "educator's commitment" was fundamentally different than the commitment of local community members both anticipated community control activists' critiques and signaled a problem of definition that UFT members were already beginning to confront from outside the union and within, from teachers both liberal and conservative. What was an "educator's commitment" and how were teachers to balance between serving others and attending to their own interests? For some New York City teachers who volunteered in the freedom schools, such as Sandra Adickes and Norma Becker, the project was an entry into a longer teaching career dedicated to political activism and social justice. Adickes filed a suit against a Hattiesburg lunch counter that refused to serve her because she brought six of her students. In 1970, the case appeared before the Supreme Court. Becker founded the Teachers' Committee against the War in Vietnam in 1965 and became a leader of the New Caucus of the UFT, formed in 1968 to counterprotest the strikes in Ocean Hill-Brownsville. Teachers like Adickes and Becker served as leaders in the UFT's civil rights projects and saw no distinction between being an effective teacher and being a committed civil rights activist. Liberal teachers who participated in the projects and some who did not pushed the union to do more. "Isn't it easy to send station wagons to Selma?" wrote Richard Rampell to Shanker in

1965. "How about sending good teachers to the ghetto?"[66] Rampell exposed the ways in which it was, in fact, easier for the union to participate in Southern civil rights projects than in local ones. Improving schools in the ghetto would require the effort of more than just forty teachers, and such teachers historically had proved difficult to find.

While most liberal teachers supported the UFT's civil rights efforts, conservative teachers voiced concern that the union was doing too much. By the fall of 1965, after twenty teachers had participated in the 1965 Mississippi freedom schools and the union had contributed $40,000 to Martin Luther King's voter registration drive, members were forthright in their criticisms. In the pages of the union press, conservative teachers questioned the motives of their liberal brethren and saw the UFT involvement in freedom schools as a distraction from the real issues that teacher unions were responsible for: the improvement of working conditions and teachers' agency in the school bureaucracy. To these teachers, an educator's commitment was distinct from social justice work. "I cannot remain silent," protested Joseph Hassid. The union newspaper had "taken on the overtones of a civil rights organization newspaper," he contended, but "the U.F.T. was formed to represent teachers in N.Y.C. on teacher issues in N.Y.C., not . . . Mississippi." Hassid objected to what he saw as the union's distraction from the issues that mattered most to teachers and bid the union to remember that "teachers should speak for teachers" not for civil rights organizations or causes, abroad or at home.[67] Like Hassid, other members found that they could not remain silent, and they wrote to the United Teacher about the ways in which the union's participation in civil rights campaigns compromised its energies and attention and offended its members' sensibilities. Such offense stemmed from the fact that the UFT did not consult with its membership before "shell[ing] out" money to "'rabble-rousing' groups."[68] "I do not want anyone to speak for me on matters on social conscious [sic]," warned member Jacob Shushuk. "If I wish to support the Civil Rights movement, I can join the NAACP or CORE."[69] In addition to embracing conservative political positions on race reform, such unionists also reflected an anxiety that in expanding its work beyond the most traditional territory of teacher unions, the UFT was sacrificing teachers' interests and most commonly shared concerns. Again and again, conservative teachers, many of whom identified as newer members, argued that allegiance to political movements distracted from the real issues on the table and, at the same time, threatened to divide teachers. These arguments were made also by UFT local chapters, such as that of George Washington High School, which voted 62–7 in 1966 against any endorsement of "national and international political and foreign affairs not directly related to the UFT as a teachers' union." Instead, the chapter advocated that "such political activity and partisanship" be "subordinated to the more immediate, local tasks of teacher welfare."[70]

In addition to communicating teachers' views of particular social issues, the conservative response to the UFT's civil rights projects also may have reflected anxieties about the divisions between teachers on race issues at home. In April 1965, the Board of Education again issued an intention to a begin a program of teacher transfers, one that the UFT immediately responded to as a "cruel hoax" that worked to convince parents that "inferior education in ghetto schools is to be blamed on teachers rather than on large classes, dilapidated buildings, short-time instruction, inadequate textbooks and supplies and failure to provide adequate resources for children with special problems." Shanker assured his chapter chairs that it was unrealistic for "the Board [to] expect any teacher to accept assignment in these schools knowing they will be blamed for conditions beyond their control . . . [and] for [the Board's] own negligence."[71] Shanker's censure of the plan earned the praises of teachers who felt that the Board, along with parents, had long misrepresented their work conditions and their abilities. Teachers like Clara Isaacs thanked Shanker for his "defense of teachers in the ghetto schools"; as with other teachers, Shanker's call for "rallies, meetings, and demonstrations" in response to the Board's plan made her "proud [to be] a member of the U.F.T."[72] To Isaacs, the union was defending teachers in a situation in which they "ha[d] been treated with contempt" and disregard for their point of view.[73]

Many teachers' responses this time around were focused on what the transfer plan implied about the quality of teachers in minority schools. Because so many more white teachers were working in minority schools in 1965 than even a decade prior, the transfer issue was less important for where it threatened to assign them as for what it said about their work. "The truth is that the atmosphere in these schools is not conducive to 'excellence of instruction,'" contended junior high school teacher Nicholas Neuhas, responding to just this concern. As with other teachers, Neuhas saw the challenge of teaching in minority schools as an issue both of basic resources and of educational values. "The community as a whole does not lend much help to teachers in the form of granting either prestige, authority, or respect, nor does it seem to show much concern."[74] Marjorie Drabkin considered the "senseless attacks" on teachers in minority schools from a different perspective. While it was common knowledge that teachers who scored well on their teaching examinations were given appointments in white, middle-class schools, Drabkin explained, it was frequently forgotten that many teachers with high scores chose to teach in minority schools, "either because they were substitutes there, or were persuaded to accept the challenge offered by principals who pursued them."[75]

But the expanded number of teachers in minority schools had another surprising and important effect on the teacher transfer issue: a greater number of teachers expressing their favor for transfers than in the past. In short, the growing percentage of minority schools in the city gave teachers incentive to improve such schools if they also wanted to improve their work conditions. As a result, unlike in the previous decade when the transfer issue drew teachers to unions, it now loomed, in the words of one unionist, as "an excellent device to splinter the union" if UFT leadership was not "forthright in expressing the union's opposition to the rotation."[76] For some teachers, a commitment to improving minority schools clearly stemmed from liberal political beliefs and an interest in social justice. The union's public commitment to "suppor[t] the quest for excellence in all our schools," wrote a junior high school teacher to Shanker, meant "it should be ready to negotiate an equitable system of staff rotation."[77] Sixty-six teachers at another minority school reminded Shanker that "[s]tudents in disadvantaged schools, too, demand experience in their fight for equal education" and implored him not to turn "a professional union into a protective one."[78] Such teachers reflected an awareness of a conservative political strain in the union that fought teacher transfers and framed beliefs about minority students as arguments about professionalism. Still others reflected the ways in which teachers in minority schools lost out in the union's lack of commitment to improving them. The faculty of a Harlem elementary school explained, "Our school is housed in a beautiful new building. We have considerably more supplies and more help than before. And yet, our problems persist! Much more than half of our staff is completely inexperienced!"[79] The severe imbalance between experienced and novice teachers in minority schools was not just a problem for students and parents, this group of teachers pointed out, but for faculty as well. Conservative-driven union policy, they suggested, risked the professional welfare of its own members.

While white unionists debated about the nature of teachers' commitment to civil rights, black educators, too, experienced division in mediating their commitment to civil rights and to teacher unionism. By mid decade, black teachers of a range of political persuasions found themselves at the intersection of a more radical black rights movement and more militant unionist ideologies. Layle Lane, former Guild member and civil rights activist, wrote to the UFT newspaper that she was sorry she was now long retired and not able to participate in the Ocean Hill-Brownsville strikes. "It's unfortunate that the adherents of 'Black Power' are getting support . . . that has only increased their intransigence," Lane lamented to her UFT brethren. For teachers such as herself, who had long fought for recognition of their "ability, integrity, and vision," regardless of race, the new emphasis on color could only be seen as a disastrous turn.[80] Kenneth Clark, like Lane, belonged to an earlier generation of activists, one devoted to integration and one that believed that a merito-cratic approach to professionalism promised the most effective way to equal-ize white and black teachers. Calling black power "a bitter retreat" from the principles of integration, Clark admitted that the goals of blacks and whites "fight[ing] the formidable forces of irrationality and immortality as allies" just might not be an idea "consistent with the passions of our times."[81]

Black teachers who shared Lane's and Clark's increasingly outdated views faced a new sense of criticism from activists and radical teachers who accused them of distancing themselves from the black community. "Black teachers must begin to identify with and speak the language of the black community," contended principal Leslie Campbell in 1967. They must "protect black chil-dren against educational injustice and systematic genocide" without bringing their leadership and skills "to the community like a 'stranger bearing gifts'" but instead should "join in and work with the community."[82] To be a success-ful teacher, in this view, was to work for community improvement, but this ap-proach toward defining an educator's commitment put black teachers in a dif-ficult situation. It made their racial identity a professional prerequisite as well as a new kind of burden in demanding more of them. Albert Vann, who with Campbell had cofounded the ATA, reported receiving complaints from black teachers who were threatened or harassed by their principals for work that appeared to overstep the classroom's boundaries. "Teachers who seek to co-operate with parents and the community to help develop better community re-lations," Vann reported, "become the victims of the education establishment. These teachers are being threatened with transfers, unfair class placement, isolation from fellow workers, and unsatisfactory ratings."[83] To educators like Vann and members of the ATA, the UFT not only left black teachers vulnerable to these kinds of penalties but endorsed them.

Still, color-blind theories of meritocracy became harder for black teach-ers to maintain, especially as they witnessed more overt hostility within the union toward linking race and professionalism. UFT treasurer Richard Par-rish remained committed to the union even as he saw the events leading up to the strikes as "the frustration of black people over some thirty or forty years brought to the fore." In contrast to Vann's and Campbell's conclusions, for Parrish, it was precisely because of the impossibility to distinguish between the work of teaching and the struggle for race equity that he urged black teach-ers to remain members of the UFT in the months leading up to the strikes and to fight for better education for minority students from within rather than without. Increasingly, however, he found his own views at odds with the UFT's policies and attitudes in addressing race issues. In 1963, Parrish had helped to form the UFT Committee on African-American history in response to the underrepresentation of black Americans and their achievements in the curriculum. In June 1968, the committee—composed of an equal number of black and white teachers—wanted to organize a regional conference on racism in education that would span topics from integrating black studies into the science and mathematics classrooms to discussions of the community control movement. But the UFT Administrative Committee registered hesitations that "the conference would be overrun by black militants and would embarrass the union" and called for the committee to develop a "tighter structure so teachers would be in control." In addition, Committee on African-American history leaders Joyce Haynes and Parrish questioned the union leadership's barring of black radicals in the new social studies curriculum and preference to include only certain types of black heroes and achievements, like Martin Luther King and Thurgood Marshall, both of whom had befriended the union in the past.[84] Haynes and Parrish saw their efforts rebuffed out of the union's fears of certain types of black activism that union leadership—and much of the membership—saw as incompatible with professionalism.

The strikes in Ocean Hill-Brownsville pushed Parrish to do something more radical and to create a Black Caucus within the UFT. His mission was to expose the hypocrisy of an organization that only four years earlier had supported Mississippi freedom schools but was now "unwilling to initiate experimental programs in disadvantaged schools in Ocean Hill-Brownsville or Harlem." Rather than disbanding from the UFT, Parrish urged black teachers to stay involved and to bring the union "in pace with the modern civil rights movement" not just in its strategies but also in its objectives. To accomplish this, Parrish argued, the UFT would have to "give community control not only within the schools, but within its own institutions."[85] To fight community control, Parrish argued, was to fight the democratic principle at the very core of civil rights movements and of unionism. Unionist Leo Shapiro wrote to the *United Teacher* to protest the "sad irony" that Parrish, who had "demonstrated for years that his rationality, logic, and ability, are not based on his skin color," now "[found] it necessary to introduce the factor of skin color into the reasoning process."[86] Even if insecurity in the face of a "pluralistic and alienated society," caused people to join groups like "the Black Caucus, the Knights of Columbus, [and] the Emerald Society," Rod MacKenzie wrote, "I don't think we should encourage it in the UFT."[87] MacKenzie's implication that black Americans were just like ethnic Americans, such as the Irish who might have joined the Emerald Society, sounded a popular conservative point of view in American thought that sought to prevent blacks from receiving special privileges; this line of thought proved to be popular in the UFT as well. Positions like Shapiro's and MacKenzie's left little room for a black teacher to see his commitment to civil rights issues as unique and necessary and, at the same time, to remain a dedicated member of the union.

Throughout the 1960s, the debates and disagreements over an educator's commitment to her students and union only increased as the UFT attracted more teachers to its ranks. But while many of the debates took place in the union newspapers and in the course of union activities, they were no secret. In September 1967, *New York Times* education reporter Fred Hechinger wrote that "the UFT faces new issues of divisiveness of its own members," and "for racial reasons of their own or out of sympathy with the arguments of minority parents, may break ranks." Such divisiveness, he added, "could be a test of union solidarity."[88] The threat of such divisions became all the more important as the union's power and influence grew and as unionized teachers stood at the center of an embroiled battle about teachers' commitment to minority students. The strikes of 1968 deepened these divisions and, at the same time, called for a union strategy that would make them less visible.

Crafting Solidarity in Ocean Hill-Brownsville

By the second half of the decade, black Americans across the urban North might have agreed with the assessment that "the majority of [white] educators . . . have stood aside and watched with little interest as civil rights and other civic groups made futile demands and proposals to counter *de facto* patterns of segregation."[89] To be certain, the UFT did not accomplish what black activists and even some of its own members desired. But, as both liberal and conservative members' writings reflect, the union had not been watching the civil rights movement passively or without interest. Nationally, 80 percent of all schools days that had been lost to strikes since 1940 had occurred in the 1967–68 academic year.[90] Accounting for the increased number of strikes and the growing number of teachers who participated in strikes late in the decade, one unionist explained that "[t]eachers have been afraid of committing illegal acts, and that is why the civil rights movement has been so important." The civil rights movement, the unionist argued, brought "legitimacy to breaking the law when the law is immoral."[91] The Ocean Hill-Brownsville strikes and coordinating demonstrations served as the greatest example of how the civil rights movement had come to impact a growing teachers' rights movement. From their observations of civil rights demonstrations, and some unionists' participation in them, union leaders and membership alike recognized the ways in which the movement offered them ideas and strategies that could be adapted to their own professional cause.

By the mid-1960s, it was clear that teachers' growing commitment to unionism could not be divorced from the larger social politics of the time, especially the changes in the black civil rights movement. A 1967 *New York Times* report explained that just as "Black nationalists no longer depend on the white man . . . militant teachers believe that they should no longer rely on school boards or principals but should have a major voice in policymaking." This belief was just one sign of how "in recent years many teachers have become obsessed with their 'powerlessness,' just as many Negroes now are."[92] Although the spirit of this observation was true, the union was careful to avoid labeling itself as militant in its quest for teachers' rights; the phrase "teacher power" would become popular in the 1970s, but it was not a phrase the union embraced in the 1960s. Rather, union leadership worked to characterize black power activists as "militants" and "extremists" and to distinguish their "vigilantism" from the efforts of integrationists and union allies, including the late Martin Luther King and labor leader Bayard Rustin, who backed the UFT throughout the strikes. Like those integrationists, Shanker insisted, teachers were a newly organized group, one that had "only recently struggled for a voice" and therefore "support[ed] others in this struggle."[93]

The arguments and strategies of the 1950s and early 1960s civil rights movement, including those of King and Rustin, appealed to many unionists' desire for moderation in civil rights demands and strategies. Such moderation also offered a model for standardizing and professionalizing the image a social movement could offer to the public. Unionists urged President Albert Shanker to consider forbidding all but UFT-approved signs at union rallies and, "[just] as civil rights organizations brief[ed] demonstrators on dress and decorum," to also brief teachers on what to wear. Such tactics, unionists such as Ruth Isquith warned, would prevent the kind of "ugly picture on the front page of the *New York Times* and the accompanying barbed article" that tended to appear whenever teachers protested. Just as nonviolence worked in civil rights activists' favor, unionists realized that the public perception of themselves as "dignified, learned, and rather conservative" was a useful one for creating empathy and support for their cause.[94] Closely tied to these professional images was the role of the press in disseminating them. Even before the 1968 strikes, the UFT had begun to explore the possibility of using the press to assuage tensions between teacher unionists and black New Yorkers. Ted Bleecker, the editor of the *United Teacher*, the UFT's newspaper, in 1966 suggested that Shanker explore writing a Sunday *New York Times* supplement to address teachers' image in public culture. In a piece that might be titled, "UFT Involvement in the Community," Bleecker recommended, Shanker could list all of the union's contributions to the black civil rights movement, including their participation in the freedom schools and their support of school boycotts in the South.[95] Publishing these supplements in local editions of the newspaper would allow the union to clarify policy, rally enthusiasm for its goals, and remind black readers of the ways in which their two movements were complementary.

Rhetorically, the most important way in which unionists were influenced by the civil rights movement was in their conceptualization and framing of the events at the center of the strikes as a fight against injustice and for human rights. While the Ocean Hill-Brownsville community control board only had the power to transfer the nineteen educators out of their district and into another, the UFT continually referred to the events as a firing. "Teachers, like any other jobholder, must be assured of job security and union rights," the UFT claimed in a $200,000 series of media advertisements geared toward gaining public support. "How would you react if you could be fired or removed from your job or forced to transfer to another section without any charges or any procedure for hearing your objections?"[96] The protection the union sought was more than a contractual procedure but an "irreducible measure of human dignity," the union asserted, one that was "almost universally recognized wherever people are employed under civilized conditions."[97] The efforts of the community control board, it followed, were uncivilized and did not follow basic, democratic codes of conduct, either in their policies or in their actions. "Whether verbal or physical, subtle or crude," the UFT contended, "harassment and intimidation of teachers cannot be tolerated."[98] The "freedom from harassment, intimidation, and violent assault on the job," it further reminded city residents, "are not subtle and disputable rights. They are elementary."[99] In configuring themselves as victims of militants' "terror," unionists also made themselves into heroes, resisting "submission to vigilantism" in order to protect the further terrorization of school boards, parent groups, and children. In all of these arguments, the union invoked a rhetoric of human rights as well as specific images of terror, especially of incidents in the South, that had pushed even moderate white Americans to support black civil rights.

These calls for teachers' rights antagonized black New Yorkers, both because they confused or obscured several issues at the heart of the strikes and because they drew comparisons to civil rights violations that Ocean Hill-Brownsville residents saw themselves still battling. In addition, the union's call for due process and constitutional rights often oversimplified more than clarified the issues at hand. In fact, the union's contract failed to outline any process or procedures for responding to a community's desire that a teacher be transferred.[100] Thus, the union's argument that its members' due process rights were violated was more complicated, and fundamentally less true, than black Americans' arguments that laws were applied differently for whites and blacks. In addition, no one on the Ocean Hill-Brownsville board, or in the schools, argued that the teachers in question were ineffective or incompetent in the classroom. Rather, the community control board's objection was to their frequent leadership roles in the UFT and their political beliefs about community control and teacher professionalism, something that had become indistinguishable from teacher quality for many blacks. While the union might have highlighted these distinctions more, it instead reduced philosophical arguments to one about process. In avoiding many of the most important disagreements at hand, the UFT solidified and deepened a fracture between white teachers and black parents. By the time the strikes began, unionists and black activists had exchanged their shared critiques of racist Board of Education policies for accusations of each other. In losing this common ground, they also obscured many of the most tangible and empirical factors in school inequity, from school funding to racial segregation to teacher assignments. While these factors had certainly not proved easy to remedy in the past, they were nevertheless easier to monitor and assess than teachers' or parents' attitudes and beliefs.

Strategically, the UFT also borrowed from 1960s-style civil rights activism; the strikes were often crafted to invoke scenes with which news readers would have been familiar. Throughout the strikes, the UFT and its supporters organized demonstrations to capture media attention for their cause and to present a unified message to the public. A rally at city hall in September was attended by fifteen thousand people. The following month, an estimated seventy-five thousand unionists and supporters marched on city hall. The *New York Times* quoted a police officer as saying he had "never seen anything like it"; an attendee described the event as "the largest civil rights demonstration since the March on Washington." In contrast, the largest procommunity control demonstrations were attended by approximately six thousand participants.[101] The UFT's demonstrations and its members' commentaries on them were constructed to parallel teachers' efforts with black civil rights demonstrations, gain support for their cause, and mask the political differences that existed among the membership, including in its responses to the strikes themselves. In addition, following both the smaller 1967 strikes over MES and the disruptive-child issue and the 1968 strikes, Shanker was ordered to serve a fifteen-day jail sentence. While these jailings echoed the experiences of King and many others in the civil rights movement, Shanker argued that they also put forth a lesson that "the image of the good old dedicated teacher who gets kicked around and, once a year, on Teacher Recognition Day, is handed a flower for his lapel" had come to an end.[102]

Throughout the strikes then, unionists had to appear assertive enough to dismantle the image of the helpless, ineffectual teacher while not so defiant as to lose public support. They did this by positioning their own rights demonstrations against those of black parents and activists, whom they hoped to portray as chaotic and possibly dangerous. In November 1968, at the end of the UFT's third strike, a group of forty parents and nonunionized teachers, including Albert Vann and Leslie Campbell, tried to bar the reentry of eight union teachers back into J.H.S. 271, the school where the controversy first began. One of those unionists was Fred Nauman, the most recognized of the original nineteen teachers to receive a transfer notice and, in the words of Ocean Hill-Brownsville administrator Rhody McCoy, "a bad symbol for [the] community." The next day, the front page of the *New York Times* featured a photograph of the disruptive parents and of even more police, who were ordered to arrest the parents if they did not back away.[103]

In contrast to the image of the school's parents and other similar events that occurred across the city, the UFT created its own media images, including one of individual UFT teachers escorted by forty police officers back into a school in East Harlem in early December. In reality, the police escort was just a media event; the school was empty. Although the strikes had ended, parents continued to boycott the school and keep their children from attending because of several controversial UFT teachers employed at the school. Even so, the photographs, also featured on the front page of the *Times*, contrasted with earlier pictures of disorderly parents and invoked some of the most famous images to come out of the civil rights movement, including the use of National Guard troops in the 1957 integration of Little Rock's Central High.[104] The parallels between the photographs of white teachers and seminal civil rights events boosted teachers' positioning of themselves as victims and served to remind newspaper readers that black students and community members were not the only people in need of protecting their rights.

But these tactics did not sit well with all members, including some who had participated in the strikes. While "due process for teachers can and should be defended by trade union methods," argued a group of teachers at one of the city's elementary schools, "calling upon the Board of Education and the Mayor to use the police does not seem to us an acceptable trade union policy."[105] Multiple groups of organized teachers, many of whom remained UFT members, actively protested the UFT's actions. The New Caucus, led by Norma Becker, argued that the UFT ignored the legitimate goals of minority parents and community activists. The union may have been "rightly for due process for teachers," the caucus argued, but it ignored "due process for children in its racist demand for the contractual right to eliminate the 'disruptive child' from the classroom."[106] Nonstriking teachers, the majority of whom were white, reported having their time cards stolen, their names and phone numbers being distributed among picketing teachers, and death threats.[107] Jewish Teachers for Community Control, a group of five hundred that included former Teachers Unionists, charged Shanker and members with exaggerating claims that black community control activists were spreading anti-Semitic propaganda and questioned whether some of the literature was not being leaked by the UFT itself.[108] Yet all of these groups usually found themselves relegated to the editorial pages of the *Times* while the UFT made front-page news.

Despite its efforts, the UFT also drew criticism from city residents who saw the union's response as disproportionate to its problems, even if they also feared black activism. Shanker's focus on the transferred teachers, one city resident argued, was just "a lever to insure the permanent defeat of decentralization."[109] This defeat, another echoed, constituted a "fight against equality for the long-suffering black population of our city," situating one rights battle against another.[110] Even white New Yorkers who originally empathized with the UFT's aversion to community control were made uncomfortable by the strikes. "To force the closing of one school," one local editorial commented, "the union has struck 800 schools. . . . To get rid of seven principals" it organized "50,000 teachers."[111] More than the ethical questions that the strikes begged about race politics, however, readers disputed the new brand of unionism that the UFT represented; rather than the "dignified" and "conservative" professionals they used to be, teachers now actively sought out disorder and rebellion for their own gain. "Mr. Shanker would do well to remember he is not striking a button factory," advised one parent, "[but] an essential public service."[112] The result of teacher unions that operated like trade unions in the minds of many readers was simply "disruption, intimidation, and insubordination" and the deprivation of "a huge urban population of . . . services they [paid] taxes" to support.[113]

But even with this widespread public skepticism, the union's efforts proved successful. When the strikes ended in November 1968, the Ocean Hill-Brownsville board was left under the control of a state trustee. When members of the board went to court to protest, the presiding judge ruled that community control boards were "no more than an unofficial body of citizen advisors without power to transfer and suspend."[114] In April 1969, facing pressure from the UFT, the New York State legislature passed a decentralization law that prohibited teacher transfers by local school boards and reorganized the city's community control districts into thirty larger school districts, diluting the power of neighborhood boards like those in Ocean Hill-Brownsville. The same year, the UFT won an effort with the Board of Education to have union dues collected from all teachers' paychecks, union members or not.[115] The policy sent a powerful message about the unmatched authority of the union to define the profession and what would constitute professional issues. Black city residents received this message clearly; in 1970, only 4 percent of Ocean Hill-Brownsville residents voted in the local school board elections, down from 25 percent in 1967.[116] While the UFT greatly increased its number of minority members when it allowed paraprofessionals—teacher assistants—to join the union in 1969, it did little to increase the percentage of black and Latino teachers. By the mid-1970s, city schools looked much as they had a decade earlier.

In many ways, the strikes successfully distracted teachers from the issue of rethinking their relationship and commitment to black students, something that the union had construed as submission to activists' demands. Even radical teachers, Ted Gold, leader of the small group Teachers for a Democratic Society, explained in 1968, had failed to "redefine their jobs" in the way that black activists and white supporters had hoped for. The obstacle to doing so, Gold argued, was the "'professionalism' which causes teachers to misidentify the source of their own oppression." The key to improving teachers' work, for Gold and many activists, was to change the state of teacher-student relationships, but so much of the discourse about professionalism in the union positioned students, especially minority students, as oppressive in their directing of teachers' energies away from academic matters and toward discipline issues. This then prevented teachers from acting on their professional training and expertise. Instead, Gold contended, the real source of teachers' oppression was the belief that "when a teacher goes into a classroom and closes the door behind him, what goes on in the room is up to him." This attitude left teachers feeling miserable and responsible for "the fault of the ways the whole education system is set up."[117] Gold claimed that if teachers went more public with their work, if they tried to work with the communities they served rather than in isolation from them, they would ultimately be able to overcome the very obstacles that they had been lamenting within their professional writing and the union. But the union's public demonstrations for their rights had been for the right to teach free from the influence of black parents and interested community members.

Instead of opening classroom doors, the post-1968 union sought to further craft and standardize the public image of the unionized teacher. The public relations strategies the union had once borrowed from the civil rights movement to professionalize its public image had been so manipulated into mechanisms of self-protection that they had lost any of their original political significance. Professional teachers, UFT leadership contested, were unionized teachers and they were of one mind. Many ordinary unionists reflected the same point of view as they criticized strikebreakers and counterprotesters in the union press. To Susan Mandel, teachers who objected to the strike appeared to think only of "their own personal, immediate wants" rather than "thinking of themselves as a professional group."[118] In contrast to the kinds of economic "personal wants" that might have compelled workers to serve as strikebreakers or scabs in more traditional labor strikes, the educators who tried to break the Ocean Hill-Brownsville strikes were driven by political conviction. This was particularly problematic to some unionists because such convictions caused some members to "execute[e] union busting maneuvers with unbelievable enthusiasm."[119] Mandel and other unionists who wrote to share similar points of view suggested that professionalism and political beliefs were incompatible, at least when one's politics differed from the union majority's point of view.

This belief was one that much of the UFT leadership shared and acted upon in the name of union solidarity. In 1969, for example, the Committee of African-American History finally published its lesson plans, something they had spent two years researching, writing, and revising. When it came time for publication, however, the individual names of the committee members were omitted, and the lesson plans were published with the UFT listed as author and publisher. Committee chairs Richard Parrish and Joyce Haynes argued that this policy departed from typical procedures for union publications, and they contested the fact that a follow-up to the original plans was in progress and none of the original committee members had been consulted. The real issue, Haynes argued, was that "the UFT felt threatened" and that listing "the names of the committee members might prove an embarrassment" since so many of them had spoken out against the strikes.[120] The publication of the plans, an important step in the union's attempt to repair its image on race issues, also reflected the importance of its new emphasis on professional solidarity. The retribution against the African-American History Committee—and other teacher groups in similar positions—highlighted the costs of this solidarity to many teachers.

Before the strikes had ended, activists, unionists, journalists, and academics began to write about and interpret the events, not just in terms of what they meant to the city and the nation at the time, but in terms of the meaning they would hold for future generations and for a history of civil rights battles over education. Ocean Hill-Brownsville, chief Times education reporter Fred Hechinger summarized, had constituted an urban conflict of "teacher power versus community power," one that by the following year was spreading to other big cities across the nation.[121] Throughout the strikes, Hechinger and the Times, generally considered the most sympathetic to the union of the city's newspapers, portrayed the UFT's tactics as increasingly coercive, where every union demand served as "the equivalent of an unconditional surrender" and each strike a "power play" that "left one million children victims."[122] Shanker was treated equally unfavorably by the *Times*' chief labor reporter A. H. Raskin. Brownsville, Raskin contended, was a test of whether municipal unions could adapt to "the explosive pressure of Negroes and Puerto Ricans for more city jobs." On this account, the UFT failed, just as it failed to see how its own political tactics contributed to "the heedlessness of law exhibited by ghetto militants when they clash[ed] with the police on school steps or streets."[123]

For black New Yorkers, the strikes substantiated many of their fears and doubts that their children were systematically disserved in the city's public schools, by Board policies and thousands of individual teachers. When the strike was over, the *New York Amsterdam News* claimed, "the issues that have given rise to it are still with us. The deep wounds of racial hostility and community bitterness . . . will take a long time to heal." High school student Dana Driskell concurred. "As far as black people are concerned, the UFT is dead," she contended. "It will never be trusted again."[124] Most clearly, the strikes had confirmed to many blacks that white teachers lacked a professional commitment to minority students. The events at Ocean Hill-Brownsville, the Teachers for Community Control argued, "made many students, especially Black students, feel victimized by teachers."[125] Just as dangerous, argued Rhody McCoy, administrator of the Ocean Hill-Brownsville demonstration district, teachers submitted to the union rhetoric without investigating what they were fighting for or against. "You don't know what is going on in your profession," McCoy spoke out in the year following the strike. "Your profession doesn't start at nine o'clock in the morning and end at three o'clock. There are many more things involved other than payday and sick days and school holidays." Most teachers, McCoy chided, "don't even know the transfer process," the issue at the center of the strike, or "what the union has negotiated supposedly for them."[126]

The UFT's successful construction of parental and community involvement as unearned and undeserved was one of the most significant results of the decade's events. Shanker's high visibility in public life—through his publications and a charismatic style of leadership that played well to media attention—along with the greater centralization of union publications and public relations materials meant that his point of view frequently came to represent his membership's point of view. The kind of fracturing that became publicly evident, if not politically significant, in Ocean Hill-Brownsville, was no longer easy to see, even as members such as Richard Parrish pressed for his union brethren to reject the "modern form of red-baiting" that blamed the strikes on black extremists and to push for improved civil rights within the UFT. Until black and Puerto Rican members were made a part of the union staff, Parrish argued, the union would be unable to "survive as a force for social change." With this call for diversity within the leadership of the UFT, Parrish hoped to achieve a new way of thinking about the relationship between teacher unions and the communities that the city's public schools served. Parrish and others who had broken ranks with union leadership over the strikes hoped for "a genuine partnership between the UFT and the black and poor communities" to provide minority students with a high-quality, equal education.[127]

The events of the decade leading up to the strikes, however, reveal that the belief in teachers' rights and freedom from the influence of parents and activists was not just a limitation among UFT leaders but among many ordinary teachers and unionists. Unionists expressed these beliefs more openly than teachers had in the past in part because they were shared by a greater number of members. But a rights-conscious culture—one that led teachers to cast professional challenges as human rights violations and black parents' activism as a political annoyance—gave weight and shape to a teachers' movement that would have been unimaginable just a decade before. In 1968, teachers won the rights they had been seeking. In the following decades, they would need to prove they could do something productive with those rights and that they were well deserved. Given the import and severity of the issues teachers had claimed that only they were best suited to resolve, the challenges ahead would be vast and great, and the questions over teachers' commitment to minority children would remain central to any discussions of professionalism or school reform.

CHAPTER 5

From Teachers' Rights to Teacher Power

Albert Shanker emerged from the Ocean Hill-Brownsville strikes with unprecedented power for a teacher union leader, but not all teachers saw his rise in status as an asset. "I think now Mr. Shanker is more self-serving and more power-hungry," one city teacher argued in a nationally televised Bill Moyers' special on teacher unionism. "I don't think he's interested anymore in the little teacher . . . He has made our union into—not a teachers union anymore—but just a union after big salaries."[1] Shanker "makes statements," claimed another teacher, "but he has not taken that fight into the schools."[2] To Shanker, these kinds of criticisms missed the mark, both in terms of his leadership and what teacher unionism had become. "For over one hundred years in this country, teachers were powerless," Shanker responded to those who doubted teacher unionism. "I can remember the nice editorials we used to get—editorials about how teachers are overworked and underpaid. . . . full of sympathy for the powerless. Things are a little different now."[3] To Shanker, teachers demonstrated for their rights not just to change their influence in education policy but to change their image in public culture. The 1960s embrace of civil disobedience inspired teachers because they, "like so many others, became tired of having things done for them," he explained. If historically for teachers to "act like a professional" meant to "obey orders and refrain from rocking the boat," post-1960s teachers sought a new definition of professionalism, Shanker argued, one that centered on a "high degree of decision-making power" and a rejection of the "right of others . . . to make decisions for them."[4] This quest for a different kind of political influence was central to a new definition of teacher professionalism, and it marked a shift to what critics and advocates of teacher unionism alike would come to call teacher power.

Teachers like those Moyers interviewed revised the fundamental question of what constituted the terrain of teacher unions. While the question dated back to the split of the Teachers Union and Guild, unionists in the 1970s operated in a strikingly different context than those who preceded them. Undoubt-edly, the success of collective bargaining in the 1960s established that teacher unions could effect certain types of change. Within a decade of the United Federation of Teachers' (UFT's) first contract, the starting salary for teachers had doubled.[5] In addition, the 1968 strikes proved that the UFT could use its size and ability to strike as political leverage. Gaining public support, however, was a different matter. The scars of Ocean Hill-Brownsville "have never been erased," the New York Times reported in 1973, and "its heritage has been a wors-ening of the 'us' versus 'them' rift between the city's whites and minorities."[6] In addition to advocating for traditional union platforms in the 1970s, the UFT also had to contend with the popularly held view that it was responsible for, if not fully in control of, the city's eroding civic culture. Skeptics of teacher unionism—including many unionized teachers themselves—wondered if the UFT could be as devoted to fighting for social and political advances that could improve minority student achievement as they were to fighting for higher sala-ries and other bread-and-butter gains.

This chapter examines the growth of a teacher power movement in the 1970s and 1980s, its relationship to the education of racial minority students, and its dependence on teacher unionism's changing relationship with public opinion. While teacher power was built on the growing number of teachers who joined the UFT and other union locals in the 1960s, it was made possible by Shanker's ability to transform those numbers into public and political influence, largely through his careful and savvy use of the press. In December 1970, Shanker wrote his first of approximately thirteen hundred installments of "Where We Stand," a paid union advertisement framed to look like an editorial column in the Week in Review section of the Sunday New York Times. Over time and writing in a vocabulary any reader could understand, Shanker documented his meet-ings with education experts and politicians, translated his readings of the lat-est education reports and theories, and sounded responses to the latest school reform initiatives, from decentralization to school vouchers. In so doing, he saw himself as using the "column" to counter "the unfair treatment [teachers] received" in the press and in public debate. Claiming that unionized teachers "received plenty of coverage during strikes" and "during negotiations—when the possibility of a strike threatened" but little otherwise, Shanker saw that news outlets such as the New York Times played a key role in representing his union members to a skeptical public.[7] He responded to the ongoing criticism by arguing that city teachers needed someone to bring "to the public the story of thousands . . . who are struggling against great odds" and "to lead a crusade against the destructive and irresponsible critics of our schools, our teachers, and public education."[8] Far outlasting many of his political contemporaries—

both rivals and allies — Shanker determined the person best suited for this role was himself.

This new, singular medium by which Shanker brought teachers to the public eye was enabled by important changes in school reform itself. In the two decades that followed the Ocean Hill-Brownsville strikes, both teacher unionism and school reform movements transformed in important ways to become the highly standardized, quality-focused movements we recognize them as today. In part, this standardization stemmed from important changes in civil rights campaigns. Across the nation, white resistance to desegregation, from violent protests over busing to a quieter but equally powerful suburbanization and opting out of public schools, again called for federal mediation. Several grassroots-driven movements against busing that began in cities as diverse as Charlotte, North Carolina, and Detroit, Michigan, required resolution in the Supreme Court.[9] At the same time, the 1970s saw the expansion of rights campaigns for a widening number of student identity groups, including limited or non-English-speaking students and the disabled.[10] These campaigns also necessitated federal intervention, via both the Supreme Court and Congress. In contrast to the previous decade, the variety of stakeholders in locally waged equity battles had expanded while the number of mechanisms for seeking and enforcing equality had grown more standardized and centralized.

Because of an increased federalism, school reform battles looked fundamentally different by the 1980s than they had in the 1960s, even as the achievement gap between middle-class white students and low-income minority ones remained fairly static. For example, between 1960 and 1985, the percentage of federal contributions to funds spent on public education increased from 8 to 16 percent, while local contributions waned from 51 to 31 percent.[11] President Nixon was uniquely important to this change. Throughout his presidency, he directed more federal funds to economically disadvantaged schools even as he opposed busing and other desegregation strategies. In fact, the 1972 Equal Educational Opportunities Act marked the beginning of a new approach to equalizing schools, which was to exchange the integration efforts of the 1960s for new revenue streams for schools that, without federal government support and enforcement, would remain racially and economically segregated. President Carter's creation of the Department of Education in 1979 both cemented the growing role of federalism in education and provided the government with an official and more powerful institution to investigate education issues. Even President Reagan, who vowed to reduce the federal government's role in education, including school funding, made a significant contribution to school reform. In 1983, the increased visibility of public education as a national political issue compelled his administration to commission A Nation at Risk. The controversial study would help set the course for a national, standards-based approach to issues of teacher quality and accountability that succeeding presidents, Republican and Democrat alike, would maintain.[12]

Growing federal intervention in school reform over the 1970s and 1980s serves as an important context for a changing teacher union movement, one that also needed to grow more unified and centralized to participate in what was becoming a national conversation about race and the schools. Increasingly over the two decades, concerns that teachers previously would have addressed within their union locals were subordinate to federal law. As a result, "the rights of UFT members," Shanker charged in 1978, "are, increasingly, political decisions."[13] Yet changes within teacher unionism itself, frequently made possible by Shanker, also encouraged greater centralization. Nearly thirty years after Ocean Hill-Brownsville, the UFT had clearly become the representative organization for all teachers in New York City—growing from fifty-seven thousand members in 1968 to 140,000 in 1995.[14] Throughout the period, the UFT served as the wealthiest and largest local in the American Federation of Teachers (AFT). Nationwide, over 80 percent of teachers belonged to unions by the mid-1970s.[15] With approximately 940,000 members by the mid-1990s, the AFT had long been the largest union in the AFL-CIO.[16] Teachers not only had become a more organized professional force but led other organized workers as they never had before, and this new influence called for a singular, coherent message and a familiar, visible representative. Shanker, who served as president of the UFT until 1986 and president of the AFT from 1974 until his death in 1997, acted as this representative.

"Teacher power," a term that Shanker and journalists alike used to name a more expansive post-1960s unionism, described the UFT's and AFT's twin goals of gaining further authority in public schools and further influence in education politics at large. Even though Shanker—and most teacher unionists— rejected the militancy of black power, teacher power resonated with the other movement in multiple ways. Black power sought to link local and international black civil rights movements and defined its quest for racial solidarity and self-determination with what Peniel Joseph has characterized as an "urgent rhetoric." This rhetoric was easily captured into media sound bites that emphasized its militaristic images, oversimplified its ideologies, and obscured its entry into mainstream municipal politics in many cities across the nation.[17] Imagistic associations between black power and the Black Panther paramilitaries, for example, made a diverse, often localized political movement appear more coherent to insiders and outsiders alike. Much of the same can be said about teacher power. Even before he became president of the AFT in 1974, Shanker proved willing to exploit his unparalleled public recognition to make broad claims about teacher professionalism and education politics. Teacher power served to organize these claims and to produce a singular narrative that distinguished an earlier, decentralized teachers' rights movement from a new one focused on the relationship between professional agency and political influence.

Despite this new rhetoric, to the public, teacher power appeared just to be a continued, if heightened, version of UFT tactics in the 1960s. On the whole, teachers in the 1970s played a vital role in turning New York into "Strike City," a moniker earned by the city's vast number of municipal strikes during the decade. Many of these strikes were waged in response to a fiscal crisis that would leave New York City more than five billion dollars in debt and teetering on the brink of bankruptcy for three years. Severe budget cuts slashed public sector jobs citywide and, from 1974 to 1976, led to the layoff of approximately fifteen thousand of the city's teachers. The layoffs created radical changes in city schools, from class size, which increased to forty or more students in many classrooms, to the average age of teachers, which rose from twenty-eight to forty-one.[18] Elective courses in the high schools, including foreign languages, mathematics, and social studies, were eliminated. As Mayor Beame and other municipal officials requested teachers' pension funds to pay off the city's debt, union members were forced to defend their own economic security against that of the city. In September 1975, when teachers who had retained their jobs returned to classrooms that often matched Depression-era classes in size, UFT members voted 22,870 to nine hundred to strike for better contracts and improved school conditions.[19] Unionists quickly discovered, however, what Shanker had already told them: there was little to negotiate during an economic collapse.

Throughout the fiscal crisis, the New York Times would later report, "a battle for public perceptions" on the part of the municipal officials who struggled to keep the city operational "eclipsed even the search for money."[20] This assessment summarized the situation of Shanker and UFT members as well, who repeatedly found that public opinion was the only currency to be gained or lost in the mid-1970s. After initially resisting lending money to the city from the union's pension fund, Shanker relented, claiming the mayor's and governor's threat that the city would spiral into bankruptcy otherwise "was blackmail and unfair, but the price of not acceding . . . would have been the destruction of the city."[21] To many, however, the city's dependency on Shanker's decision only proved how much power he and the UFT held. Since Ocean Hill-Brownsville, many people saw the union as a bully that exploited city residents for its own gain. Americans from Rhode Island to California wrote letters to Shanker to express their outrage about the union's continued willingness to strike. To them, Shanker and his "outlaw band" made "hostages of the public safety, health, and economic well-being, . . . exploited the poor and unorganized," and exhibited "absolutely no regard for the pupils or people of [the] city."[22] In their letters, the writers exhibited a range of anxieties, from a worry that the UFT was "warping all pay scales by exhorting higher pay for moron's work" to a greater concern that teachers would forever place their own interests over those of their students and the public good.[23]

Teachers, too, voiced concern over a teacher power movement that, even though limited by fiscal crisis, threatened to eclipse the very teachers who constituted it. Specifically, teachers like those Moyers interviewed in his special report and the many who wrote to Shanker weekly in response to his column revealed that they were fearful of the way in which teacher power threatened to forget the "little teacher," whose concerns may or may not have echoed the union's own. Their worry that Shanker could only speak effectively to the issue of salaries and political clout also suggested that teachers' everyday concerns, and the image they wanted to cultivate within their local communities, did not always align with the quest for greater control and authority over education policy that teacher power was about. In short, such teachers, however representative they were, echoed the doubts dissenting teacher groups had registered during the Ocean Hill-Brownsville strikes. Yet the rhetoric of teacher power—and the actual political power that teachers as an organized force earned in the twenty years following the Ocean Hill-Brownsville strikes—suggested that these doubts were inconsequential to the movement itself. "We are willing to go to the press to explain our case to the public," Shanker contended, and critics could "cry all they want; they can try to bring back the good old days when docile teachers obeyed every edict . . . but it's too late. Those days are gone forever."[24] With or without the endorsement of individual teachers, teacher power appeared here to stay.

A Matter of Justice

The Ocean Hill-Brownsville strikes highlighted the degree to which education equity had become one of the most important and controversial issues in 1960s civil rights campaigns. If black parents lost the battle in Ocean Hill-Brownsville, they did not lose the argument that minority schools were second-class institutions. City teachers' organized response to black concerns created a public portrait of a teaching corps that, because of its lack of interest, was incapable of enabling black students to succeed. As black New Yorkers in the 1970s remained focused on what transpired in segregated classrooms, they began to look for new avenues by which to influence the quality of teachers who taught their children. More expansively, black Americans' focus on teacher quality, coupled with an ongoing minority achievement gap across the nation and a lack of judicial or popular support for the desegregation policies of the 1960s, impacted the reform strategies and objectives of both black parents and unionized teachers. The case of New York City schools in the 1970s reflects the trajectory of civil rights–based school reform in the period and the ways in which greater federal intervention in education policy would plant the seeds for a more coherent teacher power movement in response.

The conclusion of the strikes in Ocean Hill-Brownsville brought little resolution to the tensions that developed between black parents and a unionized teaching force that was largely white. The strikes and the immediate events leading up to them had created an identifiable shift in minority school activists' views about the role of teachers in improving their city schools. In the 1950s, black parents and activists had argued that they wanted better, more effective teachers transferred to their children's schools. By the 1970s, it was no longer clear that they believed such teachers even existed. In 1971, the United Parents Association (UPA) declared that "parents have been moved into the front line in the fight to reform and restructure our schools." "Like it or not," UPA President Blanche Lewis attested, "it is from here we must wage our battle for the survival and success of our schools."[25] Black parents saw themselves in a battle with white teachers' conscious or unconscious presumptions that black children were incapable of succeeding in school. To be sure, minority children were not succeeding; in 1973, 68 percent of the city's public school students tested below the national average in reading. "The blame for such a shabby performance," the New York Amsterdam News declared, "must be placed squarely on the teachers of the New York City school system."[26] To minority activists, the problem resided in the fact that while half of the city's public school students were black and Puerto Rican, less than 10 percent of teachers were. In an effort to gain better quality teachers, parents petitioned for more minority teachers and administrators and for white teachers and supervisors to undergo massive retraining that would bring about a "change in attitude and re-thinking of some traditional practices."[27] Local school boards in minority neighborhoods, including Ocean Hill-Brownsville, endorsed plans for white teachers to visit black students in their homes in order to gain a stronger understanding of what black families and black lifestyles were like.[28]

None of this sat well with many UFT members, who saw these kinds of critiques and plans as a continued threat to their expertise. But they also saw that continuing to dismiss activists' concerns without any specific, alternative plan to address them would only lead to a continued racial divide between the city's minority residents and its mostly white teaching corps. In May 1970, from a jail cell where he was being held for his role in leading strikes, Albert Shanker

wrote a letter to his union members, asking them to vote to include paraprofessionals in the union. Paras, as they are known, mostly low-income black
and Latina mothers, had worked in the nation's classrooms as aides since the
fall of 1967, when their positions were funded by Title I of the Elementary and
Secondary Education Act. To be sure, when Shanker first proposed the idea,
many teachers balked. Including paraprofessionals—parents who frequently
lacked even a high school degree—stood at odds with the union's definition of
itself as an organization for professionals with specialized expertise. Shanker,
however, believed that paras could potentially resolve the union's image problem on race relations and repair its relationship with black city residents. Organizing the paras, he maintained, would mean that "when our contract and
grievance procedures are attacked, there will be over 10,000 minority group
members who will stand up to attacks," and this would show that union advocacy was "not a matter of race" but "a matter of justice."[29]

UFT leaders sought to maintain the union's color-blind, merit-based arguments in organizing the paras in other ways as well. Shanker and other UFT
leaders saw that the union could advocate for a number of improvements for
the paraprofessionals, including a contract that would raise their salaries, a
stipend for them to return to school and complete their high school or college degree, and, most importantly, a licensing system that would give them
greater legitimacy. Licensing, union literature reminded UFT members,
means a merit system and would better regulate who was working in the classroom alongside teachers. Professionalizing the black and Latina women who
constituted most of the paraprofessionals would protect them and teachers
alike from "all kinds of political pressures" and would stymie "outside groups
[who] may try to use para-professionals to further their own 'revolutionary'
ends."[30] The arguments made by UFT leadership through direct appeals from
Shanker and a series of union publications worked, both on resistant teachers
and reluctant paraprofessionals. In May 1970, UFT delegates voted three to
one to include the paras in the union. That August, paras voted 1,461–42 to
ratify the contract proposed by the UFT, including a salary increase, release
time, and stipends to complete their educations.[31] Immediately, paraprofes-
sional salaries almost doubled, and UFT membership included several thousand more minority women.

In addition to this important change in union policy, one that improved
both the economic status of thousands of black women and the public image
of unionized teachers, the UFT took a demonstrable stand on civil rights in
Canarsie, Brooklyn. In the fall of 1972, white parents in the Jewish and Italian neighborhood greeted the arrival of twenty-nine black and Puerto Rican
students bused from Brownsville to a local junior high schools with shouts of

"Go back to the zoo!" and "Go get your welfare checks!"[32] Out of their fear that the students would tip the school's existing balance of white and minority students, the parents shut the school down for weeks, citing community control as their legal and entitled avenue to determining who would and would not attend their area schools. Teachers were divided on the issue; some sympathized with the students, but others clearly sided with the protesting white parents. "It's not skin color they're worried about," one such teacher insisted, "it's just that there are definite problems the kids bring to school."[33] Shanker rejected such arguments and the "mob rule" that shut down the schools; he ordered UFT members to break the picket lines and escorted a group of teachers into the school himself. In addition to its support of desegregation, the union's position represented a consistency in its position against community control. This furthered the UFT's argument that its actions in Ocean Hill-Brownsville had been race-neutral all along.

But despite these advances in the UFT's relationship with black parents and students, city residents who still questioned the union's intentions could find plenty of evidence to support their doubts. In 1974, the union defended six teachers accused of corporal punishment and improper licensing in two Harlem elementary schools.[34] The UFT's stance in the case was the same as it had been in Ocean Hill-Brownsville. "The issue is not whether these teachers are good or bad," claimed union spokesman Ned Hopkins, "it's their right to due process."[35] The union's actions rang equally out of tune two years later when the UFT waged a campaign against Ocean Hill-Brownsville principal Carlos Edwards. In his time as principal, Edwards had raised his students' reading scores to the highest in the district and had maintained an 88 percent student attendance rate, higher than the city's average. But despite significant evidence that Edwards was raising the quality of education in the school, the UFT petitioned the Board of Education, accusing Edwards of creating hostility between black and white teachers.

To minority parents, the motivations behind these actions were clear. After Edwards was fired, three hundred of the school's four hundred families participated in protests, a percentage that far exceeded the community's political participation otherwise.[36] Going after a principal for racial bias when he was raising student performance appeared to many parents to put teachers' feelings before their children's needs. Even more, many organized black parents agreed with Edwards in his assessment that white teachers were problematic, if not inferior. Several parent groups argued that city teachers were "not concerned with quality education" but instead "only [with] higher salaries."[37] The liberal but certainly not radical *New York Amsterdam News* claimed that the UFT, in opposing setting standards of accountability, endorsed and encouraged teachers' racism and "remained indifferent to the failure of children to read."[38] Babette Edwards, cochair of the Harlem Parents Union, proposed that teachers who lacked a "vested interest in quality education" should have their salary and performance assessed "by the criteria of a child's academic accomplishments."[39] These critiques introduced a new term to the debates over education equity: accountability. If teachers could not be made to care about black students, parents argued, they would nevertheless care about their professional rewards.

Black teacher groups, too, argued that the city's white teaching force was ill equipped to respond to—or even respect—minority students' needs. The African-American Teachers Association (ATA) continued to argue that the UFT purposefully suppressed "the organization of Black people" and "the legitimate aspirations of the Black Community to improve the quality of education in their schools."[40] To the ATA, the black teachers who remained in the UFT after Ocean Hill-Brownsville and who otherwise rejected their radical view were part of the problem. In "parrot[ing] the whites' term ('quality education')," the ATA argued, such teachers failed to see that "Blacks have a different value system from the value system of the whites, and that 'quality education' for Black folks means something altogether different in our systems of values."[41] This other set of values was less individualistic, more communalistic, and decidedly more focused on black achievement and uplift. Even Richard Parrish, who in the 1960s had advocated that black teachers work within the UFT, now called for a more assertive confrontation of "the most oppressive educational system in the country." In 1970, Parrish had been expelled from the UFT Unity Committee along with several other UFT leaders sympathetic to black parents. Although he continued to head the United Black Caucus within the AFT, the expulsion convinced him that "so many 'Negro' teachers have been brainwashed by the white educational system." Only "if you can change the thinking of minority teachers," and their supposed complacency with the system, he contested, could "the educational system . . . be changed."[42] In a contrasting argument to the one he made just several years before, Parrish contended that teachers needed to put their racial identification before their professional associations.

Activists' arguments to hire more minority teachers and that minority teachers held a different professional value because of their racial or ethnic identification were bound to fall flat with most UFT members, given the union's historic belief in color-blind professionalism. Its continued desire to hold fast to this belief was made especially clear in its response not just to black parents' call for more sensitive teachers but also to Puerto Rican school reformers' efforts. More specifically, in the 1972 case of *Aspira v. the Board of Education of*

New York City, Puerto Rican activists argued that until the city's schools offered more bilingual programs for Spanish-speaking students, Puerto Rican children could not possibly succeed. The case was resolved two years later when the Board and Aspira negotiated a consent decree that ordered more bilingual courses for second-language students. In order to implement the decree, however, the Board first had to employ thousands more Spanish-speaking teachers, a development that obviated the need to hire more Latino/a teachers at a time when thousands of white teachers were being laid off.[43] The UFT protested the entire bilingual program, with Shanker critiquing both separate classes for bilingual students and separate bilingual teaching licenses. While the UFT eventually proposed a different instructional program for Spanish-speaking students, the issue of who would teach the courses continued to engender conflict between the union and the city's Puerto Rican community. Thus, even in a case in which racial and ethnic identity undeniably qualified some teachers with a unique skill set, the union was unwilling to yield to the idea that professionalism and race could or should intersect.[44]

Historically, the Guild and the UFT were committed to a belief in color-blind professionalism because doing so favored most union members and because both unions located their primary source of public support in the city's middle-class white power structure. After the militancy of the 1960s, however, the union's public image was problematic with the city's white and black residents alike. In response, Shanker focused on a strategy that had been first suggested to him by the editor of the UFT newspaper before the Ocean Hill-Brownsville strikes: to use the media to address the "new wave of social consciousness" in teacher unionism and "the possible examination of teachers' own self-image."[45] The first several years of "Where We Stand" columns indicate that Shanker was focused on discrediting his critics rather than repairing his relationship with them and on developing a new concept of teacher professionalism and teacher power that would help unionists to win the debates. Specifically, he used the column to critique his opponents in the community control movement, to advertise their eventual concessions, and to promote his own brand of civil rights rhetoric.[46] He blamed the Urban Coalition for "foster[ing] urban confrontation" and for supporting groups such as the United Bronx Parents and the ATA, both of which had "no scruples about sacrificing the children in their own communities for a 'longer-range' goal— getting into their own hands the money used to run the schools."[47] He depicted local civil rights groups as not just competing with the UFT for political power but diametrically opposed to the UFT in their values, which he characterized as "violently revolutionary, anti-brotherhood, anti-union, and anti-American."[48] In defining UFT principles as both prounion and pro-American, Shanker drew on a Guild philosophy of professionalism, one that countered local militant groups' revolutionary fervor and usual style of "promot[ing] confrontation" and "produc[ing] disaster" with a different model of power and democracy.[49] In contrast to those who fought for community control, he argued, UFT members were activists, not militants, a "creative alliance" of members that constituted a majority and acted on a careful and intelligent consensus of opinion.[50] Few city residents likely saw the UFT's willingness to strike as either consensual or creative, but Shanker's continued characterizations of black activists as violent and radical echoed with the sentiments of enough readers who held their own fears about black militancy and a changed urban demographic.

For unionists who had long held to a color-blind philosophy of school reform, including Shanker, the clear solution to the problems of equity that Ocean Hill-Brownsville raised was to trade race-based community organizations for community group coalitions organized around the UFT. Shanker admitted that the "urban crisis grows every day" but believed that the city schools' problems could "only be solved by a genuine coalition powerful enough to bring about governmental commitment."[51] In calling for this coalition, Shanker had in mind race-progress organizations such as the A. Philip Randolph Institute that were less radical than community control groups and were focused on labor. Above all, Shanker contended, black activists learned in Ocean Hill-Brownsville "that their interests are not served when invoked for the purpose of breaking unions . . . on the contrary, their interests are better served when they themselves join unions and reap the benefits of organization."[52] The experiences of the 1960s, he contended, had "left their mark" both on institutions and the people who worked within them and on "the general climate of political expression."[53] Instead of suggesting specific reforms geared toward improving schools in communities like Ocean Hill-Brownsville, he focused on trying to change the conversation. "The conflict over who should hire teachers," Shanker contended, referring to the event that set the Ocean Hill-Brownsville strikes in motion, "misse[d] the point."[54] More than misguided, the struggle for the "power to hire and fire professionals," was a "replay of an old tune."[55] Yet he had difficulty in presenting solid options to the kinds of specific policies community control activists had in mind. In response to charges that public schools were failing their students, he maintained a historic Guild argument that shifted the focus from failing teachers to failing schools. "Teachers do not deny that some of their colleagues are ineffective," he argued, but failure could not be divided from "poor conditions in the schools." For education problems to be mitigated, educators would need to see a solution to issues such as "tax reform, aid to education, national health insurance, better housing, and the elimination of poverty and discrimination."[56] While black parents saw accountability as a redress to teachers' lack of motivation in serving their children, Shanker defined teacher accountability as immeasurable in isolation and instead dependent on alliances that would support teachers' improved working conditions.

True to Shanker's word, teachers made vast strides in the 1970s in becoming an interest group that local, state, and federal governments would need to address and contend with. From their neighborhoods to the national scene, Shanker explained, teachers had experienced a "rapid political maturation," one that led them to take a stand not just on local education legislation but also on a general economic program, national health security legislation, and other policies that would have seemed like distant issues to teachers unionists in the past.[57] The 1974 election between Gerald Ford and Jimmy Carter, the *New York Times* reported the following year, showed that "in money, campaign manpower and vote-corralling effectiveness, organized teachers—only a few years ago strangers to politics—outdid every other interest group." Labor reporter A. H. Raskin traced this radical change to Shanker and the UFT's actions a decade before and to a steady increase since Ocean Hill-Brownsville in "the primacy of politics in teacher unionism."[58]

Despite this newfound import teacher unions held for the Democratic Party, however, the Carter administration sided with minority parents' concerns about teacher quality and saw the issue of minority teacher hires as one of the more efficient starting points in addressing those concerns. In 1973, following on the heels of the violent protests in Canarsie, President Carter commissioned the Department of Health, Education, and Welfare's Office of Civil Rights (OCR) to begin an investigation into school segregation in five large cities, starting with New York. After three years of investigations, the OCR charged New York City with noncompliance with the Civil Rights Act of 1964. More specifically, it found that both black students and black teachers in New York City were marginalized, more so, in fact, than in Los Angeles, Chicago, Philadelphia, Houston, or Detroit. Even in integrated schools, at least 20 percent of classrooms were segregated in ways "that could not have occurred by chance alone."[59] Overall, the study found what local parents had documented for decades: minority students were much more likely to be tracked in remedial courses, to be underrepresented in advanced placement coursework, and to be disciplined more harshly and frequently than their white counterparts. On the issue of minority teachers, the OCR report also found real imbalances. While minority teachers were grossly underrepresented based on the minority population in the city (the minority student population in the city's high schools was 62.6 percent, but the minority teacher population for high schools was only 8.3 percent), they were highly concentrated in minority schools. Finally, the report concluded that black and Hispanic teachers were "channeled" to black and Hispanic schools rather than choosing these teaching assignments.[60] In contrast to some black activists' claims that minority teachers were best suited to teach minority children, the OCR report argued that the Jim Crowing of minority teachers was as problematic as the segregation of students.

While none of the facts revealed in the OCR report were new, as both the National Association for the Advancement of Colored People and Puerto Rican Legal Defense and Education Fund maintained, the claim that New York City was breaking federal law and the resulting demand that the city do something about it marked a difference.[61] Novel too was the report's attention to the twin marginalization of teachers and students at once, something that had not been studied closely since the collapse of the Teachers Union. Both Shanker and the Board of Education responded to the report by blaming decentralization for the segregation of minority teachers; give racial minority districts the power to hire whom they wish, they maintained, and they will hire minority teachers. While many black parents might have concurred with this argument, to OCR secretary Martin Gerry and local school reform organizations such as the UPA, Shanker's claims absolved educators of any responsibility and instead placed it in the hands of the community members who also suffered the consequences of education inequality.[62] But neither the Board of Education's contention that the OCR "reduced [the problem] to a chart" nor Shanker's contention that quotas were "unconstitutional" could stand up to the federal government's findings. Shanker, claiming that the OCR "held a gun to [his] head" by threatening to withhold two hundred million dollars of federal aid per year until the situation was remedied, had no choice but to yield.[63]

By September 1977, the New York City Board of Education had developed a plan for black and Hispanic teachers to select their teaching assignments from one list and white teachers to select from another. The racial makeup of the schools each group was given to choose from contrasted with the teachers' own racial identification. The method allowed the Board to distribute teachers in the schools based on their race without having to alter its long-standing color-blind approach to teacher hiring or to adopt an affirmative action policy. In effect, the Board put the onus of school desegregation on teacher assignments, while also setting out some policies to draw more minorities into teaching. The strategy was awkward at best, and the OCR was quick to point out that the Board had chosen the particular method of resolution and that it had not been the only possible choice.[64] But educators' responses to it suggested that they found the avenue to desegregation more problematic than the original problem of teacher segregation. A group of fifteen black teachers who were transferred from a minority school to a white one were greeted by a white superintendent who declared, "We didn't ask for any of you." One black teacher noted that under the new system "you can't go where you are needed in the schools, you have to go to a place where they want another black face." Yet another argued that the policy ignored that "black role models are important in the school . . . and that the kids were losing these role models." The Board of Education's Director of Personnel correctly summarized that the new policy represented a clash of two liberal doctrines, that of integration and that of the black role model. [65] Ironically, this clash brought new attention and import to black teachers yet did nothing to enfranchise them.

The response of teachers to the New York City Board's new hiring policy illuminated the ways in which neither white nor black teachers had been consulted in discussions of how to improve the city's schools or the education offered to minority students. The Board's decision certainly did not appear to address teachers' concerns as a professional body, particularly given that the teachers who spoke out most forcefully about job assignments in the early 1970s were black teachers who favored separatism. Nor was it clear that this solution appealed to parents; one of the resources black parents had been most vocal about was the importance of black teachers in black schools. Indeed, a 1983 survey of New Yorkers' assessment of their public schools revealed that black parents were still markedly less satisfied with their children's schools than were white parents. While 70 percent of white parents gave their schools a grade of A or B, only 56 percent of black parents did the same. [66] Clearly, the OCR's statistical approach to addressing education equity had not demonstrably improved black students' education in their parents' eyes. That is, acts of justice did not necessarily bring about better schools.

While the intervention of the federal government in teacher quality debates in the mid-1970s seems like it would have marked progress, it is unclear who benefited from it. New York City teacher unionists found that they could not always pressure their way through a situation they opposed and that their increased power in political lobbying did not necessarily amount to improving the political status of individual teachers. To Shanker, who would substitute much of his ire toward community control in early *Times* columns with a passionate and frequent critique of quotas in the late 1970s, the event proved that teacher unions would need to operate differently if they were to compete with federal law. The clearest lesson learned by the OCR intervention in the New York City schools was that school reform, in Shanker's words, was not based on "the right or wrong thing to do but, rather, on who has the power to tell whom what to do." [67] Only with a more convincing teacher power movement, he and many other unionists concluded, would teachers' assessment of the right thing to do have any authority in education politics.

Teacher Power and a Nation at Risk

Contrary to popular sentiment, New York City teacher Roy Pellicano asserted in 1980, the UFT really was "becoming a professional organization with goals for peer development and self-improvement." While Pellicano was in favor of this shift, he was nevertheless troubled by what he saw as a top-down implementation of these efforts. Union leaders, he explained, "have decided upon a strategy or a set of strategies and have attempted to institutionalize them by decree" without soliciting the rank and file. While leaders' strategies may have positioned the "collective teacher" as central to school reform, they did so at the cost of the professional autonomy and participation of the individual teacher. Just as much, he argued, an ever more top-down union organization created a system of patronage that ensured the viability and longevity of professional union leaders. Union elections had become "marked by a campaign of the incumbents emphasizing their 'experience' and 'professionalism' over those who challenge (primarily classroom teachers)." After twenty years of remarkably stable UFT leadership, he concluded, "it becomes a nearly impossible task to unseat the 'experience' and 'professionalism' of the union's central office."[68] UFT member Gloria Channon agreed. "We have become compliant, perhaps even contemptible dues payers in the eyes of our union representatives," she contended. Contrary to Shanker's claims, teachers' subordination to the union organ made them "helpless, divested of any authority, in the eyes of the parents and children with whom we work."[69] Teacher power and teachers' power, these two unionists suggested, were not one and the same.

This distinction would serve as a powerful context for union responses to teacher quality concerns. The OCR case had proved to Shanker and other union leaders that neither the UFT nor the AFT could take on the federal government, particularly without powerful allies. The 1980s, Lawrence McAndrews has argued, was a pivotal decade for school reform movements, one in which teacher unions shifted from offense to defense on school reform and from "feckless confrontation to guarded collaboration" with policy makers.[70] Pellicano, and the New York City teachers who shared his sentiments about their own marginality, described some of the factors that made this shift possible, including the development of the professional unionist who may or may not have self-identified as a professional teacher. As teacher unions grew more powerful and more centralized, many teachers found that union projects were often less than democratic in their implementation than they appeared to be.

No event in the 1980s did more to entrench and heighten this tension than the publication of *A Nation at Risk* and the events that unfolded from it. Commissioned by the Reagan administration, the seminal report was published in April 1983 out of an 18-month investigation by the National Committee on

Excellence in Education (NCEE).[71] Calling on policy papers, academic reports, and hearings with educators, parents, and education experts, A Nation at Risk charged American schools with "being eroded by a rising tide of mediocrity" and argued that lagging schools threatened American security and the nation's standing as a world power. Yet while it drew highly politicized conclusions about the need for school reform, its analysis of the schools was largely apolitical. In contrast to debates in earlier decades, which squarely located the source of school failure either with ineffective teachers or delinquent youth, A Nation at Risk claimed that mediocre schools were something Americans "have allowed . . . to happen to ourselves" and the product of a general "weakness of purpose, confusion of vision, underuse of talent, and lack of leadership," rather than "conditions beyond our control." In its claims, the report focused on the failure of American public schools as a whole, drawing no distinction between schools in which students achieved and those in which they did not. The facts that it cited as evidence of school failure—including adult illiteracy rates, a decline in standardized test scores since the 1960s, and an increase in remedial mathematics courses at public colleges—suggested that all schools were equally deficient no matter whom they served. School failure, it maintained, "cuts across ages, generations, races, and political and economic groups." The report's claim that up to 40 percent of minority youth might test as functionally illiterate was its most specific about minority student achievement.[72] Instead, A Nation at Risk often alluded to issues that were inextricable from race, all the while ignoring the issue at hand.

This generalizing of public schools can best be understood in the context of several federal political developments of the time. The first of these was the politics of the Reagan administration itself, which, far more interested in international issues than social politics, effectively was compelled into addressing education because of the prominence it had achieved as a national political issue in the previous decade. The rhetoric of the report, and its argument that poor education performance represented a threat first and foremost to the nation's position in the global arena, frequently echoed this outlook. Second, Carter's use of the OCR notwithstanding, since the 1960s, the federal government had declined to enforce racial balance in the schools. Thus, A Nation at Risk's inattention to the singular problems that minority schools faced echoed a larger federal color-blindness.

While the report failed to contend with social inequities, it did draw important connections between school accountability and teacher quality, both long-standing issues central to black activists' vision for education reform. As it did so, however, it sympathized with teachers more than it critiqued them and sounded little of the sense of urgency that minority activists had expressed. The NCEE warned of making "beleaguered teachers" into scapegoats and considered one of the most essential tools in school reform "the dedication, against all odds, that keeps teachers serving in schools and colleges, even as the rewards diminish."[73] The policy statements on teacher quality that came out of the report argued that the profession needed more training and regulation, yet many of these statements called for improving teachers' standing more than diminishing it. For example, the report called for increased salaries for all teachers and for increasing teachers' influence on teacher education programs, both conditions the union favored. It also called for several developments that unions had not historically supported, including overhauling teacher evaluation systems, introducing performance-based pay, and extending teachers' contracts to eleven months per year to secure more time for in-service and professional development.

Given that the report was commissioned by the Reagan administration, many educators and political analysts expected that Shanker would dismiss it summarily. In contrast, and in what the *Times* reported as a "startling" break from teacher unions' tendency to "appeal to the members by protecting the status quo," Shanker announced he was pleasantly surprised by its findings.[74] Four days after the publication of *A Nation at Risk*, he came out in favor of it at a meeting of the New York State Teachers Union in Albany, New York. He would continue to praise its findings in "Where We Stand" for over a decade. Shanker saw that his position was unexpected and confessed that when the report came out he "decided to take a big risk." While his "normal and expected reaction would have been to express the views of many of our members . . . to blast the repor[t] whenever we thought they were wrong," he instead expressed his own view, that *A Nation at Risk* offered a "golden opportunity for teachers and public education" because schools were in trouble. Candidly, Shanker admitted, his opposition "would have been taken as evidence that 'the school bureaucracy' would never change," but, just as much, it would have fueled beliefs that Shanker himself was incapable of yielding to his opponents.[75] In "Where We Stand," Shanker extolled *A Nation at Risk* for focusing on "strengthening public education as a national necessity" while making "a series of strong recommendations on curriculum, homework, the school day and year, the discipline question, teacher quality, training and salaries." Most importantly, the report paired these recommendations with promises of "support needed from all levels of government, including and most especially the federal government."[76] As New York City teachers and Shanker had learned in the late 1970s, winning the support of the federal government was far better than trying to fight it. In response to these promises, Shanker argued for greater centralization and standardization in education reform, from curricula design to teacher training. "Strong, content based standards," he contended, were the "best hope" for privileged and disenfranchised students alike, both in terms of what they studied and, to some degree, of how they studied it.[77] This movement toward standardization, in Shanker's vision, would be created and enforced by unionized teachers, the federal government, and the business leaders whose companies depended on public school graduates.

While Shanker's response may have surprised many, in fact, several aspects of the report made it ready for his approval, particularly given the political events of the previous two decades. Most notably, the report's skimming over of race issues and its focus on teachers' skills rather than their motivations offered Shanker an opportunity to take a position on teacher performance without having to directly confront the political issues that had haunted the UFT for over two decades. Instead, he considered the accountability that the report called for—on the part of both the federal government and educators—as a "welcome tightening up of the looseness that crept into our schools in the late 60s and early 70s."[78] In contextualizing the move toward accountability in these specific terms, he alluded to the community control movement, which sought to give community leaders and parents local control over who would teach in the schools and over curricula. In contrast, A Nation at Risk promised to place both the responsibility for improving schools and the power to do so in educators' hands. To assume greater responsibility, Shanker argued, was to gain greater authority in education policy, which was the ultimate goal of teacher unionism and teacher power.

While he continued to fight merit or performance-based pay, an idea that appealed greatly to the Reagan administration, Shanker did put forth a number of realizable goals to improve teacher quality. One of the most significant of these was his argument for a national teacher exam and federal teaching standards so as to avoid a situation in some states where "the passing mark is set so low that many who become teachers are at the same level of competence as the students they're supposed to teach."[79] But he was not willing for teachers to accept all of the blame for their lack of mastery. The current safeguards for teacher quality were clearly insufficient, he argued. For example, data indicated that in some states, up to 40 percent of students were taught by teachers who were licensed in a different subject area than that which they taught. He blamed this fact on principals and supervisors who misunderstood the profession and, faced with teacher shortages, figured that a good teacher could teach anything well.[80] What Shanker did not emphasize, perhaps because it would have put teacher unions in the same position to respond to the problem as they had been in the 1950s, was that teachers in low-income and minority schools were far more likely to be teaching in subject areas in which they were unlicensed than were other teachers. Just as *A Nation at Risk* avoided addressing issues of education equity, so too did Shanker in his responses.

Shanker realized that his proposals would be controversial, even if they were consistent in many ways with his past political views. He predicted that they would create "a great national debate amongst teachers" and that while some teachers would "push for a new and better role," others, "out of fear and cynicism, [would] cling to the status quo or to a program of slow and incremental change."[81] In short, writing about accountability required Shanker to address the issues of those who were ill equipped to be a teacher, even if, in contrast to how black activists had framed such arguments, he focused on skill and merit over motivation and empathy. Doing so, in his mind, did not conflict with historic union claims of professionalism but, in fact, was essential to revising the public's view of teachers. Yet even as he upheld positions that he had articulated from the beginning—that the "old ritualistic practices" of education reform "continue even after they no longer make much sense" and that teachers' morale sinks because "they know it is not real quality that is recognized but, instead, the eye-catching"—his critiques of teacher performance represented a significant shift from his previous focus on school conditions.[82] More constant was his distrust of identity politics as Shanker charged the feminist movement with "making the teaching job less attractive to the talented." In addition, he argued, the increased number of tasks that the profession demanded without compensation encouraged many college-educated people to seek better jobs than teaching. The result was a lessening of teacher preparation and, in many districts, "the public being fooled into believing that they have qualified teachers when they only have people who have been able to pass ridiculously easy tests."[83]

On the whole, Shanker saw the changes for which he was advocating, including a national teacher exam, as a pragmatic and expedient means to further professionalize teachers and heighten union power at the same time. Professionalism, as he had long argued, was typically based on a sense of freedom from lay influence and by a preparation process that earned its participants that freedom. Creating a new examination system, he argued, would raise the standards of entry into the profession, bolster teacher professionalism, and afford teachers the ability to "recognize excellence without needing some principal or superintendent to point it out to us."[84] Embracing more rigorous professional development standards would reveal that, while teacher unions fought for "protection and security and economic well-being," all essential "part[s] of the American way of life," they also stood for "standards and excellence, and professionalism, which includes participation and self-governance."[85] Shanker's frank discussions of and proposals for improving teacher quality worked. By September 1985, over two hundred newspapers across the nation had endorsed his proposal for a national teacher exam.[86]

The educators who responded to the ideas Shanker advanced in his column also held strong convictions. While some chided Shanker for "add[ing] to the chorus of criticism" toward teachers in his suggestions, in fact many supported and were even grateful for the position he took on A Nation at Risk.[87] "Your definition of 'professionalism' is a breath of fresh air," wrote one such New York City teacher. She hoped that a national exam for teachers would not only improve "the status of the profession" but more specifically the status of elementary school teachers such as herself, who often found themselves at the bottom of a professional hierarchy.[88] "This is an unabashed fan letter," began another letter by a teacher from North Carolina. "I only hope people read and employ your philosophy before all the dedicated people have gone the way of the back door. The replacements who are filling positions vacated by the pros are little more than instructors."[89] Teachers who supported Shanker suggested that they believed upholding more rigorous standards would benefit them in earning both public respect and professional rewards.

But if most teachers supported the idea of improving teacher quality in theory, turning Shanker's philosophies into action was a different, more complicated story. As had been the case in previous decades, organized black teachers especially feared the costs of implementing ideas that they had not helped to design. Throughout the 1980s, the AFT's United Black Caucus spoke out against reforms that it saw as hierarchical, including the continued practice of education tracking and a national teacher exam.[90] The caucus feared that teacher testing was a quick fix that failed to produce real reform and was "only one measure of how competent a teacher is or will be." Even more, it worried that "the possibility of a two tier category of teachers could leave many black teachers in the bottom tier," as teaching exams had historically done, including in New York City.[91] In union locals as well, organized black teachers protested some of their unions' implementation of Shanker's goals. One of the most important examples of such took place in the Cincinnati Federation of Teachers (CFT), an AFT local that had developed an extensive peer review system. Shanker embraced peer review, which was designed to provide struggling teachers with mentorship and to give experienced, successful teachers greater control over who was and was not advancing in the profession, but only a relative handful of locals shared that embrace. Cincinnati was one of the leading locals in this project, but not all Cincinnati teachers were in favor of it. When three black teachers were rated unsatisfactory by their peers and recommended for dismissal, Dorothy Coleman, president of the Cincinnati Black Teachers' Caucus, wrote to Shanker in protest. "The CFT cannot afford to wage a battle against Black teachers because our system needs Black role models and we must assist these teachers to remain in the classroom," she argued. To Coleman, the unsatisfactory rating of the black teachers, certain to result in their termination, showed that the peer review process constituted the "harass[ment of] Black females."[92]

Peer review put Shanker's view of accountability to the test even more than instituting entry-level teacher exams because it risked the livelihood of practicing teachers rather than prospective ones. For the Black Caucus of the CFT, there was no way to separate this risk from race politics. Tom Mooney, president of the CFT, saw things differently from Coleman. He noted to Shanker that the CFT had "substantial black representation in its leadership and policy making structure" and that while 28 percent of CFT members were black, 40 percent of the teachers who sat on the peer review panel were. The percentages of teachers referred for peer review aligned almost exactly with the racial composition of the teaching force in Cincinnati as a whole, even though of the six teachers who were recommended for dismissal in the round of peer review that Coleman protested, half were black. In short, Mooney argued, the review process could not have been fairer to teachers or produce more positive results while still being accountable to the problems it was created to resolve. The CFT "provide[d] more due process in the appraisal process itself than is offered in the traditional appraisal by administrators," he explained to Shanker and "did everything possible to build in safeguards to protect teacher rights, guarantee due process, and arrive at sound decisions."[93] To be certain, Mooney's own teaching career and his local's relationship with black Cincinnati residents were more positive than Shanker's teaching career and the UFT's relationship with black city residents. But Coleman's protest, as much as it was a response to a specific situation, also reflected a larger concern that in a system in which teachers were ranked and measured, black teachers were bound to lose. Neither Shanker nor many other union leaders had proved especially adept at addressing race-specific concerns; to add to this problem, Black Caucus teachers' fears appeared to hinder reform rather than propel it forward.

On the one hand then, the move toward peer review reflected a new tension between black teachers and teacher unions. At the same time, however, peer review provoked an even larger question about the increasingly hierarchal organizational structure that unions were adopting. Roy Pellicano and Gloria Channon had critiqued a class of professional union leaders who held few ties to the classroom and, at the same time, had devised a self-sustaining tier of leadership. Peer review, as Patrick Daly of the Dearborn, Michigan, local of the AFT explained, gave classroom teachers a leadership role in education reform, but this did not always prove to be an easy or satisfactory development either.

"We've always said that anybody who has the power to hire and fire, should not be in the AFT, you've got to be in something else," Daly reflected. "Well [a] teacher sitting on an intern committee is not the power, but it's a voice."[94] The dilemma Daly pinpointed suggested two further challenges for the union in the 1980s. First, the AFT needed to rethink leadership structures to address the fact that many of the most significant advances in school reform were taking place at the local level and by teachers who simultaneously accepted leadership roles in their locals and in their schools. Second, teachers needed to adapt to a system of reform that developed new professional hierarchies and created new ways for teachers to be responsible not just to their students but to the profession. In Daly's experience, most teachers preferred to be evaluated by their principals rather than by their peers.[95] While this would seem to conflict with teachers' historic, often adversarial relationship with administrators, the teachers with whom Daly worked suggested they found their principals either to hold simpler standards or to possess a less critical eye than their colleagues. Even if peer review promised to strengthen the profession in terms of developing better teachers and more teacher leadership roles, teachers expressed that this group interest worked against their individual interests.

More broadly, the conflicts that took place between unionists supported Shanker aide Eugenia Kemble's contention that while Shanker succeeded at "making people understand 'the line' on various issues and stands, implementation remain[ed] a problem."[96] A final important example of this challenge occurred in 1991, when the AFT designed a project entitled "Leadership for Reform." The project invited a select group of union local leaders to work with Shanker on "generat[ing] a common understanding" of how to restructure schools to encourage more teacher governance over school policies and faculty professional development.[97] Its goal was to build on the kinds of changes being proposed and implemented in locals such as Toledo, Cincinnati, and Rochester and to consider how reorganizing schools could both empower teachers and create more productive and successful classrooms. From the beginning, the leaders selected for the project found the questions it provoked to be valuable yet complicated. They debated whether the union "could take the political risk of creating new professional leadership roles and structures" in the schools, much as successful peer review programs had started to do. Even more, they wondered how the union could "remain connected to such structures once they take on a life of their own."[98] In short, they saw that many of the advances for which Shanker advocated encouraged a professional autonomy and decentralization for union locals and their members that frequently conflicted with the political structures of teacher power. Shanker resolved these complications with a simplistic answer. A year after it began, he cancelled Leadership for Reform, not even notifying some members that he did so. Instead, he claimed to *Education Week* that the group's conclusions were "the kind of thing that could have come out of any group of students at a teacher/training institution over the last 50 years."[99] The project had included some of the most accomplished and visible AFT local leaders in the nation, hardly the run-of-the-mill types that Shanker suggested they were. But, if some of the project's conclusions were not new, its proposals, including rethinking academic tracking, nevertheless surpassed what Shanker was willing to advocate for.

The experiences of both organized black teachers and Leadership for Reform members reflected that school reform was a much more complicated process than Shanker's rhetoric and leadership style at times indicated. In 1991, Robert Perlman, a former consultant to the AFT, confided to Shanker that he knew the union president had tried to used his "'bully pulpit' to give intellectual leadership to these reform efforts" but that ultimately his proclamations "did not transform the AFT" and "when the union got the chance it retreated."[100] Perlman might have been referring to union locals like the Rochester Teachers Association (RTA), which adopted some of the most original and far-reaching programs for teacher mentorship and peer review. In fact, RTA president Adam Urbanski's idea for teachers' shared governance of schools gave teachers more authority—and more accountability—than Shanker had ever supported. Within several years of adopting this plan, however, tensions developed between the city's white and black teachers and between teachers and parents. Each group held different visions for their schools and the role of each other in ensuring student success. After years of infighting, Urbanski confessed, "I seem to be watching myself go more and more towards the old unionism."[101] Urbanski, like Black Caucus members and the members of Leadership for Reform, discovered that teacher power was a much messier, more complex process than the rhetoric fully accounted for. As a professional body, teachers disagreed on what they wanted to assume responsibility for, to whom they were accountable, and how to best improve public education. In short, they did not appear to agree on whether teacher power was even a suitable or attractive professional goal.

New York City's earliest organized teachers, both Teacher Unionists and Guild members, likely could not have conceived of the kinds of changes that Urbanski, Mooney, and other union leaders successfully petitioned for nationally. Programs like peer review and shared leadership structures in the schools would have seemed worlds away from what teachers who had virtually no control over their teaching assignments or their job security could have hoped to aspire to. Yet ironically, unionized teachers in the 1980s often argued that they wanted less authority, not more. For some teachers, assuming accountability over the profession required them to take responsibility for their students' and colleagues' performances, while offering them no real support or stronger relationship with the parents and communities that played an equally important role in school success. For others, accountability served as just another avenue by which to rank and marginalize teachers based on their race. Teacher power had been founded on the collaborations Shanker deemed important—especially that with the federal government—without creating a more collaborative culture among teachers or between teachers and other education stakeholders. Whether these kinds of collaborations were possible to create and how to forge them would be left for another generation of teacher unionists to determine.

Paper Teachers?

In 1989, Shanker summarized the advances teacher unionism had made in the previous decade when he claimed that education reform was "a new form of union militancy."[102] To be sure, transforming a nation of teachers and teacher unions from a largely industrial model of unionism—one in which the locals' greatest achievements were in bread-and-butter issues—to one in which school reform measures became part of union contracts with their school boards had not been easy. Nor had all locals yet made this transition. Despite examples of locals that had taken risks and fought for important reforms, Shanker concluded, "it's time for more local unions—and superintendents, and school boards and civic groups—to become militant."[103] His embrace of the term "militancy" marked a striking contrast from his writing in the 1970s, when problematic black parents were political "militants" and his own union members constituted education "activists." The contrast marked the distance that the union had traveled, both in what Shanker conceived of as its presiding mission and in public culture. The UFT in the 1960s was hardly passive. But while unionists in the 1960s and 1970s denied that they embraced militant political views, by the 1990s they welcomed a view of themselves as soldiers in a battle for better schools, primarily because Shanker and other AFT leaders made such an image a plausible one.

From his very beginnings as a teacher and teacher unionist, Shanker understood professionalism to be indelibly tied to public image. When he joined the Guild in the 1950s, he recalled, members wanted the union newspaper delivered to them at home and in plain, unmarked envelopes.[104] He pushed to get the newspaper delivered to teachers in their school mailboxes; to him, this move was not as much about union pride as it was about the visibility that successful unionism required. This seemingly minor decision on Shanker's part anticipated both the value he would hold for the press in building a professional advocacy movement and, at the same time, his willingness to prioritize what he thought was best for union members over what they thought was best for themselves. He defined a successful union as "an organization that figures out what people's hopes are, what their dreams are, and what they want . . . it shows them that the difference between dreams and reality is in making the dreams shared."[105] After determining his members' "shared dreams," both in terms of workplace concerns and in terms of heightening teacher professionalism, Shanker used "Where We Stand" to transmit his interpretation of those dreams and to build the relationships and alliances needed to make them happen.

Even more specifically, Shanker understood from early on that New Yorkers' and Americans' image of teachers and teacher unionists was intrinsically tied to his own. He traced his decision to develop the column to seeing a particular photograph published in the Sunday *New York Times*. The photograph, in which Shanker was shot from below, making a speech through a megaphone to teachers while standing on the roof on a van, portrayed him as a ringleader rather than a professional. Shanker claimed to have looked at the picture for "about an hour and I just couldn't recognize who I was." But readers' ability to recognize Shanker and to find this image consistent with what they thought about the UFT was just the point. In response to this photo, and likely to a wealth of other indicators, Shanker realized that he would need to alter the perception of himself as "some kind of madman who was only interested in power or confrontation or who somehow had a personal need to shut the schools down." At stake was not just his personal reputation but the potential "tremendous impact on public education in New York City."[106] In turn, he decided he needed to "devote some time and energy to letting the public know the union's president was someone who read books and had ideas about how to fix the schools."[107] To offer "a translation and analysis of some of the more interesting research findings in education," he called on education articles, books, and polls, often dedicating entire columns to the findings of experts in the field.[108] Relying on anecdotes of his own early teaching experiences as parables, he strove to capture the widest possible audience while still covering much of the same content as traditional union literature, including curriculum and school reform initiatives, teacher preparation and state certification battles, and a continued call for the import of collective bargaining. Shanker's attention to these subjects reflected his goals: to unite teachers and solidify membership, to register political positions, and to advertise teacher power.

While Shanker's image in the late 1960s as a militant leader made him news, his ability to transform his own image, the public perception of teachers unions, and the political issues that preoccupied teacher unions on the pages of the New York Times kept him a central public figure in the decades to follow. Yet, while "Where We Stand" enabled him to "refashio[n] the notion of union solidarity into an individual persona," as Kate Rousmaniere has argued, the decline of teacher-based journals and newspapers in New York City at the time Shanker began his column aided in this refashioning.[109] The city's fiscal crisis in the 1970s led to the cancellation of The Bulletin of High Points, the city's only mass disseminated, nonunion publication written by teachers. By the time Shanker conceived of "Where We Stand" in 1970, political conversations about city schools that, decades earlier, had been initiated and maintained by New York City teachers across a number of journalistic forums were now run largely by education experts and lawmakers. Teachers were now getting their information from a narrower group of sources and, much of the time, from Shanker himself. If historically teacher publications had empowered educators by building communities of readers and writers, Shanker's power was defined by his unique role in representing an entire community of teachers to the public and, critics would say, by equating teacher power with Shanker power.[110]

Within just a few years of Ocean Hill-Brownsville, many of Shanker's and the UFT's critics maintained that the New York Times had moderated its position on him. Writers such as Times education reporter Fred Hechinger critiqued Shanker off of the newspapers' pages, claiming that "[m]any of the things the schools need and help [Shanker] could give them would not, as he seems to think, in any way reduce his union's power or his teachers' power, but would immeasurably add to their standing."[111] But most news pieces rang a different chord. Analyses that described Shanker as a "soft-spoken, 45-year-old former mathematics teacher, steeped in the philosophy of Spinoza, Hegel, and John Dewey" painted him as more of a thinker than an activist.[112] If many accused Shanker of being a "power-hungry . . . slippery, two-faced, phony white liberal," another Times piece ventured, they might misread Shanker's visionary abilities and his dedication to making "the possible" happen.[113] In these reports, Shanker was no longer a militant but mainstream, not a man with a megaphone on a van but an education philosopher who was dedicated to the pragmatic. This change in tone frustrated union critics. Former community control rivals accused Shanker of "using newspeak to accomplish his purposes," a strategy that had become "a familiar blight on the public life of this city."[114] Other adversaries protested the ability of "Where We Stand" to serve as the sole voice over issues that were once debated between teachers and local education activists, explaining that "the presentation of union views and arguments [in the column] are plausible. They go unchallenged and unanswered because no one else has comparable resources to afford responses." The "unique national advertising campaign" Shanker embarked on "proclaim[ed] UFT wealth and power."[115] As early as three years into "Where We Stand," it was clear that the column was significant as much for what it represented about teacher power as for what it actually said.

Shanker himself noticed a change both in his treatment in the press and in teacher unions' image more largely. Teachers and schools faced a "peculiar alliance of critics," he described in 1973, including "liberal academics, giant foundations, profit-minded businessmen, and conservative public officials."[116] But while the number of critics did not diminish, the ability of teachers to address them as a collectivized force of professionals did. "For over one hundred years teachers in this country were powerless," Shanker wrote the following year, "but things are a little different now. . . . Teachers *have* a voice. Not a controlling one. We can't do everything we want. But, for the first time, we're *heard* and we get a *response*."[117] To explain this change, Shanker called on both the noticeable growth in teacher unionism and his own contributions as a leader and voice of teachers. More important to Shanker than the increasingly flattering media representations of him was what he saw as increased evidence of teacher power on the pages of the *Times* and other outlets. As brash and unyielding as Shanker himself, teacher power served as a formidable opponent to critiques of teacher performance by giving teachers the ability to speak back.

When asked about "Where We Stand," Shanker frequently cited as evidence of its influence its "readers all over the world" and the "thousands of people" who had written to him "to express their appreciation."[118] The column did indeed generate thousands of responses, from teachers—retired and practicing—common citizens, and political leaders. To be sure, the sheer number of letters that Shanker received attested to its significance and influence in teachers' eyes. This significance could often be as complicated a phenomenon as Shanker himself. Despite his often prickly persona, many fans portrayed him as not just a hero but a friend in a profession that often felt isolating. "Almost always after reading your articles, I feel so good knowing that someone understands how I feel," wrote a teacher from Livingston, New Jersey.[119] "Please keep on writing," pleaded another teacher from New York City. "As long as I read what you write, I don't feel alone."[120] Letters such as these suggested that even as most American teachers joined unions in the 1970s and 1980s, few felt part of a professional community in their everyday work lives. Teachers, even if they could not identify with Shanker, felt he could identify with them, in no small part because of his positions on school reform, high-quality teaching, and improving teachers' standing in the public eye.

While "Where We Stand" clearly set the tone for a new, growing teacher power movement, it did not clearly resolve the union's image problems—or its real tensions—with black city residents. In 1973, Shanker proposed to the *New York Amsterdam News* that he also publish his column in the black newspaper. While the paper continued to critique the performance of city teachers in the classroom, the events in Canarsie had softened its position on the UFT; one editorial even argued that the "consistency of the Union's Canarsie and Ocean Hill-Brownsville positions" proved that "UFT concerns had been, all along, quite legitimate."[121] Yet when the editors announced the forthcoming syndication of "Where We Stand," readers responded so viscerally that only one column was ever published. Even as some important black individuals and institutions altered their view of Shanker, or, at least, their willingness to work with him, other black city residents, including UFT members, did not, arguing that "Shanker and the UFT are merely interested in control of black schools for the purpose of maintaining their own economic security" and now sought "to control the minds of black readers."[122]

Shanker and his column earned criticism not just from black New Yorkers but, increasingly, from teachers as well. Shanker's attention had often been focused on addressing those who criticized him for being too closely connected with the trade labor movement, yet his mail reflected that many teachers believed he was out of touch with ordinary teachers not because he was too laborcentric but because he had become too much a part of the political establishment. To be certain, the local and national unions that Shanker led and represented often came under their fair share of criticism as they became real participants in urban education reform and in municipal, state, and federal politics. This criticism echoed a growing belief that unions were becoming just another bureaucratic institution. "Teachers are downtrodden and frustrated because their Union has failed them," explained one teacher from New York. "Whenever I have looked to my union for help—I have gotten sharp, derisive remarks similar to those I have gotten from the N.Y.C. Board of Ed."[123] But more than teacher unions coming under fire, Shanker himself drew frustration and resentment. "How interesting that you feel like patting your own back is in order," wrote one teacher. "The sixties are long gone; what have you done for us lately? We all know what we have done for you, we see it, every two weeks, on our pay stubs."[124] "I really wonder whether your old zeal for improving education hasn't waned considerably," questioned yet another. "I don't see you challenging the 'establishment' in these columns the way you should."[125] In letter after letter, teachers across the nation accused Shanker of not being knowledgeable or interested enough about the work and plight of teachers, of having lost touch with the rank and file, and of looking out for his own gain before theirs.

To such critics, Shanker's very column stood not as a political tool to improve teachers' daily work lives but as further evidence that teacher power and teachers' power were two different phenomena. Many remarked on the lack of teachers' direct voices in Shanker's column and his willingness to direct union policy from afar. The column's readers have "very little sense that you have recently been near a school, much less a classroom," critiqued one such teacher. "It is easy to be philosophical from a distance."[126] "We are doing the job while you and others pontificate," argued another.[127] Such teachers may have been responding to specific aspects of Shanker's policy or his personality, but they also responded to the fact that increasingly, throughout the 1970s and 1980s, being a teacher union leader was a position that required Shanker to spend more time with politicians than with teachers and more closely resembled the work of a lobbyist than a classroom practitioner. Column readers complained that Shanker quoted business leaders and politicians when they really wanted to hear from "those in the 'trenches.'"[128] The result, one such reader explained, was that Shanker demonstrated a "lack of concern for real teachers" as opposed to the "paper teachers who appear[ed] in [his] syndicated column."[129] To some Shanker appeared to transform teachers into just another rhetorical device by which to reach objectives that were more about professionalism and teacher power as theoretical or political concepts than the actual people in the classroom.

Teacher unionists, like teachers as a whole, were also often excluded from the production of Shanker's column. In 1986, Shanker's public relations assistant suggested that he assign twelve columns per year to be written by notable local union leaders, including Tom Mooney and Adam Urbanski, both of whom had led some of the AFT's most important strides in their locals to improve teacher quality.[130] Shanker rejected the suggestion. He often purposefully overshadowed the accomplishments of other teacher unionists who matched him in dedication, present and past. For example, in a 1985 column, "Taking a Walk down Memory Lane," Shanker reminisced on the twenty-fifth anniversary of the UFT and charted his memories as a novice teacher in 1953, when "teachers had no one empowered to represent them." He contrasted this decade with the political actions of the UFT in the 1960s, including when he was jailed, an experience that taught him "for the first time what it really means to be deprived of liberty." Part labor epic, part self-hagiography, the column ended with Shanker's promise that he would "be around, sounding off in this column and elsewhere on the unfinished business of American education and the importance of teachers controlling their own destiny."[131]

Two weeks later, Tess Gloster, an early and lifelong Guild member, composed a response. The column "might have been a remarkable one had you really remembered and paid tribute to the not small number of selfless people, impelled by their enthusiasm to encompass the real promise of teaching, who constituted the Teachers' Guild," wrote an aging Gloster, who recited a long list of Guild members and the accomplishments they had earned on workplace issues before the advent of collective bargaining. "Only Harriet Winburne and I are still alive," she concluded. "I cannot be silent while your rewriting of history commits them to oblivion."[132] The letter, concerned with rescuing the memory of the group of Guild members who predated Shanker and the union he would help to create, spoke to the way in which his column had often obscured the efforts of the many teachers he represented and who set the groundwork for modern teacher unionism. In the column's twenty-six years, Shanker had created a compelling story about teacher unions that caught public interest and attention unlike anything before. But the story Shanker told was, invariably, the view of its author, and its author had consistently fought for a singular, centralized, and uncomplicated narrative of UFT and AFT triumph.

Shanker's testimonies and writing in venues other than "Where We Stand" suggest that he believed this narrative was true. Just as important, however, he recognized that the narrative—as well as the column itself—was politically expedient. As "Where We Stand" reached more and more significant anniversaries, Shanker grew increasingly focused on addressing his celebrity and the relationship between his changed place in American political life and the role of his column. "Of course writing a weekly column is also a pain in the neck," he confessed to readers in his twentieth anniversary issue. "I travel often, and taking time away from a meeting in Kyoto or Nairobi to write or call in the column is no fun," he explained. "But whenever I start thinking this way, someone stops me at the airport in Akron or at a restaurant in Budapest and praises or criticizes what I wrote a week ago. . . . And I'm hooked again."[133] In his ruminations, Shanker constructed the column not as one man speaking to his union members and the public but as an interactive experience between a columnist and his readers. The power of "Where We Stand," he suggested repeatedly, came not from its author but from its popular demand and appeal. "There is no question," he claimed often, "that the column . . . enhanced the political power of teachers and the UFT" by focusing widespread attention on the professionals he represented.[134] Yet the story of the AFT outside of the column offers a more complicated narrative. As even his fan mail indicates, seeing Shanker as an ally or a friend was not the same as feeling satisfied in one's job. If the letters Shanker received in response to "Where We Stand" attested to its public import, they did not always prove the power of the column to improve the everyday work lives of those in the profession.

This was not the only dilemma in teacher power and the increased authority of teacher unions that the column revealed. "Where We Stand" both reflected and enabled a changed means of going about school reform, one that was closely tied to the way in which reform was debated, discussed, and legislated by the end of the 1980s. More significant than any marked change in the quality of education offered to minority students in the last quarter of the century was a changed relationship between education stakeholders. The increased federalization of school reform and teacher unionism's own centralization under the banner of teacher power altered the ways in which educators and the public communicated. Writing in 1987, Amy Gutmann argued that these changes had created "layers of administrative decisions [that] now insulate the policies of school boards and the preferences of ethnic communities within local school districts from the potentially critical perspective of teachers, and vice versa." This insulation quelled the kinds of public schisms that were so visible in 1960s New York City, but, as Gutmann argued, it also overrode "a potentially creative tension within democratic education between communal and professional authority, whereby communities and teachers are encouraged to take each others' educational priorities and programs seriously."[135] Many times, as the history of New York City teachers reflects, a tension between professionals and community members was less than creative or productive, as teachers and activists often diminished the concerns of each other. But although the strikes in Ocean Hill-Brownsville may not have presented the most flattering portrait of democracy, they attested to the seriousness with which both organized black parents and city teachers viewed the project of public education and their role within it. In contrast, by the time of Shanker's death in 1997, for reasons that both included and surpassed his vision of and strategies for teacher power, the viewpoints of parents and teachers were much more difficult to interpret, largely because they were more difficult to hear.

Gutmann's analysis touches on the most important distinction between the teacher power movement that union leaders created in the 1970s and 1980s and the relationship among teachers, professionalism, and civil rights in the four decades preceding. Teachers, parents, and citizens may have written letters to Shanker in great numbers in response to *A Nation at Risk* and his column, but their beliefs often went unrecognized in Shanker's own writing. Instead, many educators suggested they believed they had become "paper teachers," an invention of Shanker's imagination used to propel particular kinds of reform. Teacher unions had made measurable strides in political power, but the advances they had made in the classroom were much less certain. By the 1990s, public schools were as segregated as they were at the time of *Brown v. Board of Education*; minority public schools employed double the percentage of new and inexperienced teachers than did majority white schools.[136] Teachers had built the most robust and influential union movement in the nation in response to these kinds of problems, but their relationship to civil rights—which ranged from participatory to supportive to dismissive—had more radically altered their professional rights' campaigns than it had their students' welfare. In this way, teacher power may have produced important changes in unions' recognition and influence in education policy in its time, but it left many of teachers' most fundamental and long-lived professional questions unanswered.

Conclusion: Moving beyond Rights?
Teacher Professionalism and Civil Rights in the Era of No Child Left Behind

Walk into a low-income, minority school today, and you are likely to see halls plastered with the same optimistic slogans that have come to serve as fixtures in most American public schools. Walk into a classroom, however, and you are likely to see two unique realities that undermine those clichés: students mechanically preparing for standardized tests and teachers "teaching" from mandated instructional packages, otherwise known as scripted curricula. Written by private corporations that also serve as powerful lobbyists for school reform policy, these "teacher-proof" plans prescribe not just the content of a given lesson but every sentence that teachers will read off to their students in the course of a class. Accounts of teachers' work with these curricula run from the ridiculous (the scripts allotting no time for teachers to repeat themselves) to the perverse (the common technique of call-and-response drills, a system of militaristic hand signals that accompanies one such program). In the words of Robert Slavin, creator of the Success for All Foundation, a supplier of premade curricula, scripted lessons promise not to "leave very much to chance" and instead offer a "relentless" approach to ensure productive activities "down to the level of minute-by-minute in the classroom."[1] The prevalent use of scripted curricula in many urban districts nationwide suggests that because poor children come to school less prepared than middle-class children, they must sacrifice discovery and innovation for efficiency, regimentation, and routine. For teachers, districts' adoption of such curricula has produced unique professional and ethical challenges. Teaching from scripted lessons is like working in an "intellectual straightjacket," explained one teacher. "I know that teaching Success for All is a charade," confessed another, but "if I don't do it I won't be permitted to teach these children."[2] In a situation in which the educators who teach the most disadvantaged children possess the least opportunity to design creative and intellectually rewarding classrooms, students' and teachers' rights alike have been sacrificed.

Today, teachers are in the precarious position of needing to win back the professional "right" to control their work more than ever before. How did they arrive in this position? Eighty years ago, in the midst of the Great Depression, the concept of teachers' rights reflected academic freedom issues and bread-

and-butter concerns, particularly salary, tenure, and promotion. That concept grew more complex as midcentury teacher unionists linked professional rights campaigns to new sets of issues, including job assignments, the right to discipline students as they saw fit, and the right to teach without parental interference. Inextricable from larger conversations about racial discrimination and civil rights, these later understandings of teachers' rights linked students' welfare and teachers' interests in broad yet often incompatible ways. Parents, education activists, and community organizations became the targets of these campaigns as much as education administrators, leaving unionized teachers an isolated if nevertheless sizeable interest group. Today, we have entered a new era in a story of teachers' rights. For many educators, current mandates that require them to focus on test preparation and use prepackaged curricula ensure that their students are offered a second-class education and leave teachers as the disseminators of it. In addition to the negative impact this system has had on students, then, are the complex questions it poses to the profession: Does designing one's own curriculum or determining the course content in one's classroom constitute a professional right? Are teachers' rights violated when they are mandated to treat students in ways they find unethical? What is the role of teacher unions in improving teacher quality? And to what degree does it make sense to frame professional decisions and performance in terms of a discourse of rights?

These questions are all the more vital precisely because we live in another momentous period in a long-standing struggle to create education equity. The No Child Left Behind Act (NCLB), a reauthorization of the 1965 Elementary and Secondary Education Act (ESEA), is not solely the result of teachers' failure to prove themselves accountable to minority students, but it does address black parents' historic concern that their children were taught by a high percentage of unmotivated or unskilled teachers. Federal leaders have capitalized on black parents' historical call for greater accountability and have set in place a wide array of measures intended to regulate school and teacher quality. In contrast to the ESEA, however, which was one law in a body of Great Society legislation designed to address issues of poverty and social inequity, NCLB stands alone, leaving schools, teachers, and students as the exclusive bearers of wide-ranging social reform.[3] This stark fact can only make sense as a policy because of a wide public distrust of teachers and a belief that teacher incompetence is one of the broadest and most important problems in public education. "Money is never going to be the entire answer in education," Secretary of Education Duncan has maintained, because "adult dysfunction," especially that of teachers, "has hindered students' ability to learn."[4] Ridding schools of that dysfunction is not simply a problem of economics, he has argued, but of professionalism.

In addition to this distrust of teachers, a discourse of rights has made possible a platform for education reform that centers on teacher quality at the cost of so many other contributors to an achievement gap that is as profound today as it was in the 1960s. Education equity, Duncan has announced, "is the civil rights issue of our generation."[5] Standing on the Edmund Pettus Bridge in Selma, Alabama, on the forty-fifth anniversary of Bloody Sunday, he proclaimed that equalizing education was the "next bridge to cross" in civil rights and that "if you cannot read, you are not truly free."[6] To be sure, nearly eight decades after black parents' equal school campaigns first began, there is much to suggest that minority students are still being denied a fair and equal education. Northern schools are as segregated as they were at the time of *Brown v. Board of Education*; black students in the Northeast are among the most profoundly segregated in the nation. Nationwide, just over half of black and Latino students graduate from high school; for males, the percentages are as low as 33 percent in some states.[7] Black students continue to be tracked in disproportionate numbers to special education programs, where they exhibit less progress than their white counterparts.[8] The gravity and complexity of these facts, however, are too often elided in a rhetoric that represents disenfranchisement as a product of interactions between individual students and teachers without attending to the overlapping and systematic inequalities that come to hinder both.

Because of this important truth, it is critical to assess what is at stake in framing contemporary school reform efforts as civil rights initiatives, particularly when the history of school reform and civil rights has proved fraught with tension and challenges. From a positive standpoint, framing these projects as civil rights measures projects a strong message about the federal government's commitment to improving minority education. Situating education equity in the context of one of the most pivotal and publicly recognizable events in our national history—the 1960s civil rights movement—links contemporary schools to a period that many Americans consider sacred ground. More troubling, however, and as this book has argued, because both the achievements of the period and the costs of those achievements were so great, they often have defied a closer, more complete analysis. Aligning school reform with this period promises to hold the same effect. That is, justifying contemporary reform efforts as civil rights work allows some of the most problematic aspects of contemporary school reform, including scripted curricula, to go unquestioned in the search of a greater good. This equation often has been successful. In the last two decades, fundamental changes have taken place in how schools educate and who makes decisions about teaching and learning. But while these changes have been critiqued by scholars and experts, they exist on a daily basis without popular protest.

And yet, as corporations continue to create teacher-proof lessons, and as states continue to mandate their use, there is much to suggest that students and teachers in minority schools are less free because of current school reforms, not more. This dual disenfranchisement of racial minority students and the teachers who teach them is nothing new; one of the most important lessons to be learned from the example of New York City teachers is that they nevertheless had and made choices in how they confronted their shared marginalization. In the 1930s, the Teachers Union and the Guild developed different responses to these challenges and, in so doing, represented two different strands in American liberal thought: the first, a faith in the power of coalitions of organized individuals to effect change; the second, a belief that institutions were color-blind and, therefore, the best medium to promote equality, justice, and social advancement. To be certain, the Guild's philosophy often confirmed its members' own life trajectories in which schools enabled them to become the first professionals in their families. That is, Guild members' life stories echoed a greater stock narrative about American democracy and opportunity that, although conceptually limited, also stood at the very center of public school design. While troubling in their race-tinged connotations, Guild arguments were important nevertheless in their refusal to locate teachers as the source of inequalities that were first and foremost rooted in expansive economic and political disparities. Their argument that school institutions needed to be made equal before teachers could provide an equal education countered the Board of Education's conservative-driven policies. While the Guild clearly prioritized teachers' welfare over students' welfare in its transfer policies, it also suggested that when students were disenfranchised, teachers necessarily were too.

The Teachers Union recognized these institutional shortcomings as well, although it projected more faith in individual teachers to overcome them. Teacher Unionists committed themselves to protesting widespread forms of economic discrimination, and they believed that teachers could make a significant difference in the quality of children's lives until society changed. Their ability to ally themselves with the oppressed communities they served offers an important example of how liberal whites and blacks worked collaboratively to reform schools. One of the most affecting themes in minority parents' accounts of their work with the Teachers Union was the way in which Unionist teachers taught them "what can happen when teachers voice their protests, when they don't just stay for two terms."[9] To many black parents, teacher accountability and teacher quality were inextricable from working conditions that promoted professional commitment, including teachers' freedom to comment and dissent.

These two models of teacher unionism are all the more important to revisit now in a political and educational climate that appears to hold little faith either in schools as public institutions or in the individuals who teach in them. One of the lesser recognized effects of this lack of faith is the way in which it has curtailed teachers' ability to dissent from practices and philosophies they find unproductive, unethical, and unprofessional. Former Minnesota Federation of Teachers president Louise Sundin has compellingly explained how NCLB has set teacher unions back. "We spent 20 years trying to professionalize teachers," she has argued, "and now we're getting thrown back into the industrial model, because it's top down, it's organized around hierarchy, and it's line supervisor oriented. You do the curriculum this way because that's the way we've decided it's going to be better."[10] Sundin contends that unions have met top-down, contemporary reforms that prioritize regulation over professional agency and aspiration with much of the same. A strong advocate of peer review and the kinds of teacher leadership roles with which union locals experimented in the 1980s and early 1990s, Sundin sees the current undoing as a threat to the profession and to teacher unions, which have often been ineffective in countering the reforms mandated by NCLB.[11]

Since the debates over teacher transfers in the 1940s, unions' commitment to a particular notion of teachers' rights has often operated defensively and reactively to inadequate social policy rather than setting forth a proactive agenda that fosters and rewards teacher quality despite it. As a result, unionists like Sundin have faced difficulty in creating a more nuanced conversation about education equity, in part because their opinion is less consequential in compensatory school policy than in the most traditional terrain of teachers' rights: salary, tenure, and pension.[12] State governors, for-profit education foundations, and lobbyists representing private corporations have gained unprecedented influence in shaping the content and implementation of school reform regulations. Education interest groups such as teacher unions, which in Shanker's era had an opportunity to participate in reform decisions, largely have been shut out from the process.[13] To union critics, this alienation is a product of unions' unwillingness to look beyond teachers' rights and their proclivity to excuse poor teacher quality. The very concept of "reform unionism," Terry M. Moe has argued, constitutes a "fanciful notion, based on a fatal misconception: that the unions can be counted on not to pursue their own interests." Moe's interpretation of union policies and his definition of union interests as "securing benefits and protections for members, increasing the demand for teachers, supporting higher taxes, regularizing the flow of resources into union coffers, minimizing competition, and seeking political power" echo the arguments of many critics, including minority parents, who have viewed unions as intransigent, self-interested organizations.[14]

Yet the history of the Teachers Union, and moments in the Guild's history, contest a popular interpretation of teacher unions as purely reactionary and divisive. Critiques of unions as solely self-interested exclude all of the public works that teachers have performed through their unions, including designing multicultural curricula, petitioning for black school board representatives, fighting for better school facilities and other resources for black students, teaching in freedom schools, and risking their job security to speak out on behalf of black children's civil rights. Some of teachers' most important professional achievements in the past century occurred when they overcame a fear that their professionalism could be sacrificed or compromised by minority students and the problems that minority schools presented. In these instances, unions served as an important source of support for these teachers and, in so doing, made such works possible. Whether unions can work on behalf of a larger, more expanded and connected sense of teachers' and students' interests is not truly the question then. History tells us that the answer is yes. Whether unions will, and if the more than one million teachers who count themselves as union members will expect and demand for them to do so, remains to be seen.

If contemporary education politics poses new challenges for disenfranchised students and the teachers who serve them, it might also indicate new grounds on which to be hopeful for change—and, more specifically, ideas for how teachers may play an important role in this change. To be certain, the education of poor, minority students holds a different kind of political currency now than it has in the past; at stake in the debates over how to improve minority schools is not just the welfare of minority communities but of American public schools themselves. In 2003, nearly 40 percent of all American public school students belonged to racial minority groups, a percentage that will increase in the coming decades.[15] Reforming minority schools is no longer a marginal concern; improving disadvantaged schools has become one of the nation's most important domestic policy issues. But as the implementation of NCLB and the current realities of minority schools signal, real reform and real equity must make the actors at hand part of the equation, not disinvite them from it because they are complex or risky or unpredictable. In this light, making sense of the relationship between teachers and the minority communities they serve takes on an even broader significance. If we can understand the historic challenges to cooperation between these two groups and learn from the ways in which students' and teachers' interests were polarized in the past, we will have a stronger basis on which to remedy these factors and ensure student welfare and teacher welfare at once.

In the context of early civil rights efforts for school equity, teacher quality was one of a number of factors by which black parents and activists measured the overall quality of their schools. Teachers were seen as an important resource, but not necessarily the primary or most strategic one in this fight. Civil rights campaigns in the 1930s were at least equally focused on the unsafe and unsatisfactory conditions of neighborhood school buildings, conditions that led to more widespread and documentable inequities than did individual teachers. With the growth of teacher unions and unions' frequent evasion, if not obstruction, of black parents' critiques and objectives, the issue of teacher quality gained prominence in civil rights campaigns. By the 1960s, black children's reading and math scores remained well below the city average, and black students were disproportionately assigned to remedial classes and juvenile courts. These systematic problems were not solely a product of unequal economic resources, parents concluded, but of the people who were teaching their children, many of whom were vocal about their displeasure in doing so. The more militant and organized movement that developed around a concern over teacher quality is one of the most powerful legacies to have grown out of the history of teacher unions. Black parents won some and lost many school policy battles in the 1960s; more certainly, they won a sense of public empathy in what became a struggle against teacher unions as much as Board policy.

Since then, few of black activists' historic concerns about education equality have been resolved, while public interest in teacher quality has grown all the more wide-ranging.[16] Policy makers and education analysts across the political spectrum have argued that teacher quality determines the kind of education students receive more than any other school resource, even as they disagree on what constitutes quality and how to measure it.[17] Closely tied to this development is another. In the decades since Shanker endorsed A Nation at Risk, civil rights measures focused on closing the achievement gap have concentrated on academic excellence—or the absolute quality of education—rather than on equity, the relative quality of education provided to different groups of students. As a result, "accountability" has come to define the central mission of good schools in contemporary legislation and, Lawrence McAndrews has argued, has "supplanted 'opportunity' as the major buzzword of school policy."[18] Accountability is an important term, one first employed by black parents. Today, policy makers use "accountability" to signify a theoretically objective set of education measurements in which the bottom line is easier to quantify, failure is easier to name, and professional skill is easier to evaluate. At the same time, to be accountable is to be accountable to someone or something. For schools to become accountable requires the people who work within them to be answerable to the communities they serve, not to stand as the self-regulating actors they at times have claimed to be.

Yet teacher quality has become no easier to define or, even more, to regulate. This is all the more so in the case of the novice teachers who are overrepresented on faculty rosters in minority schools.[19] The history of New York City shows that parents frequently developed their own standards and factors for assessing teacher quality—including teachers' feelings of job satisfaction and the retention required to promote teacher development within particular school settings—that may or may not have echoed those of the Board or teachers themselves. Today, the measurement systems endorsed by federal and state laws frequently underscore the complexity of the profession more than they offer evidence by which to strengthen it. Efforts on the part of most states to count years of service as an indicator of teacher quality have led to the designation of almost all experienced teachers as highly qualified, regardless of their actual skills and abilities.[20] Nationwide, less than 1 percent of teachers rank as unsatisfactory on their evaluations, a trend that disguises excellence as much as it does failure.[21] Parents, teachers, education experts, and administrators have concluded that the best teachers are those who possess mastery of a broad range of pedagogical practices that can be adapted to different students, but most teacher evaluations are standardized, one-time affairs that conflict with those essentials of good teaching. Teacher unions, which recently have lagged in advancing better alternatives, are now starting to advocate for more holistic and in-depth models of evaluation, but the ability of schools to radically transform the culture of evaluation and professional development, and the effectiveness of federal law to promote such changes, remains to be seen.[22]

Altogether, the challenges in defining and documenting teacher quality are just one example of Kathryn Neckerman's larger argument that NCLB "is symbolically quite important, but it is coupled with too thin an understanding of how schools work."[23] With this thin understanding, lawmakers have turned to standardized test scores as a universal indicator of teacher performance and quality. Objective accountability measures like test scores, lawmakers have argued, are the best insurance that minority children are being offered an equitable education. But, as most teachers in such schools can testify, the resulting effect on classrooms is hardly equitable. Tracing a year in a low-income minority school in Maryland, journalist Linda Perlstein found that "everything was judged on its effect on the scores."[24] The result, Perlstein recounts in *Tested*, echoes what many teachers in struggling minority schools witness every day: teachers pushed to focus first (and, often, solely) on training students to improve their test performances, largely out of administrative pressure, but also because nearly a decade into NCLB, many novice teachers have few professional models of anything else. What Perlstein tracked in one school is common to urban, high-poverty, and high-minority schools. Teachers in these schools report that they dedicate a month and more of class time solely to test preparation and that they regularly make pedagogical decisions based on their students' performance on exams rather than on what they believe would be most relevant or helpful for students to learn.[25] If anything, NCLB has only intensified the stratification of pedagogical techniques in the nation's least and most privileged school districts.

At the heart of this stratification exist cultural beliefs about poor and minority students; just as important, however, are the beliefs NCLB projects about their teachers. The range of measures designed to improve teacher and school performance, Susan Moore Johnson argues, has had the effect of announcing that teachers "are not making sufficient efforts in their work and may be motivated to try harder by promises of financial rewards or threat of public embarrassment."[26] Many teachers believe that even if most Americans are not versed in the specifics of the law, they assent to these fundamental assumptions and to the correlating images of teachers as lax and unmotivated. In 2007, 38 percent of teachers in urban, minority schools reported that they did not feel respected by society.[27] Earning a graduate degree in teaching was a futile task, reported one teacher in *Tested*, although she was pursuing one nevertheless. In a school culture of scripted curricula and constant test preparation, she admitted, "anyone could walk off the street and have my job."[28] As in the past, teachers in minority schools today exhibit feelings of professional limitations and liabilities that are connected to the student populations they serve. Rather than addressing this difficulty, current policy makers have exacerbated it. To remedy the problem, however, requires teachers to respond.

To address teacher professionalism, unions must address the issue of teacher quality. The belief that minority students fail because their teachers lack sufficient motivation or dedication has been a difficult one to dispel, in part because the public image unionized teachers created in the mid-twentieth century so solidified this image. At the heart of accountability talk exists an underlying belief that teachers have not been held accountable to the students at the bottom of the achievement gap. The historic relationship between teacher unionists and civil rights activists in New York City reveals some of the reasons why this belief developed. Yet both Guild and Teachers Union members saw unionism as a pathway to being *more* engaged in the profession, not less so. Those city residents who were most aware of teacher unionists' presence—black parents—testified on behalf of Teacher Union members throughout World War II and the cold war, and they worked with the Guild on desegregation campaigns. Such parents saw teacher unionists as more influential and often more accountable to their children than many other teachers. This changed in the 1950s and 1960s, when a wider political spectrum of teachers joined the Guild and the United Federation of Teachers (UFT) and used the unions to advocate for them on an equally wide and complex range of issues, from salary concerns to setting boundaries on parents' direct presence in the classroom. In short, teachers' midcentury "freedom from" argument as a means of framing their professional rights suggested that they were above accountability, both to the communities they served and to the social issues that came to impact their classrooms. To much of the public, teacher unions appeared to protect teachers, however negligent, inadequate, or unaccountable, and to prioritize teachers' improved influence and position in the competitive and hierarchical political structure of education policy over producing better teachers.

Teacher unions' general record of achievement in the last fifty years has reinforced this narrow view of teachers' interests and rights. The UFT and the American Federation of Teachers (AFT) have been successful in their collective bargaining over tenure, salary, and pensions; teaching is a better rewarded profession that it was at the time of World War II, and teachers' salaries have changed more substantially than have the economic conditions of minority schools.[29] This success has been predicated on another: the growth and mainstream positioning of teacher unions in political culture. The anguished debates over whether or not teachers should unionize in the 1930s are inconceivable today. But unions have been far less successful in closing the achievement gap or, it would seem, in helping to produce better teachers. These objectives, central to the work of the early Teachers Union and Guild, appear to have been lost in a rhetoric of teachers' rights, largely because they did not easily fit into that rhetoric. Instead, teacher unions frequently have come under fire from conservatives and liberals alike for maintaining the status quo and obstructing the process of improving minority education. From resisting more rigorous evaluation systems for teachers to collective bargaining agreements that have made insufficient teachers almost impossible to fire, unions often appear to defy accountability even as they profess to advocate it.

Yet it is not too late to learn from history. If teacher quality has been difficult to define, teachers' concerns have not been. Teachers' greatest obstacles today both resound with and differ from the past. Nationally, teachers who resign from large urban schools to teach elsewhere list student discipline, lack of student motivation, lack of parental involvement, and lack of influence over decision making as the most important causes of their departure.[30] Each of these complaints echoes those recorded by white teachers as early as the 1930s, even though, as this book has shown, some of them, such as a lack of parental involvement, were a product of teachers' perceptions or expectations more than a reality. In an important change, however, contemporary teachers' grievances have been consistent across racial lines. Rather than indicating some kind of "postracial society," these responses reflect a shared belief among teachers that urban schools are difficult places in which to feel professional because teachers' expertise goes unvalued by students and administrators alike. Policy studies support this impression. In terms of individual school policies, teachers on the whole exert the most influence in tracking students, setting school discipline policies, and making spending decisions about their schools' budgets. They hold the least influence in establishing a schoolwide curriculum, determining the subject or source of in-service workshops they are mandated to attend, and deciding teacher assignments. This has proven most true for teachers in large urban schools.[31] In other words, most teachers have little say in the most important academic and professional decisions in their schools, including their professional development and that of their colleagues.

Just as these kinds of deficiencies in school culture do not readily lend themselves to legal solutions or rights-based campaigns, unions must also adapt to address the kinds of changes that can most powerfully improve teacher quality. American teachers' commitment to unionism remains strong: 88 percent of teachers belong to a union. But the landscape of what constitutes teachers' professional welfare has changed, and unions have thus far been slow to adapt. Contemporary teachers suggest they are ready and eager for change, with or without their unions. Most unionized teachers, 81 percent, report that their unions are most helpful at protecting them against school politics or administrators who abuse their power. But few see their unions as playing key roles in larger education issues; nearly half believe that their unions fight to protect low-quality teachers.[32] Union leaders who have "gone in and defended teachers who shouldn't even be pumping gas" receive criticism from a wide swath of teachers who see this narrow approach to defending teachers' rights as harmful to the profession.[33] Approaching professional incompetence as a civil rights issue has extracted costs from teachers and unions alike. While unions appear to their members to be doing a good job of advocating for them on an individual basis, they see their unions as doing considerably less well at raising the standards of the profession.

These critiques are important, and they may reflect a change in what contemporary teachers want from their unions. Teachers hired at the height of the civil rights movement, Julia Koppich has shown, by and large value "job security and autonomy, are wary of competition, and oppose differential job treatment." Other scholars have found similar results. Teachers hired in the 1960s and 1970s, as Morgaen Donaldson describes them, "proved to be a conservative group on the job" and have "intensely resist[ed] reforms that were intended to engage them in group work" or that have sought "to make distinctions between them, such as recognizing and rewarding individuals' special skills, strengths, or contributions."[34] The most recent generations of teachers, by contrast, continually report to value variety, collaboration, risk taking, and entrepreneurial opportunities. "The former set of values is a good fit for the type of collective bargaining that built the power of teacher unions," Koppich concludes, "the latter is not."[35] In fact, teachers' sentiments about unionism appear to bear out these central differences; the older teachers are, the more likely they are to believe that their union reflects their views and values.[36] New teachers then seem not only to hold a different view of unionism than experienced teachers, they also appear to hold a different view of professionalism. The working relationships that they describe might be said to combine the Guild's philosophy of the term "professionalism"—one focused on professional expertise—with that of the Teachers Union—one focused on teachers' relationship with other education stakeholders, including administrators, students, parents, and the local communities that schools serve.

This philosophy of professionalism is echoed in important teacher organizations that focus on professional development and advocacy at once. One such example, the largest and most significant of such, can be found in the National Writing Project (NWP), a national network of hundreds of local sites that since 1973 has focused on improving literacy instruction and providing opportunities for teachers to assume greater agency and responsibility in their professional development. As an organization, the NWP has prioritized teacher collaboration and teacher learning and has radically changed the ways in which participating educators think of professional expertise.[37] In month-long institutes each summer, thousands of NWP teachers across the nation teach experimental lessons before their peers and conduct scholarly research in response to questions that have arisen for them in the context of their classroom work. Year-round, they write professional publications about their findings and offer in-service workshops that draw on both their research and their classroom experience to teach other teachers what they know. In short, the NWP has brought value and visibility to teachers' ongoing learning and professional development, rather than arguing that "expertise" is a finished product or something that exists independently from the communities teachers serve. With over two hundred branches nationwide, some of the largest and most prolific are found in large urban areas where racial minority students constitute the majority of public school students, including New York, Philadelphia, Los Angeles, and Denver. This is the kind of work that unions might also be able to foster, and it is the kind of work, contemporary political culture suggests, that they must foster if they want to exist as something more than bread-and-butter organizations.

As teachers continue to seek out professional development organizations to find the kinds of support they are looking for, they pose important questions and challenges to teacher unions. The problems minority schools face may be as significant as they were midcentury, but teachers suggest we have entered a period in which rights talk is no longer the most desired or effective pathway to advocacy. To be sure, teachers appear to distinguish between the workplace rights for which their unions adjudicate effectively and a host of important professional, social, and political problems that are equally central to their work and that many unionists like Louise Sundin have professed they want unions also to address. The rights-based rhetoric of teacher unions that developed in the 1960s and has persisted ever since has proven too restrictive and too simplistic to address the complexities of either teaching or learning. Instead, unions must present accessible, specific, and committed arguments for improving teacher professionalism and students' well-being at the same time and lobby for the support they need to act on them. It has been done before. Fighting for the continued existence of the Teachers Union in its last decade, teacher Eugene Jackson explained to those who held too limited an understanding of what it accomplished, "I know the union ha[s] made me a better teacher," because it made him a more committed, involved, and empowered professional in the classroom, his school, and his school's community.[38] For modern unions to do more than survive but to produce meaningful changes in the ways American children are educated, they must return to this goal once again.

Abbreviations

AF   Ann Filardo Collection, American Federation of Teachers, Archives of Labor and Urban Affairs, Walter P. Reuther Library, Wayne State University.

AFTOH   AFT Oral History Collection, Archives of Labor and Urban Affairs, Walter P. Reuther Library, Wayne State University.

CB   Charles J. Bensley Papers, 1947–1954, New York City Board of Education, New York City Department of Records/Municipal Archives.

CINN   Cincinnati Federation of Teachers Collection, Archives of Labor and Urban Affairs, Walter P. Reuther Library, Wayne State University.

GUILD   New York City Teachers Guild Records, 1923–1957, Kheel Center for Labor-Management Documentation and Archives, Cornell University Library.

HNAP   Harlem Neighborhood Association Records, 1941–1978, Schomburg Center for Research in Black Culture, New York City Public Library.

HP   *The Bulletin of High Points in the Work of the High Schools of New York City.*

JB   Associate Superintendent Jacob Greenberg, Intercultural Education Course Files, 1944–1953, New York City Board of Education Records, New York City Department of Records/Municipal Archives.

JM   James Marshall Papers, 1930–1986, New York City Board of Education Records, New York City Department of Records/Municipal Archives.

NHF   Neighborhood Home Festival Folder, Miscellaneous American Letters and Papers, Schomburg Center for Research in Black Culture, New York Public Library.

OH   United Federation of Teachers Oral History Project, Tamiment Library/Robert F. Wagner Labor Archives, New York University.

RP   Richard Parrish Papers, Schomburg Center for Research in Black Culture, New York City Public Library.

SHANKER   Shanker Papers, American Federation of Teachers Collection, Archives of Labor and Urban Affairs, Walter P. Reuther Library, Wayne State University.

TU   Teachers Union of the City of New York, 1916–1964, Kheel Center for Labor-Management Documentation and Archives, Cornell University Library.

UPA   United Parents Association Records, 1919–1989, New York City Board of Education Records, New York City Department of Records/Municipal Archives.

UFT   United Federation of Teachers Records, 1916–2002, Tamiment Library/Robert F. Wagner Labor Archives, New York University.

Notes

INTRODUCTION

1. Henry Linville to the American Federation of Teachers, August 9, 1935, box 15, folder 22, UFT.

2. Henry I. Christ, "The Atomic Bomb Shakes the Classroom," HP 27 (September 1945): 5–8; "Human Relations Activity—A Cooperative Approach," HP 28 (September 1946): 38–44.

3. "Improve Difficult Schools," Guild Bulletin, September 1957, 1, 4.

4. Linda Darling-Hammond, "From 'Separate but Equal' to 'No Child Left Behind': The Collision of New Standards and Old Inequalities," in Many Children Left Behind: How the No Child Left Behind Act Is Damaging Our Children and Our Schools, ed. Deborah Meier and George Wood, 3–32 (Boston: Beacon Press, 2004); Stan Karp, "NCLB's Selective Vision of Equality: Some Gaps Count More than Others," in Many Children Left Behind, 53–78; Gary Orfield, Dismantling Desegregation: The Quiet Reversal of Brown v. Board of Education (New York: New Press, 1996); Amy Stuart Wells, "No Accountability for Diversity: Standardized Tests and the Demise of Racially Mixed Schools," in The Resegregation of the American South, ed. Jack Bogart and Gary Orfield, 187–211 (Chapel Hill: University of North Carolina Press, 2006); Gary Orfield, Schools More Separate: Consequences of a Decade of Resegregation (Cambridge, MA: The Civil Rights Project, Harvard University, July 2001).

5. Thomas J. Sugrue, Sweet Land of Liberty: The Forgotten Struggle for Civil Rights in the North (New York: Random House, 2008), 61.

6. "Guild Membership Trends," [n.d.], box 73, folder 11, UFT.

7. Rebecca C. Simonson, "The President's Corner: The Teacher's Cultural Lag," Guild Bulletin, June 1952, 2.

8. Diane Ravitch, The Great School Wars: A History of the New York City Public Schools (Baltimore: Johns Hopkins University Press, 2000), 256.

9. Teachers Guild Committee on Teacher Interests, "Statement on the Ban of Voluntary Transfers," May 1945, box 10, folder 61, UFT.

10. Martha Biondi, To Stand and Fight: The Struggle for Civil Rights in Postwar New York City (Cambridge: Harvard University Press, 2003), 3; Jerald Podair, The Strike That Changed New York (New Haven: Yale University Press, 2002), 32.

11. Eugene Maleska, "White Teacher in Harlem," HP 29 (May 1947): 5–9, 5.

12. Jim Haskins, Diary of a Harlem Teacher (New York: Grove Press, 1969), 19.

13. Jerald Podair, The Strike That Changed New York; Daniel Perlstein, Justice, Justice: Social Politics and the Eclipse of Liberalism (New York: Peter Lang, 2004); Jacquelyn Dowd Hall, "The Long Civil Rights Movement and the Political Uses of the Past," Journal of American History, 91, no. 4 (2005): 1233–63.

14. Fred M. Hechinger, "Teachers Adopting a Militant Approach," New York Times, January 9, 1969.

15. Arnold F. Fege, "Getting Ruby a Public Education: Forty-Two Years of Building the Demand for Quality Public Schools through Parental and Public Involvement," Harvard Educational Review 76, no. 4 (2006): 570–86.

16. Clara S. Goldwater, "Cultural Tensions in Schools Pose Almost Insuperable Prob-

lems," *Guild Bulletin*, December 1953, 4; Central Harlem Council for Community Planning, "Conference on P.S. 90," October 14, 1954, box 3, folder 3, HNAP.

17. Matthew Frye Jacobson, *Roots Too: White Ethnic Revival in Post–Civil Rights America* (Cambridge: Harvard University Press, 2006): 6, 319; Sara Evans, *Personal Politics* (New York: Vintage, 1980); James T. Patterson, *Grand Expectations: The United States, 1945–1974* (New York: Oxford University Press, 1996); John D. Skrentny, *The Minority Rights Revolution* (Cambridge, MA: Harvard University Press, 2002).

18. Mary Ann Glendon, *Rights Talk: The Impoverishment of Political Discourse* (New York: Free Press, 1993), 7, 9.

19. See Lani Guinier, "From Racial Liberalism to Racial Literacy: Brown v. Board of Education and the Interest-Divergence Dilemma," *Journal of American History* 91, no. 1 (2004): 92–118; James T. Patterson, *Brown v. Board of Education: A Civil Rights Milestone and Its Troubled Legacy* (New York: Oxford University Press, 2002); Jack Balkin, ed., *What Brown v. Board of Education Should Have Said: The Nation's Top Legal Experts Rewrite America's Landmark Decision* (New York: New York University Press, 2002).

20. Isaiah Berlin, "Two Concepts of Liberty," in *Liberty: Incorporating Four Essays on Liberty*, ed. Henry Hardy (Oxford: Oxford University Press, 2002), 166–217.

21. See, for example, Podair, *The Strike That Changed New York*; Perlstein, *Justice, Justice*; Richard D. Kahlenberg, *Tough Liberal: Albert Shanker and the Battle over Schools, Unions, Race, and Democracy* (New York: Columbia University Press, 2007).

CHAPTER 1

1. "Oust Principal in Beating," *New York Amsterdam News*, December 12, 1936. See also "Boy Slugged, Principal Accused," *New York Amsterdam News*, October 31, 1936; "Slugged, Boy Calls School Head Brutal, "*New York Amsterdam News*, November 7, 1936; "Principal Is Freed," *New York Amsterdam News*, January 23, 1937.

2. "Editorial Paragraphs," *New York Teacher*, December 1936, 5.

3. Cheryl Greenberg, *"Or Does It Explode?": Black Harlem in the Great Depression* (Princeton: Princeton University Press, 1991), 43–44; Celia Zitron, *The New York City Teacher Union, 1916–1964* (New York: Humanities Press, 1968), 127. Often genuinely concerned about children, teachers who were also desperate to hold onto their jobs in a period of severe cutbacks contributed over two million dollars.

4. George S. Counts, *Dare the School Build a New Social Order?* (New York: Arno Press and the New York Times, 1969), 4, 28. Within this group of scholars existed a range of opinions about the schools' specific role in social change and what that meant for teachers. Because of their unique influence on the Teachers Union and the Guild, this chapter focuses on Counts and Dewey, respectively. For more, see Herbert M. Kliebard, *The Struggle for the American Curriculum, 1893–1958* (New York: Routledge, 1995), 155–78; David Tyack, Robert Lowe, and Elizabeth Hansot, *Public Schools in Hard Times: The Great Depression and Recent Years* (Cambridge, MA: Harvard University Press, 1984); Diane Ravitch, *Left Back: A Century of Failed School Reforms* (New York: Touchstone Press, 2000), 202–37; Robert B. Westbrook, *John Dewey and American Democracy* (Ithaca, NY: Cornell University Press, 1993); Ronald K. Goodenow, "The Progressive Educator, Race and Ethnicity in the Depression Years: An Overview," *History of Education Quarterly* 15, no. 4 (1975): 365–94.

5. Frank Pierrepont Graves, "Report of a Study of New York City Schools" (Albany, 1933), pp. 48, 49, 53, subseries 2.1, folder 21, UPA.

6. "Only the Beginning," *New York Amsterdam News*, December 12, 1936.

7. See Marjorie Murphy, *Blackboard Unions: The AFT and the NEA, 1900–1980* (Ithaca, NY:

Cornell University Press, 1990); Stephen Cole, *The Unionization of Teachers: A Case Study of the UFT* (New York: Praeger Publishers, 1969); Zitron.

8. Henry Linville, "Can the Union Solve Its Left-Wing Problem?" *Union Teacher*, May 1933, 5.

9. For a fuller account, see Adina Back, "Up South in New York: The 1950s School Desegregation Struggles." PhD diss., New York University, 1997.

10. Charles J. Hendley to Principals of New York City Schools [c. 1937], box 5, folder 18a, UFT.

11. "The Schoenchen Case," *Guild Bulletin*, December 15, 1936, 1.

12. Henry R. Linville, "Newsletter from New York Sent Personally to a Limited Number," June 12, 1937, box 1, folder 7, GUILD.

13. Jacqueline Dowd Hall, "The Long Civil Rights Movement and the Political Uses of the Past," *Journal of American History* 91, no. 4 (2005): 1234–63.

14. See Tyack, Lowe, Hansot; Patricia A. Carter, *'Everybody's Paid but the Teacher': The Teaching Profession and the Women's Movement* (New York: Teachers College Press, 2002); Kate Rousmaniere, *City Teachers: Teaching and School Reform in Historical Perspective* (New York: Teachers College Press, 1997); Jonna Perrillo, "Beyond 'Progressive' Reform: Bodies, Discipline, and the Construction of the 'Professional Teacher' in Interwar America," *History of Education Quarterly* 44, no. 3 (2004): 337–63; Jackie Blount, *Destined to Rule the Schools: Women and the Superintendency, 1873–1995* (Albany: State University of New York Press, 1998); John L. Rury, *Education and Women's Work: Female Schooling and the Division of Labor in Urban America, 1870–1930* (Albany: State University of New York Press, 1991).

15. Harold Campbell, "Charting the Future of Secondary Education in the Large Urban Centers of the United States," HP 14 (November 1932): 5.

16. "How to Strengthen Schools," *Journal of the National Education Association* 14 (January 1925): 3–4, 3; Graves, "Report of a Study of New York City Schools," 57.

17. Greenberg, *Or Does It Explode?* 68. As Greenberg has argued, black youth may have stayed in school during the Depression rather than leave for work because black New Yorkers faced such severe employment discrimination.

18. David Ment, "Patterns of School Segregation, 1900–1930: A Comparative Study of New York City, New Rochelle, and New Haven," in *Schools in Cities: Consensus and Conflict in American Educational History*, ed. Ronald K. Goodenow and Diane Ravitch, 67–110 (New York: Holmes and Meier, 1983), 72; figure quoted in Greenburg, *Or Does It Explode?* 15.

19. Different percentages are cited in Mark Naison, *Communists in Harlem during the Depression* (Urbana: University of Illinois Press, 1983), 32; and Greenberg, *Or Does It Explode?* 16. A sizable black population also lived in Brooklyn at the time and shared these same characteristics. See Craig Steven Wilder, *A Covenant with Color: Race and Social Power in Brooklyn* (New York: Columbia University Press, 2000), 123–8.

20. Ment, "Patterns of School Segregation," 74, 78. Despite these figures, not all schools in Harlem were black-majority schools, especially in East Harlem. For more on East Harlem schools and the ways in which teachers dedicated themselves to improving schools for Italian-American students, see Michael C. Johanek and John L. Puckett, *Leonard Covello and the Making of Benjamin Franklin High School* (Philadelphia: Temple University Press, 2007). For more on the experiences on black students in New York before the 1930s, see Frances Blascoer, *Colored School Children in New York* (New York: Public Education Association of the City of New York, 1915); and Marcy S. Sacks, *Before Harlem: The Black Experience in New York City before World War I* (Philadelphia: University of Pennsylvania Press, 2006), 154–8.

21. Gerald Markowitz and David Rosner, *Children, Race, and Power: Kenneth and Mamie*

Clark's Northside Center (Charlottesville: University of Virginia Press, 1996), 83; Ment, "Patterns of School Segregation," 91.

22. Blascoer, Colored School Children in New York, 93.

23. Blascoer, Colored School Children in New York, 19.

24. Graves, "Report of a Study of New York City Schools," 92.

25. Committee for the Study of Retardation, Truancy, and the Problems of Personality and Conduct, Retardation, Truancy, and the Problems of Personality and Conduct (Board of Education of the City of NY: October 1931). New York City Board of Education Archives, Series 554, Committee for the Study of Retardation, Truancy, and the Problems of Personality and Conduct. New York City Department of Records/Municipal Archives.

26. Quoted in Ment, "Patterns of School Segregation," 84. This pattern in New York City was typical of the increased segregation of schools concomitant with an increased black population in urban centers across the North. See Davison M. Douglas, Jim Crow Moves North: The Battle over Northern School Segregation, 1865–1954 (New York: Cambridge University Press, 2005), 125 and following.

27. Langston Hughes, "The Negro Artist and the Racial Mountain," Nation, June 23, 1926.

28. "Harlem Launches Campaign for School Board Member," New York Amsterdam News, April 18, 1936.

29. "Wadleigh Still 'Melting Pot,'" New York Amsterdam News, December 18, 1937.

30. See "Police Shoot into Rioters; Kill Negro in Harlem Mob," New York Times, March 20, 1935; Naison, Communists in Harlem, 140–43.

31. "Complete Riot Report Bared," New York Amsterdam News, July 18, 1936.

32. Charles H. Roberts, Oswald Garrison Villard, and Eunice Hunton Carter to Mayor Fiorello La Guardia, May 22, 1935, box 1, folder 1, GUILD.

33. The Mayor's Commission on Conditions in Harlem, The Complete Report of Mayor LaGuardia's Commission on the Harlem Riot of March 19, 1935 (New York: Arno Press, 1969), 84–86.

34. "Demand New Schools for Harlem Children," New York Amsterdam News, March 28, 1936.

35. "Improvement in Harlem's Schools Asked by Education Survey Group," New York Amsterdam News, June 3, 1931.

36. A similar group to the Harlem Committee, the Bedford-Stuyvesant Regional Committee of the Teachers Union, was established in Bedford-Stuyvesant, Brooklyn, in 1936. For more on that group, see Lauri Johnson, "'Making Democracy Real': Teacher Union and Community Activism to Promote Diversity in the New York City Public Schools, 1935–1950," Urban Education 37, no. 5 (2002): 566–87.

37. The Mayor's Commission on Conditions in Harlem to Mayor Fiorello LaGuardia, May 22, 1935, Box 1, Folder 1, TU.

38. W.N. Huggins, "The Negro Teacher and the Student Go to School," New York Amsterdam News, December 22, 1934; Herbert L. Bruce, "Score Failure to Assign Negro Teachers to P.S. 68," New York Amsterdam News, September 24, 1938.

39. On Ayer's struggle, see Lauri Johnson, "A Generation of Women Activists: African American Female Educators in Harlem, 1930–1950," Journal of African American History 89, no. 3 (2004): 223–40. For a wider discussion of the discriminatory practices, see Christina Collins, "Ethnically Qualified": Race, Merit, and the Selection of Urban Teachers, 1920–1980 (New York: Teachers College Press, 2011).

40. "Negro WPA Teachers Find Jobs Difficult to Get," New York Amsterdam News, October 5, 1940.

41. "Harlem to Bare Evil at Schools," New York Post, April 11, 1935.

42. *The Complete Report of Mayor LaGuardia's Commission on the Harlem Riot of March 19, 1935* (New York: Arno Press, 1969), 81–82.

43. *The Complete Report of Mayor LaGuardia's Commission*, 88.

44. *The Complete Report of Mayor LaGuardia's Commission*, 85–86.

45. *The Complete Report of Mayor LaGuardia's Commission on Conditions in Harlem*, 88.

46. See "Tribute Paid to Mrs. Ayer," *New York Amsterdam News*, June 6, 1936; W.N. Huggins, "The Negro Teacher and Student Go to School."

47. "Editorial Paragraphs," *New York Teacher*, February 1936.

48. Otto Klineberg, *Negro Intelligence and Selective Migration* (New York: Columbia University Press, 1935), 28, 59. On the education of Southern blacks during and leading up to the 1930s, see James D. Anderson, *The Education of Blacks in the South, 1860–1935* (Chapel Hill: University of North Carolina Press, 1988); James L. Leloudis, *Schooling in the New South: Pedagogy, Self, and Society in North Carolina, 1880–1920* (Chapel Hill: University of North Carolina, 1996); Michael Fultz, "Teacher Training and African American Education in the South, 1900–1940," *Journal of Negro Education* 64, no. 2 (1995): 196–207; Adam Fairclough, *A Class of Their Own: Black Teachers in the Segregated South* (Cambridge, MA: Harvard, 2007).

49. See, for example, work on Lewis Terman: see JoAnne Brown, *The Definition of a Profession: The Authority of Metaphor in the History of Intelligence Testing, 1890–1930* (Princeton: Princeton University Press, 1992); Paul Davis Chapman, *Schools as Sorters: Lewis B. Terman, Applied Psychology, and the Intelligence Testing Movement, 1890–1930* (New York: New York University Press, 1988); Stephen Jay Gould, *The Mismeasure of Man* (W.W. Norton and Company, 1981); and Wendy Kline, *Building a Better Race: Gender, Sexuality, and Eugenics from the Turn of the Century to the Baby Boom* (Berkeley: University of California, 2001). For the response of black social scientists to intelligence testing, see V.P. Franklin, "Black Social Scientists and the Mental Testing Movement, 1920–1940," in *Black Psychology*, 3d ed., ed. Reginald L. Jones (Berkeley: Cobb and Henry, 1991); Carl Jorgensen, "The African American Critique of White Supremacist Science," *Journal of Negro Education* 64, no. 3 (1995): 232–42.

50. Bella M. Bator Chase, "Character Training in the Public Schools," HP 20 (February 1938): 18–22, 22. For a fuller discussion on teaching evaluations in the city schools in the Progressive Era, see Kate Rousmaniere, *City Teachers*.

51. "What Relationship Should Exist between Teacher and Pupil?" HP 18 (May 1935): 7–9, 9.

52. Hector LaGuardia, "The Teacher's Role in the Development of Student Personality," HP 20 (January 1938): 45–46, 45.

53. "Be Good-Looking, and Let Who Will Be Clever," *Newsweek*, August 3, 1935, 35.

54. *The Teacher's Handbook: A Guide for Use in the Schools of the City of New York*, 4th ed. (New York: Department of Education of the City of New York, January 1, 1928).

55. Board of Education of the City of New York, *Report and Recommendations of the Joint Committee on Maladjustment and Delinquency*, January 1938. New York City Board of Education Records, series 164, Joint Committee on Maladjustment and Delinquency, Reports, 1936–1938, box 1, folder 5. New York City Department of Records/Municipal Archives.

56. Abraham Gedulig, "Should We Indoctrinate?" HP (October 1933): 32; "Saving Energy for the Classroom: A Plea for Better Teaching," *Education* 54 (November 1933): 176.

57. Sarah Thorwald Steiglitz, "My Class Struggle," HP 20 (March 1938): 46–52, 48.

58. See Larry Cuban, *How Teachers Taught: Constancy and Change in American Classroom, 1880–1990* (New York: Teachers College Press, 1993).

59. "A Report on Conditions in the Schools in Harlem, Submitted by a Committee of Principals," January 24, 1938, p. 17, subseries 2, folder 17, JM.

60. "A Report on Conditions in the Schools in Harlem," 9, 11, 22.

61. For more on the connection between scientific knowledge and professionalism, see Magali Sarfatti Larson, *The Rise of Professionalism: A Sociological Analysis* (Berkeley: University of California Press, 1977); Thomas Haskell, ed., *The Authority of Experts: Studies in History and Theory* (Bloomington: Indiana University Press, 1984); Eliot Friedson, *Professionalism: The Third Logic* (Chicago: University of Chicago Press, 2001); and Amitai Etzioni, *The Semi-Professions and Their Organizations: Teachers, Nurses, Social Workers* (New York: Free Press, 1969).

62. On the efforts of social scientists to exhibit political neutrality at the time and their failed attempt to do so, see Darryl Michael Scott, *Contempt and Pity: Social Policy and the Image of the Damaged Black Psyche, 1880–1996* (Chapel Hill: University of North Carolina Press, 1997); John P. Jackson, Jr., *Social Scientists for Social Justice: Making the Case against Segregation* (New York: New York University Press, 2001), 17–42; Alice O'Connor, *Poverty Knowledge: Social Science, Social Policy, and the Poor in Twentieth-Century U.S. History* (Princeton: Princeton University Press, 2002); and Mark C. Smith, *Social Science in the Crucible: The American Debate over Objectivity and Purpose, 1918–1941* (Durham, NC: Duke University Press, 1994).

63. Mayor's Commission of Conditions in Harlem to Mayor Fiorello LaGuardia.

64. "A Report of Conditions in the Schools of Harlem," 4–5.

65. A Report on Conditions in the Schools in Harlem," 9.

66. Elspeth McCreary, "Low Class Brackets," HP 16 (January 1934): 20–24, 20.

67. "Row Ends Meeting of Teachers' Union," *New York Times*, May 8, 1932, 25.

68. "Editorial Paragraphs," *New York Teacher*, May 1936, 125.

69. Teachers Union, "The Constitution of the Teachers Union of the City of New York," March 10, 1916, box 13, folder 1, UFT.

70. For more on the influence of the Lusk Laws on teachers, see Murphy, *Blackboard Unions*, and Ruth Jacknow Markowitz, *My Daughter, the Teacher: Jewish Teachers in the New York City Schools* (New Brunswick, NJ: Rutgers University Press, 1993). Wayne Urban and Kate Rousmaniere show that women teachers in New York City organized before teacher unions existed to protest the treatment of women teachers. Their efforts resulted in the repeal of a ban on married women teachers in 1904 and the abolition of a separate pay scale for men and women teachers in 1911, despite opposition by organized groups of male teachers. Both victories made New York City more progressive than most American cities in its school employment policies toward women. See Rousmaniere, *City Teachers*, 18–20; Wayne J. Urban, *Why Teachers Organized* (Detroit: Wayne State University Press, 1982), 89–110.

71. Rousmaniere, *City Teachers*, 23.

72. See, for example, interviews with Edward Gottlieb, Hy Hirsch, Tess Gloster, Fanny Simon, Ray Frankel, Jack Mendel, Sarah Weiner, Samuel Wallach, and Rebecca Simonson. United Federation of Teachers Oral History Project, Tamiment Library/Robert F. Wagner Labor Archives.

73. As Ruth Jacknow Markowitz argues, many of these teachers came more specifically from leftist Jewish families. In 1930, 44 percent of the city's new teachers were Jewish. The percentage of Jewish teachers increased over the course of the civil rights movement. See Markowitz, *My Daughter, the Teacher*, 2.

74. For more on who became teachers in the period, see Rousmaniere, *City Teachers*; and John L. Rury, "Who Became Teachers? The Social Characteristics of Teachers in American History," in *American Teachers: A History of a Profession at Work*, ed. Donald Warren, 9–48 (New York: Macmillan Publishing, 1989).

75. Douglas C. Rossinow, *Visions of Progress: The Left-Liberal Tradition in American* (Philadelphia: University of Pennsylvania Press, 2007).

76. Gary Gerstle, "The Protean Character of American Liberalism," *American Historical Review* 99, no. 4 (1994): 1044–7.

77. Henry R. Linville to the Union members in P.S. 43 Bronx, 21 May 1930, box 1, folder 2, GUILD.

78. The Teachers Union of the City of New York, *A Proposal to Establish an Experimental School within the Public School System of the City of New York* (New York: The Teachers Union of the City of New York, 1924).

79. In future decades—as following chapters will show—the two unions' membership expressed more distinct views about race. In this period, it is often difficult to assess what most Guild members thought about race and civil rights because they were so unwilling to discuss it as part of their union work.

80. Charles J. Hendley, Press Release, October 3, 1938, box 74, folder 3, TU.

81. "The Situation in the Teachers Union," [c. 1936], box 74, folder 3, TU.

82. "Progressive Group Bulletin," November 1936, box 74, folder 3, TU.

83. Charles Hendley, "Program of the Teachers Union," March 1935, box 1, folder 2, GUILD.

84. "Cloistered Teachers," *Union Teacher*, April 1933, 3.

85. Charles Hendley, "Program of the Teachers Union," March 1935, box 1, folder 25, TU.

86. "Lester Granger Addresses Meeting of Teachers' Union," *New York Amsterdam News*, May 13, 1934.

87. "Local Groups Demand Schools Be Improved," *New York Amsterdam News*, July 4, 1936; "Demand New Schools for Harlem," *New York Amsterdam News*, March 28, 1936; "Local Teachers Demand Reforms," *New York Amsterdam News*, January 11, 1936; "Harlem Launches Campaign for School Board Member," *New York Amsterdam News*, April 18, 1936.

88. "School Head Is Criticized," *New York Amsterdam News*, April 28, 1934; "Harlem Principal Defends Policies," *New York Times*, May 9, 1935.

89. *Education for Democracy* (Program from the Annual Education Conference of the Teachers Union, 1939), pp. 57–58, box 13, folder 60, UFT.

90. *Education for Democracy*, 60.

91. John Dewey, "Can Education Share in Social Reconstruction?" *Teachers College Record* 1 (November 1, 1934): 11–12.

92. Henry Linville to the American Federation of Teachers, August 9, 1935, box 15, folder 22, UFT.

93. Henry Linville to Principal Arthur Hughson, April 20, 1940, box 5, folder 10, UFT.

94. Henry Linville to American Federation of Teachers, August 9, 1935, box 15, folder 22, UFT.

95. "Teachers Protest School Budget Cut," *New York Times*, April 10, 1939.

96. "Teachers Ask New Test System," *New York Times*, February 15, 1937; "Teachers Guild Plea Is Heard at Albany," *New York Times*, June 14, 1939.

97. Pauline Michel Papke, "Are Married Women People, or Have They Forfeited Democratic Freedom?" *Guild Bulletin*, September 26, 1939, 3.

98. "1,500 City Teachers Held Unbalanced," *New York Times*, March 27, 1934; "250 Teachers Held Unfit for Service," *New York Times*, August 12, 1939.

99. Henry Linville to Commissioner Frank P. Graves, [n.d.]; Henry Linville to Commissioner Frank P. Graves, December 3, 1935, box 10, folder 55, UFT.

100. Henry R. Linville, "Newsletter from New York Sent Personally to a Limited Number," June 12, 1937, box 1, folder 7, GUILD.

101. Guild Committee on Professional Status, "A Professional Code for Teachers," March 23 1939, box 5, folder 10, GUILD.

102. Linville, "Newsletter from New York."

103. "How the Teachers Union and the Teachers Guild Differ," [n.d.] box 1, folder 22, GUILD.

104. "An Open Letter to Non-Members," *Guild Bulletin*, January 18, 1938, 1.

105. Linville, "Newsletter from New York."

106. "Local Groups Demand Schools Be Improved," 5.

107. Counts, *Dare the School Build a New Social Order*, 7–8, 4.

108. "Better Teaching in the High Schools of New York City" (Annual Report of Superintendent of the High Schools John Tildsley), HP 9 (October 1927): 3–148, 134, 142.

109. Teachers Union, *Handbook*, 1939, box 1, folder 5, GUILD.

110. "A Report on the Conditions in Harlem," 15–16.

111. "Harlem School Fight Gains Supporters," *New York Amsterdam News*, October 3, 1936.

112. Charles Hendley, "Program of the Teachers Union," March 1935, box 1, folder 25, GUILD.

113. Guild Committee on Professional Status, "A Professional Code for Teachers."

114. Quoted in Naison, *Communists in Harlem*, 309.

115. Former member, Harlem, letter to the editor, *New York Amsterdam News*, November 26, 1938.

116. Linville, "Newsletter from New York."

117. "Under Union Methods," [n.d.], box 1, folder 7, GUILD.

118. "How the Teachers Union and the Teachers Guild Differ," [n.d.], box 1, folder 22, GUILD.

119. Kliebard, *The Struggle for the American Curriculum*, 163.

120. "Where the Guild Stands," *Guild Bulletin*, April 8, 1938, 1.

CHAPTER 2

1. Rebecca C. Simonson, "Muscular Democracy," *Guild Bulletin*, May 1949, 2.

2. Rebecca C. Simonson, "The President's Column," *Guild Bulletin*, February 19, 1946, 2.

3. For more on American racism and foreign relations in the time, see Michael Sherry, *In the Shadow of War: The United States Since the 1930s* (New Haven: Yale University Press, 1995); Mary L. Dudziak, *Cold War Civil Rights: Race and the Image of American Democracy: Race and the Image of American Democracy* (Princeton: Princeton University Press, 2000); Brenda Gayle Plummer, ed., *Window on Freedom: Race, Civil Rights, and Foreign Affairs, 1945–1988* (Chapel Hill: University of North Carolina Press, 1988).

4. Thomas J. Sugrue, *Sweet Land of Liberty: The Forgotten Struggle for Civil Rights in the North* (New York: Random House, 2008), 66

5. Gary Gerstle, "The Protean Character of American Liberalism," *American Historical Review* 99, no. 4 (1994): 1043–73; Gary Gerstle, *American Crucible: Race and Nation in the Twentieth Century* (Princeton: Princeton University Press, 2001), 187–237; and Paula Fass, *Outside In: Minorities and the Transformation of American Education* (New York: Oxford University Press, 1989); Walter A. Jackson, *Gunnar Myrdal and America's Conscience: Social Engineering and Racial Liberalism, 1938–1987* (Chapel Hill: University of North Carolina Press, 1994), 274.

6. Benjamin Fine, "Schools to Open Tolerance Drive," *New York Times*, January 16, 1938; "Schools Ordered to Teach 'Tolerance' Twice Monthly," *New York Times*, December 22, 1938.

7. Constance Curtis, "Air Wadleigh Problem," *New York Amsterdam News*, November 23, 1946, 1.

8. Risa L. Goluboff, *The Lost Promise of Civil Rights* (Cambridge: Harvard University Press, 2007), 5.

9. "A City's Shame," *Time*, April 5, 1948, 69.

10. *Report on the Harlem Project by the Research Committee: A Project Sponsored Jointly by the New York Foundation and the Board of Education of the City of New York, September 1943–June 1945* (New York: Board of Education of the City of New York, December 1947), 106.

11. Lillian Leon to Rebecca Simonson, November 16, 1940, box 10, folder 61, UFT.

12. Quoted in "How Democratic Is Your School?" *Strengthening Democracy* 1 (May 1949): 3. New York City Board of Education Records, series 664: Division of Curriculum, "Strengthening Democracy," 1948–1965. NYC Department of Records/Municipal Archives.

13. The Committee for the Study of Practical Democracy in Education, "Practical Democracy in Education" (Board of Education of the City of New York, 1943). New York City Board of Education Records, series 175: Committee for the Study of Practical Democracy in Education, Report, 1943. NYC Department of Records. Municipal Archives.

14. Robert Korstad and Nelson Lichtenstein, "Opportunities Found and Lost: Labor, Radicals, and the Early Civil Rights Movement," *Journal of American History* 75, no. 3 (1988): 811. On the import of labor to wartime civil rights, see also Goluboff, *The Lost Promise of Civil Rights*; Paul Frymer, *Black and Blue: African Americans, the Labor Movement, and the Decline of the Democratic Party* (Princeton: Princeton University Press, 2008); Paul Burstein, *Discrimination, Jobs, and Politics: The Struggle for Equal Employment Opportunity in the United States since the New Deal* (Chicago: University of Chicago Press, 1998); Robin D.G. Kelley, *Race Rebels: Culture, Politics, and the Black Working Class* (New York: Free Press, 1994); Nelson Lichtenstein, *State of the Union: A Century of American Labor* (Princeton: Princeton University Press, 2002); Margaret C. Rung, *Servants of the State: Managing Diversity and Democracy in the Federal Workforce, 1933–1953* (Athens: University of Georgia Press, 2002); Martha Biondi, *To Stand and Fight: The Struggle for Civil Rights in Postwar New York City* (Cambridge: Harvard University Press, 2003), 17–37; Kathryn M. Neckerman, *Schools Betrayed: Roots of Failure in Inner-City Education* (Chicago: University of Chicago Press, 2007), 32–59.

15. Sugrue, *Sweet Land of Liberty*, 77.

16. Statistics quoted from Sugrue, *Sweet Land of Liberty*, 77, and Goluboff, *The Lost Promise of Civil Rights*, 83.

17. Estella Unna, "The Thrill of Conquest," HP 27 (October 1945): 60–64, 63.

18. Inez C. Pollak, "Report of a Conference with Charles Smith of the Bureau of Placement and Guidance, Board of Education," January 13, 1942, box 6, folder 13, GUILD.

19. Layle Lane to Miss Woods, November 7, 1941, box 6, folder 3, GUILD.

20. "Reforms for School in Harlem Urged by Union," *New York Amsterdam News*, July 18, 1942. This marginalization of black students in the vocational curriculum was echoed in cities across the North, including the all-important war manufacturing cities of Detroit and Chicago. See David L. Angus and Jeffrey E. Mirel, *The Failed Promise of the American High School, 1890–1995* (New York: Teachers College Press, 1999), 90–92; Neckerman, 107–26.

21. Board of Education of the City of New York Emergency Training Program for National Defense Division of Trainee Personnel and Statistics, "Statistical Report on the Training of Negroes for the Period Sept. 1, 1941 to Dec. 31, 1941," February 6, 1942, box 6, folder 3, GUILD.

22. Quoted in Jack Schierenbeck, "Lost and Found: The Incredible Life and Times of (Miss) Layle Lane," *American Educator* 24, no. 4 (Winter 2000–2001): 12. Mark Naison has

identified Lane as one of the most important members of a group of black Socialists who actively and victoriously fought to exclude communists from civil rights efforts in Harlem in the early 1940s. See Naison, *Communists in Harlem during the Depression* (Urbana: University of Illinois Press, 1983), 287–310.

23. Schierenbeck, "Lost and Found," 12–16. The war and its dependence on the students who trained at trade schools also brought more attention to the status of trade schools more largely. See Herbert M. Kliebard, *Schooled to Work: Vocationalism and the American Curriculum, 1876–1946* (New York: Teachers College Press, 1999); Kliebard, *The Struggle for the American Curriculum, 1893–1958* (New York: Routledge, 1995), 206–208; Angus and Mirel, *The Failed Promise of the American High School*, 57–101.

24. "Minutes of Committee on Problem Areas," January 5, 1942, box 6, folder 3, GUILD.

25. Inez C. Pollak, "Report of a Conference with Charles Smith of the Bureau of Placement and Guidance, Board of Education," January 13, 1942, box 6, folder 3, GUILD.

26. Margaret Plaut, "Interview with Ms. Betty Hawley Donnely [sic] of the Board of Education," June 25, 1942, box 6, folder 3, GUILD.

27. Pollak, "Report of a Conference with Charles Smith."

28. "Minutes of Meeting of Committee on Problem Areas," March 3, 1942, box 6, folder 3, GUILD.

29. Andrea Friedman, "The Strange Career of Annie Lee Moss: Rethinking Race, Gender, and McCarthyism," *Journal of American History* 94, no. 2 (2007): 453. Friedman offers an extensive reading of Paul Robeson's treatment by race liberals as well. For more on black Americans and the Red Scare, see Biondi, *To Stand and Fight*, 425–45, 137–63; Gerald Horne, *Black Liberation/Red Scare: Ben Davis and the Communist Party* (Newark: University of Delaware Press, 1994); Eric Arnesen, "'No Graver Danger': Black Anticommunism, the Communist Party, and the Race Question," *Labor: Studies in Working-Class History of the Americas* 3 (Winter 2006): 13–52; Doug Rossinow, *Visions of Progress: The Left-Liberal Tradition in America* (Philadelphia: University of Pennsylvania Press, 2007), 152–58.

30. For an explanation of Count's turn in loyalties, see Marjorie Murphy, *Blackboard Unions: The AFT and the NEA, 1900–1980* (Ithaca: Cornell University Press, 1990), 150–74.

31. Benjamin Fine, "Teachers Guild Scans Records of Applicants," *New York Times*, September 21, 1941.

32. Two years later, the Teachers Union would join the Congress of Industrial Organizations, but the CIO would face its own communist purges in 1948 and 1949. For more on the Union's relationship with the CIO, see Celia Zitron, *The New York City Teachers Union, 1916–1964* (New York: Humanities Press, 1968), 36–39.

33. "Red Drive to Win Negroes Charged," *New York Times*, December 21, 1943.

34. Max Rubenstein, "Statement Made at General Conference on October 29, 1947 Re: Parents' Association," series 8, folder 124, UPA.

35. "Teacher Working with Harlem Parent, Punitively Transferred," *New York Teacher News*, December 6, 1947; Clare Baldwin to Rose Shapiro, March 24, 1948, series 8, folder 123, UPA.

36. "Transferred after 10 Years of Working with Harlem Parents," *New York Teacher News*, December 20, 1947, 5; Petition to Mr. Rubenstein, November 14, 1947, series 8, folder 124, UPA.

37. Minutes of the Delegate Assembly of United Parents Associations, Held Monday March 1, 1948, at Washington Irving High School, 40 Irving Place, New York City, New York at 8:15 p.m., p. 2, series 8, folder 123, UPA.

38. Agnes Doe, Harlem Council on Education, "Shall Parents and Teachers Be Intimidated? Do We Have Democracy in Education?" series 8, folder 123, UPA.

39. "Mayor Puts Negro in Education Post," *New York Times*, July 22, 1948; "Asks Ousting of Timone," *New York Times*, March 15, 1946; "City's School Heads Deny Infiltration by Communists," *New York Times*, September 29, 1948.

40. Rose Nurnberg, "Children of Freedom," HP 25 (September 1943): 15–18.

41. See Diana Selig, *Americans All: The Cultural Gifts Movement* (Cambridge, MA: Harvard University Press, 2008). For more on the history of interculturalism, see also Nicholas V. Montalto, *A History of the Intercultural Movement, 1924–1941* (New York: Garland Publishing, 1982); Yoon K. Pak, "'If There Is a Better Intercultural Plan in Any School System in America, I Do Not Know Where It Is': The San Diego City Schools Intercultural Education Program, 1946–1949" *Urban Education* 37, no. 5 (2002): 588–609; Robert Shafer, "Multicultural Education in New York City during World War II," *New York History* 77, no. 3 (1996): 301–32; Cherry A. McGee Banks, *Improving Multicultural Education: Lessons Learned from the Intergroup Education Movement* (New York: Teachers College Press, 2004); Michael C. Johanek and John L. Puckett, *Leonard Covello and the Making of Benjamin Franklin High School: Education as if Citizenship Mattered* (Philadelphia: Temple University Press, 2007).

42. Pearl M. Fisher, "English, Democracy, and Color," HP 24 (May 1942): 5–10, 6. While black civil rights leaders such as W.E.B. DuBois and A. Philip Randolph endorsed interculturalism, the movement operated independently of black civil rights organizations. For more on the separatism between interculturalists and black scholars and social scientists, see Cherry A. McGee Banks, *Improving Multicultural Education*; 121–23; James A. Banks, "The African American Roots of Multicultural Education," in *Multicultural Education, Transformative Knowledge and Action: Historical and Contemporary Perspectives*, ed. James A. Banks, 30–45 (New York: Teachers College Press, 1996). For more on the black response to interculturalism, see Daryl Michael Scott, "Postwar Pluralism, *Brown v. Board of Education*, and the Origins of Multicultural Education," *Journal of American History* 91, no. 1 (June 2004): 69–82; and Jonathan Zimmerman, "Brown-ing the American Textbook: History, Psychology, and the Origins of Modern Multiculturalism," *History of Education Quarterly* 44, no. 1 (Summer 2004): 46–69.

43. Rachel Davis DuBois, *All This and Something More: Pioneering in Intercultural Education* (Bryn Mawr: Dorrance, 1948), 63–84.

44. See Zoe Burkholder, "From 'Wops and Dagoes and Hunkies' to 'Caucasian': Changing Racial Discourse in American Classrooms during World War II," *History of Education Quarterly* 50, no. 3 (August 2010): 324–58; Matthew Frye Jacobson, *Whiteness of a Different Color: European Immigrants and the Alchemy of Race* (Cambridge, MA: Harvard University Press, 1998);Thomas A. Guglielmo, *White on Arrival: Italians, Race, Color, and Power in Chicago, 1890–1945* (New York: Oxford University Press, 2003); David R. Roediger, *Working toward Whiteness: How America's Immigrants Became White* (New York: Basic Books, 2005); Noel Ignatiev, *How the Irish Became White* (New York: Routledge, 1995).

45. Mary Riley, "American Harmony," HP 26 (March 1944): 15–19, 15.

46. For more on the development and effects of a therapeutic culture, see John P. Jackson, Jr., *Social Scientists for Social Justice: Making the Case against Segregation* (New York: New York University, 2001), 17–42; Ellen Herman, *The Romance of American Psychology: Political Culture in the Age of Experts* (Berkeley: University of California Press, 1995); Eve Moskowitz, *In Therapy We Trust: America's Obsession with Self-Fulfillment* (Baltimore: Johns Hopkins University Press, 2001); Wilfred M. McClay, *The Masterless: Self and Society in Modern America* (Chapel Hill: University of North Carolina Press, 1994); Ann Hulbert, *Raising America: Experts, Parents, and a Century of Advice about Children* (New York: Random House, 2003).

47. Alice O'Connor, *Poverty Knowledge: Social Science, Social Policy, and the Poor in Twentieth-Century U.S. History* (Princeton: Princeton University Press, 2001), 77 and following. Like many historians of social science in this period, O'Connor offers a perceptive critique of one of the most influential social science texts for psychologists, Gunnar Myrdal's seminal *An American Dilemma: The Negro Problem and Modern Democracy* (New York: Harpers and Row, 1944). See also Ralph Ellison's insightful critique of Myrdal in "An American Dilemma: A Review," in *Shadow and Act* (New York: Random House, 1964), 303–17; and Walter A. Jackson, *Gunnar Myrdal and America's Conscious: Social Engineering and Racial Liberalism, 1938–1987* (Chapel Hill: University of North Carolina Press, 1990). For more on the damaged black psyche, see Herman, *The Romance of American Psychology*; and Scott, "Postwar Pluralism."

48. DuBois, *Build Together Americans* (New York: Hinds, Hayden, and Eldredge, 1945), 108.

49. Stewart G. Cole, "Culture Patterns in Minority Groups," in *One America: The History, Contributions, and Present Problems of Our Racial and National Minorities*, ed. Francis J. Brown and Joseph S. Roucek (New York: Prentice-Hall, 1945), 468; Murray Eisenstadt, "Total War in the Schools," HP 25 (January 1943): 6–12, 11; Will Scarlet, "Putting the Emotions to Work for Democracy," HP 24 (June 1942): 50–51, 50.

50. "Outstanding Courses for Fall Term," *New York Teacher News*, September 15, 1945, 3.

51. Selig, *Americans All*, 223.

52. "Shine Up Your Sensitivity," *New York Teacher News*, February 9, 1946, 3.

53. "Form Committee for Negro History in the Curriculum," *New York Teacher News*, February 19, 1949, 3; The Harlem Committee of the Teachers Union, "Negro History Week and the Eight Suspended Teachers," February 1952, folder 11, box 44, GUILD.

54. Teachers Guild, "Human Relations Can Be Taught," box 1, folder 6, JB.

55. "Human Relations Can Be Taught," in-service bulletin, [c. September 1949], folder 8, box 8, GUILD.

56. Selig, *Americans All*, 107.

57. DuBois, *Build Together Americans*, 89.

58. DuBois, *Build Together Americans*, 12. Importantly, not all interculturalists were cut from the same cloth. Some, like Sabra Holbrook, noted school segregation as a major impediment to the success of the movement in the classroom. See Sabra Holbrook, "A Study of Some Relationships between Negro and White Students in New York Public Schools," HP 26 (June 1944): 5–17.

59. Alexander Breinan, "How the Teacher Can Help to Foster Intercultural Relations," HP 30 (February 1948): 52–56, 53.

60. "Human Relations Activities—A Cooperative Approach," HP 28 (September 1947): 41.

61. Blanche Schwartz, "Parranda and Program," HP 30 (September 1948): 10–16, 11.

62. Benjamin Fine, "Tolerance Aim in School Plan," *New York Times*, December 31, 1939, 28. This anxiety over the failure of tolerance education was all the more founded after the war. Clyde Miller, a Columbia University professor who specialized in the study of propaganda and participated in the Teachers Union workshops, showed that *High Points*, the city's official monthly professional journal written by teachers, published fifteen articles on interculturalism in 1946, a figure in line with the several years preceding. By 1948 and 1949, the journal published only two articles in each year. See "Intercultural Education in New York: What Has Happened to It?" *New York Teacher News*, February 7, 1953, 2.

63. Rebecca Simonson to William Jansen, March 3, 1949, box 8, folder 15, GUILD.

64. "To Fuse Racial Understanding into School Curriculum," *New York Teacher News*, May 6, 1944, 1.

65. Charles E. Slatkin, "True Confession," HP 26 (February 1944): 45–49, 47.

66. Willard Waller, "Revolt in the Classroom," HP 25 (October 1943): 5–12, 8. Claims of anti-intellectualism were not isolated to reactions against interculturalism in the postwar era but were made against other curricula changes such as life adjustment education. See Arnold Bestor, *Educational Wastelands: The Retreat from Learning in Our Public Schools*, 2d ed. (Urbana: University of Illinois Press, 1985); JoAnne Brown, "'A Is for Atom, B Is for Bomb': Civil Defense in American Public Education, 1948–1963," *Journal of American History* 75, no. 1 (1988): 68–90; Diane Ravitch, *Left Back: A Century of Battles over School Reform* (New York: Simon & Schuster, 2000), 343–52.

67. Marie Syrkin, *Your School, Your Children: A Teacher Looks at What's Wrong with Our Schools* (New York: L.B. Fisher, 1944), 193.

68. E. Harold Mason, "Report of Visits to Faculty Meeting at P.S. 89, NHF.

69. Michael Glassman, "A Practical Intercultural Education Project at Tilden," HP 31 (June 1949): 56–63, 57.

70. Central High School of Needle Trades teachers to Jacob Greenberg, November 5, 1947, folder 6, box 1, JB.

71. Quoted in "Will the Bigots Take Over Our Schools?" *New York Teacher News*, November 1, 1947, 4. For more on conservative Catholic critiques of the city's Jewish teaching force, see Ruth Jacknow Markowitz, *My Daughter the Teacher* (Newark: Rutgers University Press, 1993), 159–62.

72. As Joshua B. Freeman and Steve Rosswurm have argued, the Catholic Church came to focus on communism as a threat to its own welfare because of it represented "the most recent (and dangerous) manifestation of secularism" and because it "directly competed with Catholicism in its ability to provide a coherent set of solutions to the ongoing economic and social crisis" in the mid-1930s. Also important were the ways in which communism's gains in race rights movements threatened the Church's white, working-class base. See Freeman and Rosswurm, "The Education of an Anti-Communist: Father John F. Cronin and the Baltimore Labor Movement," *Labor History* 33, no. 2 (1992): 226.

73. The Board's growing alliance with the Catholic Church was one reason cited for its failure to fully discipline May Quinn, a Brooklyn teacher who in 1946 was tried for making anti-Semitic and racist remarks in the classroom. Quinn was fined two months' salary and transferred to a different school, but Teachers Unionists, Guild members, and thousands of other city residents argued that Quinn's license should have been revoked. In addition, in 1948 the Board banned the *Nation* magazine from all school libraries after it published an article critical of the Catholic Church. See Benjamin Fine, "Quinn Case Appeal Urged upon Wade" *New York Times*, March 1, 1946; "Miss Quinn on Job; School Is Picketed," *New York Times*, February 2, 1946; "4,000 at Protest in May Quinn Case," *New York Times*, April 5, 1946.

74. "To Probe 'Extensive' (2-Course) NYS Intercultural Education," *New York Teacher News*, March 13, 1948, 4; Murray Illson, "Superintendents Ban the *Nation* from Schools As Anti-Catholic," *New York Times*, June 24, 1968; "Ban on the *Nation* Is Put to Hearing," *New York Times*, January 25, 1949; "Schools Continue Ban on the *Nation*," *New York Times*, May 25, 1949. For more on city schools and the Catholic Church see Joshua Zeitz, *White Ethnic New York* (Chapel Hill: University of North Carolina Press, 2007).

75. William Jansen to Rebecca Simonson, March 9, 1949, folder 15, box 8, GUILD. The Teachers Union was not the only party to run into trouble with Red Scare politics in the cold war. In 1953, Rachel Davis DuBois was subpoenaed before the McCarthy Commission, although she was eventually exempted from all charges.

76. Layle Lane to Cara Cook, April 15, 1949, folder 15, box 8, GUILD.

77. Rebecca Simonson, "The President's Column," *Guild Bulletin*, May 1948, 2.

78. "Student Strikes Flare into Riots in the City Schools," *New York Times*, September 29, 1945.

79. "Athletic Coaches Scored by Mayor," *New York Times*, October 1, 1945. The fact that the fight took place in Covello's school was especially important since the school was central to interculturalism and had been founded by Covello to improve opportunities for the neighborhood's Italian American boys, often at the exclusion of its black youth. See Johanek and Puckett, *Leonard Covello*; Leonard Covello, *The Heart Is the Teacher* (New York: McGraw Hill, 1958), 242–43.

80. See Dominic Capeci, *The Harlem Riot of 1943* (Philadelphia: Temple University Press, 1977). See also Biondi, *To Stand and Fight*, 11, 70–72; Howard Sitkoff, "Racial Militancy and Interracial Violence," *Journal of American History* 58, no. 3 (1971), 661–81; and Dominic J. Capeci, Jr. and Martha Wilkerson, *Layered Violence: The Detroit Rioters of 1943* (Jackson: University of Mississippi Press, 1991).

81. Henry T. Hillson, "The Negro History and Culture Club," HP 25 (December 1943): 19–23, 21.

82. Hillson, "The Negro History and Culture Club," 21. Robert Shaffer interprets the Negro History and Culture Club at Eastern differently than I do here. He writes that, "the exploration of black history and culture at this high school in the 1940s led to interracial social contacts that would probably otherwise not have happened." I believe that this is likely true, but I do want to bring attention to the grounds upon which these contacts were made and sustained. See Robert Shaffer, "Multicultural Education in New York City during World War II," *New York History* 77 (July 1996): 316.

83. Mildred Englander, "Homemaking for Boys," HP 29 (June 1947): 67–72, 68.

84. *Report on the Harlem Project by the Research Committee*, 137

85. *Report on the Harlem Project by the Research Committee*, 106, 108.

86. Agnes E. Benedict, "Violence in the Schools," *Nation*, January 9, 1943, 51–53, 53.

87. "Harlem Problem Calls for More School Services," *Guild Bulletin*, November 1, 1941, 1.

88. "Harlem Schools Teach Democracy, but Students Find Little Outside," *New York World Telegram* November 17, 1943.

89. "Raps Smear in Juvenile Delinquency," *New York Amsterdam News*, January 23, 1943.

90. "Teachers Appeal to Police to Curb Unruly Students," *New York Times*, December 11, 1942.

91. Quoted in "Teacher in Beaten by Angry Mother as Class Looks on," *New York Times*, December 12, 1942.

92. "Teachers Appeal to Police to Curb Unruly Students," 1.

93. "Minutes of Meeting of Committee on Problem Areas."

94. *Report on the Harlem Project by the Research Committee*, 117.

95. Jackie Reemes, "School Evils Protested by Irate Council," *New York Amsterdam News*, November 24, 1945.

96. DuBois, *Build Together Americans*, 1.

97. E. Harold Mason, Report of Visit to Faculty Meeting at P.S. 89 [n.d.], NHF.

98. DuBois, *Build Together Americans*, xiv.

99. Hillson,"The Negro History and Culture Club," 21; DuBois, *Build Together Americans*, 226, 151.

100. Theodore Huebener, "How Can the Classroom Teacher Help to Foster Intercultural Relations?" HP 29 (April 1947): 36.

101. "Reduced Number of Negro Teachers Blamed on Board," *New York Teacher News*, October 22, 1949, 4.

102. "Teacher-Training for Negro Students Urged on Regents," *New York Teacher News*, November 17, 1952, 1.

103. Eugene T. Maleska, "White Teacher in Harlem," HP 29 (May 1947): 5–9, 5.

104. Statistics quote in *Report on the Harlem Project by the Research Committee*, 101.

105. *Report on the Harlem Project by the Research Committee*, 101–5.

106. Teachers Guild Committee on Teachers Interests, "Statement on the Ban of Voluntary Transfers," May 1945, box 10, folder 61, UFT.

107. Teachers Guild, "Rotation in September?" [n.d.], box 3, folder 19, GUILD.

108. Teachers Guild, "Rotation in September?"

109. Teachers Guild Committee on Teachers Interests, "Statement on the Ban of Voluntary Transfers."

110. Lillian Leon to Rebecca Simonson, November 16, 1940, box 10, folder 61, UFT.

111. Harlem School Teacher to Editor, *New York Post*, November 11, 1941.

112. *Report on the Harlem Project by the Research Committee*, vi.

113. Benjamin Fine, "New York City School System, for the First Time in Many Years, Has a Serious Teacher Shortage," *New York Times*, March 18, 1945.

114. Teachers Guild Committee on Teachers Interests, "The Problem of Teacher Rotation," January 5, 1944, box 3, folder 19, GUILD.

115. Teachers Guild Committee on Teachers Interests, "Statement on the Ban of Voluntary Transfers."

116. Esther Cahan, "National Unity through Intercultural Education," *Guild Bulletin*, February 15, 1945, 2.

117. Teachers Guild Committee on Teachers Interests, "The Problem of Teacher Rotation."

118. Teachers Guild Committee on Teachers Interests, "Statement on the Ban of Voluntary Transfers."

119. Teachers Guild Committee on Teachers Interests, "The Problem of Teacher Rotation."

120. Clare C. Baldwin, "A Progress Report on Districts 10 and 11 for the Period 1946–1949," p. 2, subseries 2, box 3, folder 17, JM.

121. Teachers Union, "Meet the Teachers Union," 1949, box 1, folder 12, CB.

122. Teachers Union, "What Kind of School for Your Child?" 1949, box 1, folder 12, CB.

123. "Address Made at the Meeting of the Board of Education on April 6, 1950, in Re Item #26, Banning Teachers Union," box 2, folder 13, CB.

124. "Address Made at the Meeting of the Board of Education on April 6, 1950, in Re Item #26, Banning Teachers Union."

CHAPTER 3

1. Statistic cited in Sara Slack, "Jansen Talks 2 Hrs. but Says Nothing," *New York Amsterdam News*, October 5, 1957.

2. Martha Biondi, *To Stand and Fight: The Struggle for Civil Rights in Postwar New York City* (Cambridge: Harvard University Press, 2003), 248; "Jansen Approves New Job Policy," *New York Times*, May 15, 1968.

3. Exie Welsch to Thomas J. Patterson, Director of the Budget, November 23, 1951, box 2, folder 3, HNAP.

4. NAACP-Brooklyn Branch, "Testimony before the Board of Education on the Reports of the Zoning and Teacher Assignment Subcommissions," January 17, 1957, box 44, folder 14, TU.

5. Michael S. Sherry, *In the Shadows of War: The United States Since the 1930s* (New Haven: Yale

University Press, 1995); Laura McEnaney, *Civil Defense Begins at Home: Miltarization Meets Every-day Life in the 50s* (Princeton: Princeton University Press, 2000); Mary L. Dudziak, *Cold War Civil Rights: Race and the Image of American Democracy: Race and the Image of American Democracy* (Princeton: Princeton University Press, 2002).

6. Harlem Council on Education for Better Schools, "Brief for a Better Education for the Children of Harlem," February 1950, box 44, folder 11, TU.

7. Kenneth Clark, "Segregated Schools in New York City," April 24, 1954, p. 8, box 8, folder 12, GUILD.

8. Public Education Association, *The Status of the Public School Education of Negro and Puerto Rican Children in the City* (New York: Public Education Association of New York City, October 1955).

9. "Report of the 1954 [AFT] Convention Committee for Democratic Human Relations." [n.d.], box 9, folder 8, GUILD.

10. Celia Lewis Zitron, *The New York City Teachers Union, 1916–1964* (New York: Humanities Press, 1968), 45.

11. David Selden, "Guild Membership Trends" [c. 1956], box 9, folder 17, GUILD.

12. C. Gerald Fraser, "What's Happening to Our Children in Public Schools?" *New York Amsterdam News*, October 17, 1953.

13. Benjamin Fine, "Teachers Oppose Integration Plan," *New York Times*, January 18, 1957.

14. "N.A.A.C.P. Rebukes City Board for All-Negro Brooklyn School," *New York Times*, November 2, 1956. For more on white parents' resistance to school integration in New York, see Diane Ravitch, *The Great School Wars: A History of the New York City Public Schools* (Baltimore: Johns Hopkins, 2000), 258–60; Thomas J. Sugrue, *Sweet Land of Liberty: The Forgotten Struggle for Civil Rights in the North* (New York: Random House, 2008), 188–99; Joshua B. Freeman, *Working-Class New York: Life and Labor since World War II* (New York: New Press, 2000).

15. Gene Currivan, "Integration Plan Is Voted by Board," *New York Times*, March 1, 1957; "Text of the Board of Education Statement on Integration," *New York Times*, February 26, 1957.

16. "Statement by Mrs. Sophia Yarnell Jacobs, President of the Urban League of Greater New York, at a Public Hearing of the NYC Board of Education on Reports of the Commission on Integration," January 17, 1957, box 44, folder 14, TU.

17. Leonard Buder, "Union Head Quits Jansen Meeting," *New York Times*, November 5, 1957.

18. "Minutes of Executive Board Meeting" March 7, 1957, box 45, folder 11, TU. Interestingly, James Madison was one of the city's almost exclusively white high schools, with a minority student population of only 1 percent. See Parents Workshop for Equality in New York City Schools, "Zoned Academic High Schools with Ethnic Composition, Index of Utilization and Zoning Variances," box 45, folder 7, TU.

19. Lawrence Lane to Albert I. Drachman, March 13, 1957, box 45, folder 11, TU.

20. "Statement Submitted by Legislative Representative, Rose Russell, at Public Hearing before the Board of Education January 17, 1957, On the Reports to the Commission on Integration by the Sub-Commissions on Teachers Assignments and Personnel (December 7, 1956) and on Zoning (December 14, 1956)," box 44, folder 14, TU.

21. Ada B. Jackson to William Jansen, January 30, 1950, box 2, folder 3, TU.

22. Teachers Union, *Bias and Prejudice in Textbooks in Use in New York City Schools* [c. 1951], box 13, folder 9, UFT.

23. "Textbooks Purging—To Exclude Insults—Backed by Parents," *New York Amsterdam News*, March 14, 1953.

24. Teachers Union, "Employment of Negro Teachers in the New York City Schools," December 18, 1951, box 45, folder 4, TU.

25. Teachers Union, "A Survey of the Employment of Negro Teachers in New York City," Spring 1955, box 45, folder 5, TU.

26. Charles Cogen, "Will New York City Learn from the South?" *Guild Bulletin*, October 1957, 2.

27. "Teachers Reject Bias Accusation," *New York Times*, November 18, 1957.

28. "Experts Say Housing Is Key to Integration Dilemma," *Guild Bulletin*, March 1957, 1–2.

29. "Improve Difficult Schools!" *Guild Bulletin*, September 1957, 1.

30. Commission on School Integration, *Public School Segregation and Integration in the North* (Washington, DC: National Association of Intergroup Relations Officials, November 1963), 30.

31. Abraham Lederman and Rose Russell to the Board of Education and Superintendent of the Schools, February 18, 1957, box 44, folder 14, TU; "Adopt School Integration Reports," *Urban League News*, March 1957, 1, box 92, folder 4, TU.

32. Urban League of Greater New York, Press Release, September 29, 1957, box 44, folder 14, TU.

33. Paul Zuber to Rose Russell, March 27, 1959, box 45, folder 1, TU.

34. Teachers Reject Bias Accusation," *New York Times*, November 18, 1957, 21.

35. Charles Cogen to Edward Lewis, May 19, 1957, box 9, folder 43, UFT.

36. "Displaced Negro Teachers Aided," *Guild Bulletin*, September 1956, 1. For more on black teachers' job losses following desegregation in the South, see Adam Fairclough, "The Costs of *Brown*: Black Teachers and School Integration," *Journal of American History* 91, no. 1 (2004): 43–55; and Michael Fultz, "The Displacement of Educators Post-*Brown*: An Overview and Analysis," *History of Education Quarterly* 44, no. 1 (2004): 11–45.

37. Rose Russell to Benjamin Fine, October 17, 1957, box 45, folder 1, TU.

38. Jacob Greenberg to Teachers Union, February 25, 1958, box 45, folder 4, TU.

39. For more on the eight teachers and the 1950s Red Scare in the schools see Marjorie Murphy, *Blackboard Unions: The AFT & the NEA, 1900–1980* (Ithaca: Cornell University Press, 1990); Zitron, *The New York City Teachers Union*; and Ruth Jacknow Markowitz, *My Daughter the Teacher: Jewish Teachers in the New York City Schools* (New Brunswick: Rutgers University Press, 1993). Martha Biondi lists the total number of teachers to have lost their jobs by the end of the 1950s Red Scare at four hundred. See Biondi, *To Stand and Fight*, 173.

40. *Conformists, Informers, or Free Teachers: Excerpts from the Trials of Seven New York City Teachers Dismissed on Thursday, January 8, 1953*, box 24, folder 1, TU.

41. "Statement by Cyril Graze in Connection with Superintendent Jansen's Inquiry into 'Subversive Activities,'" October 15, 1951, box 9, folder 8, TU. These communist firings were part of a larger Red Scare purging that happened both at the national level and in New York City and that often focused especially on labor unions and organizations. For more on the Red Scare in New York and in American labor, see Biondi, *To Stand and Fight*; Nelson Lichtenstein, *State of the Union: A Century of American Labor* (Princeton: Princeton University Press, 2002); Ellen Schrecker, *Many Are the Crimes: McCarthyism in America* (Princeton: Princeton University Press, 1999).

42. "Interview with Miss Stella Eliashaw, Teacher of English, Washington Irving High School," [c. April 1953], box 8, folder 1, TU.

43. Abraham Lederman and Rose Russell, Press Release, September 18, 1953, box 76, folder 6, TU.

44. While the long-standing political alliances between the Teachers Union and Har-

lem activists were generally positive and productive relationships, black parents at times questioned the motivations of some Union teachers. As one parent explained, teachers who actively chose to teach in Harlem could seem to parents like "missionaries" or "'do-good' type teachers [who] just want to see the Negroes here have clean streets and a nice home." This parent and others pointed out that political commitment did not mean these teachers were good teachers or were providing their children with a high-quality education. See C. Gerald Fraser, "Parents Comment on Children's Progress in School," *New York Amsterdam News*, October 31, 1953.

45. Rose Russell to Dr. William Jansen, August 19, 1954, box 44, folder 11, TU.

46. "Boys and Girls Together," *Time*, October 19, 1953, 72–80, 72. For more on juvenile delinquency and public interest in the period, see James B. Gilbert, *A Cycle of Outrage: America's Reaction to the Juvenile Delinquent in the 1950s* (New York: Oxford University Press, 1986); Erich C. Schneider, *Vampires, Dragons, and Egyptian Kings: Youth Gangs in Postwar New York* (Princeton: Princeton University Press, 1999); William Graebner, *Coming of Age in Buffalo: Youth and Authority in the Postwar Era* (Philadelphia: Temple University Press, 1990); Grace Palladino, *Teenagers: An American History* (New York: Basic Books, 1996).

47. Evan Hunter, *Blackboard Jungle* (New York: Simon and Schuster, 1954), 205.

48. "A Letter to Time Magazine," *New York Teacher News*, November 14, 1953, 2.

49. Milton Bracker, "Definitions Vary for Delinquency," *New York Times*, May 24, 1955, 24.

50. Jon B. Leder, "The Century of the Private School," HP 42 (February 1959): 15.

51. Charles A. Tonsor, "Topsies in Rebellion," HP 35 (March 1954): 16–18, 16.

52. Irma Gelber Rhodes, "A Teacher-Mother Replies," HP 36 (November 1954): 25–30; 26–17.

53. Milton Bracker, "Vitality of Schools Sapped by Delinquency Rise Here," *New York Times*, May 23, 1955.

54. Jennifer de Forest, "Tilting at Windmills? Judge Justine Wise Polier and a History of Justice and Education in New York City," *History of Education Quarterly* 49, no. 1 (2009): 76.

55. Michael M. Katzoff, quoted in "Do Our High Schools Meet Today's Challenge?" HP 42 (April 1959): 50–57, 50.

56. Milton Bracker, "Schools' Discord Traced to Homes," *New York Times*, May 25, 1955.

57. "Improve Difficult Schools!" *Guild Bulletin*, September 1957, 1, 4.

58. Carl Fichander, "Current Problems Facing the Vocational High Schools," HP 36 (June 1954): 16–20, 18.

59. William Isaacs, "Not All Slow Learners Are Slow," HP 36 (March 1954): 19–27, 22.

60. Christopher W. Schmidt, "The Children of Brown: Psychology and School Desegregation in Midcentury America," in *When Science Encounters the Child: Education, Parenting, and Child Welfare in 20-th Century America*, ed. Barbara Beatty, Emily D. Cahan, and Julia Grant, p. 177 (New York: Teachers College Press, 2006). See Darryl Michael Scott, *Contempt and Pity: Social Policy and the Image of the Damaged Black Psyche, 1880–1996* (Chapel Hill: University of North Carolina Press, 1997); Lani Guinier, "From Racial Liberalism to Radical Literacy: Brown v. Board of Education and the Interest-Divergence Dilemma," *Journal of American History* 9, no. 1 (2004): 92–118; James T. Patterson, *Brown v. the Board of Education: A Civil Rights Milestone and Its Troubled Legacy* (Oxford: Oxford University Press, 2001). Importantly, Guinier also points to the inaccuracies in Clark's research in the doll study and the conclusions he drew from his data (110–11).

61. Guinier, "From Racial Liberalism to Radical Literacy," 113.

62. Arthur T. Jersild, *When Teachers Face Themselves* (New York: Teachers College Press, 1955), 45.

63. Ida Klein Steinberg, "A Layman's Thoughts on Psychoanalysis," HP 34 (October

1952): 26–30, 30. Teachers also realized that they could employ the mainstream interest in psychology to secure other objectives. For example, argued one teacher, "Through self-analysis . . . an alert teacher can keep his technical competence at high pitch without submitting to the ever-repetitive offerings of the schools of education." Teachers had resented faculty development courses since the early 1930s; now they posited self-awareness as a potential substitute. Quoted in Charles Salkind, "Gold or Iron Pyrite?" HP 34 (May 1952): 12–22, 12.

64. Helen Hiller, "An Open Letter to 'The Most Representative Father,'" HP 34 (May 1952): 55–7, 56.

65. Clark, "Segregated Schools in New York City," 2.

66. Central Harlem Council for Community Planning, "Conference on P.S. 90," October 14, 1954, box 3, folder 3, HNAP.

67. Central Harlem Council for Community Planning, "Conference on P.S. 90."

68. Edward S. Lewis to Charles Cogen, September 26, 1957, box 9, folder 43. UFT.

69. Sophia Yarnell Jacobs and Edward Lewis to Charles Silver, November 9, 1955, box 92, folder 4, TU.

70. Ray Rosenberg, "Developmental Mathematics for Emotionally Disturbed Adolescents," HP 36 (January 1954): 63.

71. George Kaplan, "Misconceptions on Democracy and Education," HP 37 (February 1955): 28–32, 31.

72. "Teachers Decry Onerous Duties," New York Times, November 21, 1959.

73. "Some Non-Instructional Duties Which Teachers Are Required to Perform," box 37, folder 1, TU.

74. Abraham Lefkowitz, "Delinquency Marches On," HP 10 (December 1953): 29–33, 30.

75. de Forest, "Tilting at Windmills?" 76. For more on Polier, see Adina Back, "Exposing the 'Whole Segregation Myth': The Harlem Nine and New York City's Desegregation Battles," in Freedom North: Black Freedom Struggles outside the South, 1940–1980, ed. Jeanne F. Theoharis and Komozi Woodard, 65–91 (New York: Palgrave Macmillan, 2003); Justine Wise Polier, Juvenile Justice in Double Jeopardy: The Distanced Community and Vengeful Retribution (Hillsdale, NJ: Lawrence Erlbaum, 1989).

76. Lefkowitz, "Delinquency Marches On," 31.

77. "Harlem Crusade Misguided; JHS 136 Boasts Facilities," Guild Bulletin, January 1959, 2.

78. Carrie Haynes, Chair of JHS Coordinating Committee of PTA 135 and 197M, "Press Release," November 15, 1958, box 45, folder 9, TU.

79. The JHS Coordinating Committee of PTA 135 and 197M to Rose Russell [c.1958], box 45, folder 9, TU.

80. "Harlem Crusade Misguided; JHS 136 Boasts Facilities," 2.

81. Milton Bracker, "Schools' Discord Traced to Homes," New York Times, May 25, 1955.

82. Leonard Buder, "Many City Schools Listed as 'Difficult'; Entire System Hurt" New York Times, October 15, 1957.

83. Ellen Herman, The Romance of American Psychology: Political Culture in the Age of Experts (Berkeley: University of California Press, 1995), 29. See also Eve Moskowitz, In Therapy We Trust: America's Obsession with Self-Fulfillment (Baltimore: Johns Hopkins University Press, 2001); Elizabeth Quinn Lasch, Race Experts: How Racial Etiquette, Sensitivity Training, and New Age Therapy Hijacked the Civil Rights Revolution (New York: Norton, 2001).

84. Andrew G. Clauson, "The American Teacher," HP 35 (January 1953): 26–32, 27.

85. Ralph W. Heller, "Looking Backward—and Forward," HP 35 (May 1953): 26–32, 30.

86. Dorothy H. Schwartz, "Somebody Should Have Told Me," HP 39 (March 1957): 5–15, 5–7.

87. Isador Millman, "The Faculty Conference," HP 40 (October 1958): 30–37, 31.

88. Harold Wagenheim, quoted in "Morale in New York City High Schools: How Can It Be Improved?" HP 41 (January 1959): 54–68, 64.

89. Clara Goldwater, "Cultural Tensions in Schools Pose Almost Insuperable Problems," Guild Bulletin, December 1953, 4.

90. Goldwater, "Cultural Tensions in Schools," 4.

91. Fraser, "What's Happening to Our Children in Public Schools?" 14.

92. Fraser, "What's Happening to Our Children in Public Schools?" 14.

93. For more on black mothers as activists, see Back, "Exposing the 'Whole Segregation Myth'"; Ruth Feldman, "'I Wanted the Whole World to See': Race, Gender, and Constructions of Motherhood in the Death of Emmett Till," in Not June Cleaver: Women and Gender in Postwar America, 1945–1960, ed. Joanne Meyerowitz, 263–303 (Philadelphia: Temple University Press, 1994); Annelise Orleck, Storming Caesar's Palace: How Black Mothers Fought Their Own War on Poverty (Boston: Beacon Press, 2006); Vicki L. Crawford, Jacqueline Anne Rouse, Barbara Woods, eds., Women in the Civil Rights Movement: Trailblazers and Torchbearers, 1941–1965 (Bloomington: University of Indiana Press, 1993); Kathleen Blee, ed., No Middle Ground: Women and Radical Protest (New York: New York University, 1998).

94. Fraser, "Parents Comment on Children's Progress in School," 15.

95. Central Harlem Council for Community Planning, "Conference on P.S. 90," October 14, 1954, box 3, folder 3, HNAP.

96. George Barner, "Teacher Groups Oppose Integrating NY Schools," New York Amsterdam News, February 2, 1957; "Says Teachers Have Same Duty as Firemen," New York Amsterdam News, February 16, 1957.

97. "High School Morale at 'All Time Low,' Conditions 'Unbearable,' Bd Is Told," New York Teachers News, October 22, 1955, 1; "The Low State of Teacher Morale," Guild Bulletin, November 1954, 2; "Low Morale Due to Many Factors," Guild Bulletin, March 1955, 1.

98. "Integration Here, Too," New York Times, March 4, 1957.

99. Henry E. Hein, "Advances and Challenges," HP 35 (May 1953): 33–39, 36.

100. Frederick L. Redefer, "The Importance of Teacher Morale," in Problems and Practices in NYC Schools (New York: New York Education Society for the Experimental Study of Education, 1957), 19.

101. Charles Cogen to Ely Trachtenberg, May 4, 1956, box 7, folder 1, UFT.

102. "TU'ers Lead National Movement to Hire More Negro Tutors," New York Teacher News, December 6, 1952, 13.

103. Patricia Sexton, Education and Income (New York: Viking Press, 1961), 233.

104. Charles Eckstadt, "A Statement to My Fellow Teachers at Bryant High School," April 13, 1953, box 7, folder 10, TU.

105. Charles Cogen, "The President's Column," Guild Bulletin, December 1952, 2.

106. Edward Siegel to Charles Cogen, November 14, 1960, box 20, folder 40, UFT.

107. Ely Trachtenberg to Charles Cogen, April 24, 1956, box 7, folder 1, UFT.

108. David Selden, "Guild Membership Trends" [c. 1956], box 9, folder 17, GUILD.

109. "Teacher Unionism Is Fall Conference Theme," Guild Bulletin, June 1957, 4.

110. Tess Gloster, interviewed by Renee Epstein, September 26, 1986, OH.

111. Tess Gloster, interviewed by Renee Epstein.

112. Tess Gloster, interviewed by Renee Epstein.

113. Leonard Buder, "Teacher Groups Ready to Merge," New York Times, March 16, 1960; Gene Currivan, "Teachers' Group Condemns Strike," New York Times, November 21, 1960.

114. Currivan, "Teachers' Group Condemns Strike," 41.

115. Melvyn Aaronson, letter to editor, *United Teacher* [c. November 1960], box 135, folder 37, UFT.

116. Sara Slack, "School Strike a Fizzle in Harlem," *New York Amsterdam News*, November 12, 1960.

117. "Teachers Union Seeks to Disband," *New York Times*, October 22, 1963, 24.

118. Teachers Union, "Resolution of October 3, 1963," box 80, folder 8, TU.

119. Teachers Union, "Resolution of October 3, 1963."

120. Oscar Olshansky, letter to editor, *Teacher Union News*, November 19, 1963, 3.

121. Teachers Union, "Resolution of October 3, 1963."

122. Richard Parrish, "Building a National Union Movement of Teachers," August 27, 1963, box 133, folder 8, UFT.

CHAPTER 4

1. Telegram from Harlem Parents' Committee to Superintendent Calvin Gross, July 15, 1963, box 3, folder 13, HPNA; Harlem Parents Committee, "Boycott Jim Crow Schools" flyer, 1963, box 6, folder 9, HPNA.

2. "Boycott-Eve Rally Brings Deep South Flavor to the City," *New York Times*, February 3, 1964, 1.

3. Leonard Buder, "Blacklist Is Laid to School Board," *New York Times*, February 20, 1964, 26. An expanded account of the boycott, and Galamison's role in fighting for equal schools, can be found in Clarence Taylor's *Knocking at Our Own Door: Milton A. Galamison and the Struggle to Integrate New York City Schools* (Lanham, MD: Lexington Books, 2001).

4. "It's Over—But," *New York Amsterdam News*, November 30, 1968; Preston Wilcox, "The Meaning of Community Control" bulletin, 1969, box 56, folder 4, UFT.

5. Naomi Salz to Albert Shanker, October 1, 1967, box 36, folder 20, UFT.

6. "The UFT and the Battle for Human Rights," n.d. [c. 1968], box 130, folder 11, UFT; Albert Shanker to Chapter Chairmen, October 8, 1968, box 135, folder 33, UFT.

7. United Federation of Teachers, "We Are Fighting for All New Yorkers," September 19, 1968, box 135, folder 24, UFT.

8. Ad Hoc Committee to Defend the Right to Teach, "The Freedom to Teach" (advertisement), *New York Times*, September 20, 1968.

9. W.E.B. DuBois Clubs of New York, "Stop Racism! End the School Strike! Open the School Now!" flyer, n.d. [c. 1968], box 135, folder 24, UFT.

10. Jerald E. Podair, *The Strike That Changed New York: Blacks, Whites, and the Ocean Hill-Brownsville Crisis* (New Haven, CT: Yale University Press, 2002), 207, 210. By consolidation of "white" values, Podair refers to the high percentage of Jewish teachers in the New York City school system and their allegiance with other white teachers during the strikes. While Jewish/black community relations serve as an important lens on the events in Ocean Hill-Brownsville, they are less important to the view that this chapter offers on the decade's events.

11. Daniel H. Perlstein, *Justice, Justice: School Politics and the Eclipse of Liberalism* (New York: Peter Lang, 2004), 8.

12. Gary Gerstle, "Race and the Myth of the Liberal Consensus," *Journal of American History* 82, no. 2 (1995): 579–86; Ronald P. Formisano, *Boston against Busing: Race, Class, and Ethnicity in the 1960s and 1970s* (Chapel Hill: University of North Carolina Press, 1991).

13. Commission on School Integration, *Public School Segregation and Integration in the North* (Washington, DC: National Association of Intergroup Relations Officials, November 1963), 42.

14. An example of the influence of black studies in New York City public schools and the issues addressed here could be found in the School of Common Sense, a high school opened by the Brooklyn CORE. The school offered courses in Swahili and Nzimah and located its English teachers in the Department of Foreign Languages. See "New School for Blacks Opens Fall Registrations," *New York Amsterdam News*, September 28, 1968. For more on black studies see Peniel Joseph, "Dashikis and Democracy: Black Students, Student Activism, and the Black Power Movement," *Journal of African American History* 88, no. 2 (2003): 182–203.

15. Commission on School Integration, 82.

16. UFT, "We Would Rather Teach than Picket. But We Have No Choice" (advertisement), *New York Times*, October 15, 1968, 51.

17. "Statement by David Selden, Special Representative, United Federation of Teachers, AFL-CIO, at Budget Hearing, City Hall, April 20, 1960," box 22, folder 1, UFT.

18. For more on the influence of the civil rights movement on these groups, see Matthew Frye Jacobson, *Roots Too: White Ethnic Revival in Post-Civil Rights America* (Cambridge, MA: Harvard University Press, 2006): 6, 319; Sara M. Evans, *Personal Politics* (New York: Vintage, 1980); James T. Patterson, *Grand Expectations: The United States, 1945–1974* (New York: Oxford University Press, 1996); John D. Skrentny, *The Minority Rights Revolution* (Cambridge, MA: Harvard University Press, 2002).

19. Leonard Buder, "Teachers Union Re-Elects Cogen," *New York Times*, June 11, 1962; "Membership Drive Is Now Underway" *United Teacher*, March 22, 1965, 2.

20. Sol Stern, "Scab Teachers," in *Confrontation at Ocean Hill-Brownsville: The New York School Strikes of 1968*, ed. Maurice R. Berube and Marilyn Gittell, 180–81 (New York: Praeger, 1969).

21. Thomas J. Sugrue, *Sweet Land of Liberty: The Forgotten Struggle for Civil Rights in the North* (New York: Random House, 2008), 477.

22. UFT, "Help Preserve Sanity in Our Schools" (advertisement), *New York Times*, October 8, 1968, 33.

23. Harlem Youth Opportunities Unlimited, Inc. (HARYOU), *Youth in the Ghetto: A Study of the Consequences of Powerlessness and a Blueprint for Change* (New York: HARYOU, 1964), 172–84.

24. Fred Hechinger, "The City Schools—A Mixed Report Card," *New York Times Magazine*, June 14, 1964, 43.

25. Negro Teachers Association, "Crisis in Our Schools: A Conference of Educational Personnel, Community Groups, and Parents Concerned with the Situation Confronting the Schools in the Black Community Today," May 27, 1967, box 24, folder 8, UFT. These statistics account for black and Puerto Rican students, whose numbers also grew in the 1960s.

26. Harlem Parents Committee, "Questions and Answers," n.d. [c.1964], box 6, folder 9, HPNA.

27. Dan Dodson, "Public Education in New York City in the Decade Ahead," *Journal of Educational Sociology* 34, no. 6 (1961): 280.

28. HARYOU, *Youth in the Ghetto*, 430.

29. Harlem Neighborhood Association, "Parent Research Project," June 27, 1963, box 6, folder 5, HPNA.

30. Harlem Parents Committee, "Questions and Answers," n.d. [c. 1964], box 6, folder 9, HPNA

31. "A Day in the Life," *Hey Teach!* (Newspaper of Teachers for a Democratic Society), [n.d.], Tamiment Library Boxed Newspapers, periodicals 1, box 150.

32. Goldie M. Curtain, "Improving the Image of Our School," HP 47 (October 1965): 25–30, 28.

33. Jeanne Tenenbaum, "I Remember," HP 48 (May 1966): 53–57, 54.

34. David Boroff, "Report Card on New York's Teachers," *New York Times Magazine*, December 10, 1961, 15.

35. Elsa M. Voss, "On Making the Image 3-Dimensional," HP 46 (January 1964): 59–63, 61.

36. Virginia Anderson, "Teaching English to Puerto Rican Pupils," HP 46 (March 1964): 51–54.

37. Charles Savitsky, "Social Theory Advances on the Disadvantaged," HP 46 (February 1964): 54–62, 61.

38. Quoted in Fred Hechinger, "The City School—A Mixed Report Card.".

39. Jim Haskins, *Diary of a Harlem Schoolteacher* (New York: Grove Press, 1969), 19.

40. Marjorie Drabkin, letter to editor, HP 47 (October 1965): 72.

41. William Isaacs, "Dissenting Thoughts on School Integration," HP 47 (May 1965): 17–29, 23. The most significant example of white parents' organization was the growing popularity of Parents and Taxpayers (PAT) organizations, which started in Jackson Heights, Queens, in September 1963 as an alliance among Italian, Irish, and Jewish parents to resist integration efforts in their neighborhood schools. By the end of the year, over one hundred chapters of PAT existed in Queens, Brooklyn, and the Bronx, and the organization had over three thousand members. See Podair, *The Strike That Changed New York*, 24–28.

42. A.H. Raskin, "He Leads His Teachers up the Down Staircase," *New York Times*, September 3, 1967. Such reports' characterizations of black power as something both of growing annoyance and, at the same time, not fully serious would earn the *Times*, like the UFT, criticism for siding against community activists.

43. Edward Gottlieb, interview by Renee Epstein, March 1, 1986, OH.

44. Leonard Buder, "There Will Be No Teachers, No School," *New York Times*, September 10, 1967.

45. Negro Teachers Association, "Petition against the U.F.T. Agency Shop," [c.1967], box 24, folder 8, UFT.

46. Podair, *The Strike That Changed New York*, 160. News reports were also less factually supported by the publication of several popular novels and exposes that spoke to the public appeal and concern over violence and minority students. See Evan Hunter, *Blackboard Jungle* (New York: Simon and Schuster, 1954); Bel Kaufman, *Up the Down Staircase* (Englewood Cliffs, NJ: Prentice Hall, 1964); Jim Haskins, *Diary of a Harlem Schoolteacher* (New York: Grove Press, 1969); George N. Allen, *Undercover Teacher* (New York: Doubleday, 1960).

47. Sandra Adickes, "My Seven Year (H)itch: A Rambling, Discursive, Anecdotal History of the Evolution of a Radical Teacher," July 1967, folder 7, Adickes Papers, McCain Library and Archives, University of Southern Mississippi. For more on Adickes's experience in Mississippi, see Sandra E. Adickes, *Legacy of a Freedom School* (New York: Palgrave MacMillan, 2005).

48. "Resignation of Slum Teachers," *New York Times*, March 16, 1967.

49. Negro Teachers Association, Press Release, "The 'So-Called Disruptive Child,'" August 9, 1967, box 24, folder 8, UFT. Statistic found in Joshua B. Freeman, *Working-Class New York: Life and Labor Since World War II* (New York: The New Press, 2001), 204.

50. Albert Vann, Untitled Press Release, n.d. [c. August 1967], box 24, folder 8, UFT.

51. Preston Wilcox, "The Meaning of Community Control" bulletin (1969), box 56, folder 4, UFT.

52. HARYOU, *Youth in the Ghetto*, 220.

53. Negro Teachers Association, "Crisis in Our Schools: A Conference of Education

Personnel, Community Groups, and Parents Concerned with the Situation Confronting the Schools in the Black Community Today," May 27, 1967, box 24, folder 8, UFT.

54. "Teachers to Present Grievances," *New York Amsterdam News*, June 24, 1967.

55. Negro Teachers Association, "Resolutions, Negro Teachers Association," May 28, 1967, box 24, folder 8, UFT.

56. Luther W. Seabrook, "Proposal for the Recruitment and Training of Teachers for Disadvantaged Areas," n.d. [c. October 1967], box 24, folder 8, UFT.

57. NTA, "Petition against the U.F.T. Agency Shop," n.d. [c. 1967], box 24, folder 8, UFT.

58. UFT, "Statement of School Integration," July 18, 1963, box 6, folder 9, HPNA.

59. Solidarity, "No Boycott," n.d. [c. February 1964], box 130, folder 13, UFT.

60   Shalom Sperber, letter to editor, *United Teacher*, October 22, 1965, 4; Leonard Boyer, letter to editor, *United Teacher*, October 22, 1965, 4.

61. Charles Cogen and Richard Parrish to Carl Megel, April 23, 1964, box 227, folder 40, UFT.

62. COFO to Freedom School participants, n.d. [c. February 1964], box 118, folder 4, UFT.

63. For more on Day and his curriculum, see Daniel Perlstein, "Teaching Freedom: SNCC and the Creation of the Mississippi Freedom Schools," *History of Education Quarterly* 30, no. 3 (1990): 311–3.

64. Liz Fusco to Albert Shanker, February 1, 1965, box 227, folder 40, UFT.

65. Fusco's sentiments were not ones that COFO staff restricted to UFT volunteers; in fact, as Doug McAdam and Sara Evans have shown, Southern black activists were concerned about the role and responsibilities of white, middle-class volunteers before Freedom Summer began, even as they depended on these very volunteers for greater press coverage of their cause. See Evans, *Personal Politics*; Doug McAdam, *Freedom Summer* (New York: Oxford University Press, 1990).

66. Richard Rampell to Albert Shanker, May 2, 1965, box 19, folder 3, UFT.

67. Joseph Hassid, letter to editor, *United Teacher*, September 24, 1965, 4.

68. Miss H. Alexander, letter to editor, *United Teacher*, October 22, 1965, 4.

69. Jacob Shushuk, letter to editor, *United Teacher*, November 5, 1965, 2.

70. Martin Geisser, letter to editor, *United Teacher*, January 9, 1966, 4.

71. Albert Shanker to Chapter Chairmen, April 28, 1965, box 133, folder 21, UFT.

72. Clara J. Isaacs to Albert Shanker, n.d., box 64, folder 2, UFT; Albert Shanker to UFT Members, April 28, 1965, box 64, folder 2, UFT.

73. Ben Tobias to Albert Shanker, May 12, 1965, box 19, folder 13, UFT.

74. Nicholas Neuhas, letter to editor, *New York World-Telegram*, April 26, 1965.

75. Marjorie Drabkin, letter to editor, HP 47 (October 1965): 72.

76. Grace R. Donovan to Albert Shanker, May 9, 1965, box 19, folder 13, UFT.

77. Al Mathew to Albert Shanker, May 1, 1965, box 19, folder 13, UFT.

78. Letter from UFT Delegates, John S. Roberts High School to Albert Shanker, n.d., box 19, folder 13, UFT.

79. Faculty of P.S. 79 Manhattan to Albert Shanker, n.d., box 19, folder 13, UFT.

80. Layle Lane, letter to editor, *The United Teacher*, November 6, 1968, 8.

81. Kenneth Clark, "A Negro Looks at Black Power," *New York Post*, November 11, 1967.

82. Leslie Campbell, "The Black Teacher and Black Power," *African-American Teachers Association Forum*, May–August 1967, p. 2, box 24, folder 11, UFT.

83. Telegram from Albert Vann to Albert Shanker, June 7, 1967, box 24, folder 8, UFT.

84. "Minutes of Meeting of UFT Committee on African-American History," June 13, 1968, box 97, folder 25, UFT.

85. Richard Parrish, "The New York City Teacher Strikes: Blow to Education, Boon to Racism," *Labor Today* 8 (May 1969): 30–33.

86. Leo Shapiro, letter to editor, *United Teacher*, October 24, 1968, 8.

87. Rod MacKenzie, letter to editor, *United Teacher*, December 18, 1968, 5.

88. Fred Hechinger, "The Hidden Issue," *New York Times*, September 11, 1967.

89. Daniel U. Levine. "The Need for Teacher Activist Roles among Teachers in Big City School Districts," *Journal of Secondary Education* 44 (March 1969): 122–8. For more on the role of teachers in securing or troubling education equity in Northern urban centers at the time, see Jack Dougherty, *More Than One Struggle: The Evolution of Black School Reform in Milwaukee* (Chapel Hill: University of North Carolina Press, 2004); Jeffrey Mirel, *The Rise and Fall of an Urban School System: Detroit, 1907–81*, 2d ed. (Ann Arbor: University of Michigan Press, 1999); Ronald P. Formisano, *Boston against Busing: Race, Class, Ethnicity in the 1960 and 1970s* (Chapel Hill: University of North Carolina Press, 1991); John F. Lyons, *Teachers and Reform: Chicago Public Education, 1929–1970* (Urbana: University of Illinois Press, 2008).

90. Fred M. Hechinger, "Teachers Adopting a Militant Approach," *New York Times*, January 9, 1969. For more reporting on the spread of decentralization and teacher militancy, see Fred M. Hechinger, "Negroes' Priority Demand," *New York Times*, October 13, 1968; "Decentralization Snags," *New York Times*, September 18, 1968; "A Conflict with No Easy Solution," *New York Times*, September 22, 1968; Joseph Loftus, "Rising Militancy Noted in Public Employees," *New York Times*, September 3, 1968.

91. Quoted in Stephen Cole, *The Unionization of Teachers: A Case Study of the UFT* (New York: Praeger, 1969), 74.

92. J. Anthony Lukas, "Nation's Teachers Using Rights Protest Methods," *New York Times*, September 11, 1967.

93. Albert Shanker, "Sounding Board: Four Major Figures Look at the Decentralization Dispute," *New York Times*, January 9, 1969.

94. Ruth Isquith to Albert Shanker, May 30, 1965, box 85, folder 28, UFT.

95. Ted Bleecker to Albert Shanker, June 30, 1966, box 51, folder 8, UFT.

96. UFT, "An Open Letter to the Parents of New York City" (advertisement), *New York Times*, September 11, 1968. For figure on UFT spending, see "U.F.T. Spends $200,000 on Ads during Strike," *New York Times*, November 16, 1968.

97. UFT, "Help Preserve Sanity in Our Schools" (advertisement), *New York Times*, October 8, 1968.

98. UFT, "There's No Room for Extremism in Our Schools" (advertisement), *New York Times*, October 31, 1968.

99. "Ad Hoc Committee to Defend the Right to Teach" (advertisement), *New York Times*, September 20, 1968. For more on the images the UFT was footnoting and the role of the media in the success of the civil rights movement, see Melvin Small, *Covering Dissent: The Media and the Anti-War Movement* (New Brunswick: Rutgers University Press, 1994); Todd Gitlin, *The Whole World Is Watching: Mass Media in the Making and Unmaking of the New Left* (Berkeley: University of California Press, 1980); Gene Roberts and Hank Klibanoff. *The Race Beat: The Press, the Civil Rights Struggle, and the Awakening of a Nation* (New York: Alfred A. Knopf, 2006).

100. Podair offers an extensive examination of the effect of this oversight on the proceedings among the union, the Ocean Hill-Brownsville board, and the Board of Education. See Podair, *The Strike That Changed New York*, 99–102. For more on due process and teachers, see

Louis Fischer, David Schimmel, and Cynthia Kelly, *Teachers and the Law* (New York: Longman, 1981), 190–213.

101. Sylvan Fox, "40,000 Marchers Support Teachers," *New York Times*, October 18, 1968; Freeman, *Working-Class New York*, 226.

102. Leonard Buder, "Shanker Is Jailed for School Strike," *New York Times*, December 21, 1971.

103. Sylvan Fox, "8 Union Teachers Barred 3–1/2 Hours from J.H.S. 271," *New York Times*, November 22, 1968.

104. Homer Bigart, "School Is Ringed," *New York Times*, September 26, 1957; Bill Kovach, "7 Teachers Enter P.S. 39 with Police but Find It Empty," *New York Times*, December 7, 1968.

105. Members of the United Federation of Teachers, P.S. 246K, letter to editor, *United Teacher*, October 7, 1968.

106. New Caucus, "Community Control and the Future of the AFT," [1968 Convention], box 135, folder 24, UFT.

107. Theresa L. Held, "Non-Striking Teachers Harassed in School," *New York Times*, October 21, 1968.

108. "Jewish Teachers Back Ocean Hill," *New York Times*, November 2, 1968; and Stern, "'Scab' Teachers." For a more extensive look at Teachers for Community Control, see Perlstein, *Justice, Justice*, 48–64.

109. Susan Previant Lee, letter to editor, *New York Times*, October 25, 1968.

110. Eugene Jackson, letter to editor, *New York Times*, November 14, 1968.

111. "The Shame of the Schools," WABC Editorial October 2, 16, 18, 19, 1968, box 53, folder 11, UFT.

112. Lee Epstein, letter to editor, *New York Times*, November 12, 1968, 46.

113. Roy G. Seher, letter to editor, *New York Times*, October 28, 1968; Epstein, letter to editor.

114. Quoted in Diane Ravitch, *The Great School Wars: A History of the New York City Public Schools* (Baltimore: Johns Hopkins Press, 2000), 377.

115. Podair, *The Strike That Changed New York*, 146, 180.

116. Perlstein, *Justice, Justice*, 152.

117. Margie Stamberg, "NY Schools Open, but Parents Angry," *Guardian*, November 30, 1968.

118. Susan Mandel, letter to editor, *United Teacher*, December 18, 1968.

119. Nicky Feldman, letter to editor, *United Teacher*, December 4, 1968.

120. Joyce Haynes, "An Open Letter to Al Shanker and Members of the U.F.T.," n.d., box 2, folder 1, RP Additional.

121. Hechinger, "Teachers Adopting a Militant Approach."

122. Fred M. Hechinger, "Bitter Conflict Threatens Disintegration of the Schools," *New York Times*, October 15, 1968; "Third Strike," *New York Times*, October 15, 1968.

123. A.H. Raskin, "Why New York Is 'Strike City,'" *New York Times*, December 22, 1968.

124. "It's Over—But," *New York Amsterdam News*, November 30, 1968; Dana Driskell, "UFT vs. Blacks," *New York High School Free Press*, October 9–22, 1968, The Tamiment Library Boxed Newspapers, periodicals 1, box 150, New York High School Free Press folder.

125. "Opposition Slate Formed for UFT Elections," *Teachers for Community Control Newsletter*, June 1969, 1, box 94, folder 6, UFT.

126. Quoted in Melvin Urofsky, ed., *Why Teachers Strike: Teachers' Rights and Community Control* (Garden City, NY: Anchor Books, 1970).

127. Parrish, "The New York City Teacher Strikes." Shanker was originally supposed to contribute to the same volume but refused when he learned that Parrish's article was to appear.

CHAPTER 5

1. "Albert Shanker = Teacher Power," Bill Moyers' Journal, April 16, 1974, WNET, transcript, p. 6, Microfilm R-2986, reel 3, RP.

2. "Shanker's Foes Call His Rule Autocratic," New York Times, February 24, 1971.

3. Albert Shanker, "Shanker Responds: The Way It Really Is," Phi Delta Kappan 55, no. 6 (1974): 387.

4. Albert Shanker, "For Teachers, Bigger Role," New York Times, January 12, 1970.

5. A.H. Raskin, "Shanker's Great Leap," New York Times, September 1, 1973.

6. Raskin, "Shanker's Great Leap."

7. Shanker, "Shanker Responds: The Way It Really Is," 387.

8. Albert Shanker, "Where We Stand: Why This Column?" New York Times, December 13, 1970.

9. See Ronald P. Formisano, Boston against Busing: Race, Class, and Ethnicity in the 1960s and 1970s (Chapel Hill: University of North Carolina Press, 1991); Matthew Lassiter, The Sunbelt Majority: Suburban Politics in the Sunbelt South (Princeton: Princeton University Press, 2005); Rosemary C. Salomone, Equal Education under Law: Legal Rights and Federal Policy in the Post Brown Era (New York: Palgrave Macmillan, 2000); Gary Orfield and Susan E. Eaton, Dismantling Desegregation: The Quiet Reversal of Brown v. Board of Education (New York: New Press, 1997); Bernard Schwartz, Swann's Way: The School Busing Case and the Supreme Court (New York: Oxford University Press, 1986); James E. Ryan, Five Miles Away, a World Apart: One City, Two Schools, and the Story of Educational Opportunity in Modern America (New York: Oxford University Press, 2010).

10. For more on these other campaigns, see Gareth Davies, See Government Grow: Education Politics from Johnson to Reagan (Lawrence, KS: University of Kansas Press, 2007); and Adam R. Nelson, The Elusive Ideal: Equal Educational Opportunity and the Federal Role in Boston's Public School, 1950–1985 (Chicago: University of Chicago Press, 2005).

11. Patrick J. McGuinn, No Child Left Behind and the Transformation of Federal Education Policy, 1965–2005 (Lawrence, KS: University of Kansas Press, 2006).

12. McGuinn captures how the Reagan administration initially commissioned A Nation at Risk assuming the report would appease the public by commending public schools. When it did otherwise, as this chapter will later examine, it spurred enormous changes in national school reform efforts. See McGuinn, No Child Left Behind, 39–47. For more on the growing influence of the federal government in education politics from Nixon to Reagan, see Davies, See Government Grow.

13. Albert Shanker to UFT Members, "Message from the President for Spring Conference Program" [c.1978]. box 14, folder 2, SHANKER.

14. See Jerald E. Podair, The Strike That Changed New York: Blacks, Whites, and the Ocean Hill-Brownsville Crisis (New Haven: Yale University Press, 2002), 141.

15. Joshua B. Freeman, Working-Class New York: Life and Labor Since World War II (New York: The New Press, 2001), 215.

16. Jacques Steinberg, "Tears for a Union's Founder, Cheers for His Successor," New York Times, July 30, 1997.

17. Peniel E. Joseph, "The Black Power Movement: A State of the Field," Journal of American History 96, no. 3 (2009): 751–76, 753. See also Peniel E. Joseph, Waiting 'Til the Midnight

Hour: A Narrative History of Black Power in America (New York: Henry Holt, 2006); Rod Bush, *We Are Not What We Seem: Black Nationalism and Class Struggle in the American Century* (New York: New York University Press, 2000); Jeffrey O.G. Ogbar, *Black Power: Radical Politics and African American Identity* (Baltimore: Johns Hopkins Press, 2004); William L. VanDeburg, *New Day in Babylon: The Black Power Movement and American Culture, 1965–1975* (Chicago: University of Chicago Press, 1992).

18. Fred Perretti, "Financial Crisis Crippling New York's Public Schools," *New York Times*, December 12, 1976.

19. Richard D. Kahlenberg, *Tough Liberal: Albert Shanker and the Battle over Schools, Unions, Race, and Democracy* (New York: Columbia University Press, 2007), 182; Lee Dembart, "Shanker Opposed to Teachers' Strike," *New York Times*, September 30, 1975.

20. Martin Gottlieb, "New York's Rescue: The Offstage Dramas," *New York Times*, July 2, 1985.

21. Quoted, in Freeman, *Working-Class New York*, 268.

22. Murray Halwar to Albert Shanker, May 4, 1971; Jack Sherman to Albert Shanker, May 10, 1971, box 102, folder 12, UFT.

23. Richard L. Lotreck to Albert Shanker, December 19, 1971, box 102, folder 15, UFT.

24. Shanker, "Shanker Responds: The Way It *Really* Is," 387.

25. "Statement of Mrs. Blanche Lewis, President, United Parents Association, before the New York Commission on Human Rights, Public Hearings on Minority Hiring in City Schools, Wednesday January 29, 1971," series 10, folder, 81, UPA.

26. "The Teacher Flunked the Test," *New York Amsterdam News*, March 31, 1973.

27. "Statement of Mrs. Blanche Lewis."

28. J. Zambga Browne, "White Teachers Must Visit Homes of Minority Pupils," *New York Amsterdam News*, March 23, 1974.

29. "In a Letter from Jail, Shanker Asks UFT Members for a Big 'Yes" Vote on Honoring Para-Picket Lines," *United Teacher*, May 31, 1970, 2.

30. United Federation of Teachers, *Teachers and Para-Professionals: On-the-Job Partners . . . Working Together for Better Schools* [c. 1970], p. 2, box 2, folder 6, American Federation of Teachers: Human Rights and Community Relations Department, American Federation of Teachers Collection, Archives of Labor and Urban Affairs, Walter P. Reuther Library, Wayne State University.

31. Richard D. Kahlenberg, *Tough Liberal*, 131.

32. "Parents' Boycott Shuts 6 Schools in Canarsie Area," *New York Times*, October 31, 1972.

33. "Teachers at 211 Ignoring Boycott," *New York Times*, October 31, 1972.

34. "Anker Backs Shanker in Black-White Fight," *New York Amsterdam News*, October 12, 1974.

35. "Showdown with Shanker Shaping up in Harlem," *New York Amsterdam News*, October 5, 1974.

36. "Blacks Link UFT to Ouster of Principal," *New York Amsterdam News*, August 27, 1975.

37. "Schools Called Anti-Parents," *New York Amsterdam News*, April 22, 1972.

38. "Teachers Rap UFT Demands," *New York Amsterdam News*, August 5, 1972.

39. "Schools Called Anti-Parents."

40. "Black Teachers Hold 3-Day Meeting Here," *New York Amsterdam News*, April 22, 1972.

41. "Communications from the ATA," *New York Amsterdam News*, April 7, 1973.

42. 'United Black Caucus, Involved Black Teachers," *New York Amsterdam News*, April 24, 1971.

43. In the 1970–71 school year, only 803 of the city's approximately fifty-nine thousand teachers identified as Hispanic, while 22.8 percent of the student body—or 260,040 students—did so. Board of Education statistics cited in Isaura Santiago-Santiago, "Aspira v. Board of Education Revisited," *American Journal of Education*, v. 95, n. 1 (November 1986): 149–99, 172.

44. For more on the *Aspira* case and its role in the history of bilingual education, see Davies, *See Government Grow*, 141–65; Luis O. Reyes, "The Aspira Consent Decree: A Thirtieth Anniversary Retrospective of Bilingual Education in New York City," *Harvard Educational Review*, v. 76, n. 3 (Fall 2006): 369–400. Paradoxically, the success of rights campaigns for specialized classes for disabled and second-language students removed from otherwise integrated classrooms the same black and Puerto Rican students that teachers sought to expel a decade earlier. See Nelson, *The Elusive Ideal*, 121–49.

45. Ted Bleecker to Albert Shanker, June 30, 1966, box 51, folder 8, UFT.

46. One of the most obvious ways in which Shanker supported a particular civil rights platform was through the use of guest columnists. The most frequent such columnist by far was Bayard Rustin, who wrote fourteen columns between 1970 and 1981. Rustin served as Chairman of the A. Philip Randolph Institute at the time, and his columns suggest an often conservative stance on race progress and a belief that teachers unions were best suited to improve the public schools. In a column on black power, for example, Rustin wrote, "Born as it was in bitterness and frustration, black power, never a significant force in the black man's movement, has left us a powerful legacy of polarization, division, and political nonsense" ("Black Power's Legacy," November 12, 1972). Other topics Rustin wrote about for the column include "The Myths of Black Education" (April 22, 1973), "Quotas and the 'New Ethnicity'" (August 25, 1974), and "The Dangers of Ethnic Separatism" (July 6, 1975).

47. Albert Shanker, "Give a Damn," *New York Times*, February 21, 1971; Albert Shanker, "Two Absentees in the Coalition to Save Our Public Schools," *New York Times*, March 21, 1971.

48. Albert Shanker, "Luis Fuentes: Propagandist as Educator," *New York Times*, July 15, 1973.

49. Albert Shanker, "Obstacles on the Road to Accountability," *New York Times*, March 28, 1971; Albert Shanker, "Two Absentees in the Coalition to Save Our Public Schools,"; Albert Shanker, "A Salute to *Commentary* Magazine," *New York Times*, April 8, 1973.

50. Albert Shanker, "Minority Group Members Gain More as Union Members," *New York Times*, June 20, 1971.

51. Shanker, "Give a Damn."

52. Shanker, "Minority Group Members Gain More as Union Members."

53. Shanker, "A Salute to *Commentary* Magazine."

54. Albert Shanker, "Teacher Role Central," *New York Times*, January 3, 1971.

55. Albert Shanker, "Obstacles on the Road to Accountability."

56. Albert Shanker, "Teacher Unionism: A Quiet Revolution," *New York Times*, October 28, 1973.

57. Albert Shanker, "Convention Stresses Broad Economic Issues," *New York Times*, August 22, 1976.

58. A.H. Raskin, "Teachers New Lions in Political Arena," *New York Times*, January 15, 1975.

59. Office of Civil Rights, Department of Health, Education and Welfare, "Summary of Findings," October 5, 1977, p. 4, box 92, folder 8, SHANKER.

60. Martin Gerry to Chancellor Irving Anker, November 9, 1976, pp. 3, 4, series 10, folder 82, UPA.

61. David Vidal, "Christen Says U.S. Report Citing School Bias 'May Be a Disservice,'" *New York Times*, January 20, 1977.

62. John Saunders , Mary Ellen Fahs, and David Seeley to Robert Christen and Irving Anker, November 12, 1976, series 10, folder 82, UPA.

63. Roger Wilkins, "New York City Plan to Equalize Distribution of Minority Teachers Stirs Controversy," *New York Times*, October 3, 1977.

64. Wilkins, "New York City Plan to Equalize Distribution of Minority Teachers Stirs Controversy."

65. Ari L. Goldman, "Assignment of Teachers by Race: Anxiety in New York City Schools," *New York Times*, September 23, 1977.

66. The New York Alliance for the Public Schools, *New Yorkers View Their Public Schools, 1983: A Public Opinion Survey*, November 15, 1983, box 14, UFT 1983 folder, SHANKER. Interestingly, the percentage of Hispanic parents who gave their schools grades of an A or B was higher than that of black or white parents, at 72 percent. By the mid-1970s, bilingual education was an important and visible issue in education policy and teacher unionism, although this book does not attempt to address either. Because of this visibility and the distinct issues Spanish-speaking parents cared about, the history of education for Puerto Rican students in New York City calls for its own study.

67. Albert Shanker, "The Making of a Profession" (American Federation of Teachers, April 1985), 5.

68. Roy C. Pellicano, "New York City Public School Reform: A Line Teacher's View," *Phi Delta Kappan* 62, no. 3 (1980): 174.

69. Gloria Channon, "First Do No Harm," *Teachers Action Caucus Newsletter*, December 1983, p. 2, box 2, folder 3, AF.

70. Lawrence J. McAndrews, *The Era of Education: The Presidents and the Schools, 1965–2001* (Urbana, IL: University of Illinois Press, 2006), 132.

71. For more on the relationship between the Reagan administration and the commissioning of the report, see McGuinn, *No Child Left Behind*; David T. Gordon, ed., *A Nation Transformed? American Education 20 Years after A Nation at Risk* (Cambridge: Harvard Education Press, 2003); Maris A. Vinovskis, *From A Nation at Risk to No Child Left Behind: National Education Goals and the Creation of Federal Education Policy* (New York: Teachers College Press, 2009).

72. National Commission on Excellence in Education, *A Nation at Risk: The Imperative for Educational Reform* (Washington, DC: Government Printing Office, 1983), 8.

73. National Commission on Excellence in Education, *A Nation at Risk*, 12

74. Fred M. Hechinger, "A Warning from Albert Shanker," *New York Times*, March 20, 1984.

75. Albert Shanker, "What Makes Teachers Resist Change?" *New York Times*, August 18, 1985.

76. Albert Shanker, "Key Issues to Consider before Voting," *New York Times*, November 4, 1984.

77. Albert Shanker, "A Landmark Revisited," *New York Times*, May 9, 1993; Albert Shanker, "National (not Federal) Standards," *New York Times*, April 28, 1996.

78. Albert Shanker, "A Teacher's Tales out of School," *New York Times*, January 1, 1987.

79. Albert Shanker, "Real Tests, Higher Grades, Better Pay," *New York Times*, June 19, 1983.

80. Albert Shanker, "'Making Do' with Misassigned Teachers," *New York Times*, October 27, 1985.

81. Albert Shanker, "Education Report Stirs Credentials Debate" *New York Times*, June 1, 1986.

82. Albert Shanker, "Does Pavarotti Have to File an Aria Plan?" *New York Times*, February 6, 1983; Albert Shanker, "Parents, Teachers Resist Change for Its Own Sake" *New York Times*, January 4, 1981.

83. Albert Shanker, "What's Happening to Teacher Testing?" *New York Times*, November 8, 1987.

84. Albert Shanker, "State of the Union Address, AFT Convention" (August 1984), reprinted in *American Educator* 21 (Spring/Summer 1997): 26.

85. Shanker, "State of the Union Address, AFT Convention" (August 1984).

86. Scott Widemeyer to Albert Shanker, September 26, 1985, box 4, folder 24, SHANKER.

87. Edward Meyer to Albert Shanker, July 21, 1986, box 97, folder 111, SHANKER.

88. Arlene M. Donowitz to Albert Shanker, October 2, 1985, box 97, folder 104, SHANKER.

89   Mary Ellen Snodgrass to Albert Shanker, September 19, 1975, box 97, folder 104, SHANKER.

90. Barbara Mitchell to Albert Shanker, November 11, 1991, box 11, folder 8, SHANKER.

91. "Tests Discussed," *AFT Black Caucus Newsletter*, Summer 1986, 1, box 3, folder 10, AF.

92. Dorothy B. Coleman to Albert Shanker, March 15, 1989, box 20, folder 1520, SHANKER.

93. Tom Mooney to Albert Shanker, April 27, 1989, box 20, folder 1520, SHANKER.

94. Patrick Daly, Dearborn Teachers Association, interview by Dan Golodner, April 4, 1987, transcript, p. 159, AFTOH.

95. Daly, Dearborn Teachers Association, 146. In Rochester, New York, members differed with local union leaders in voting against a proposal for "diversified performance assessment," which would have improved teachers' salaries based on assessments created by teachers' colleagues, students, and students' parents. While this would have represented a radical change in teacher evaluations, unionists' votes suggest they found it too risky. See Adam Urbanski to Albert Shanker, October 17, 1990, box 17, folder 616, SHANKER.

96. Eugenia Kemble to Albert Shanker and Bob Porter, March 2, 1981, box 2, folder 2, SHANKER.

97. Eugenia Kemble to AFT Leaders, July 26, 1991, box 5, folder 17, CINN.

98. AFT Leadership for Reform, "Applying the Proposed Principles: Implications for the Local Union and Questions for Discussion with Al Shanker" [n.d.], box 5, folder 17, CINN.

99. Dana H. Brown to Albert Shanker, January 11, 1993, box 5, folder 17, CINN.

100. Robert Pearlman to Albert Shanker, June 17, 1991, box 5, folder 8, SHANKER

101. Quoted in Gerald Grant and Christine E. Murray, *Teaching in America: The Slow Revolution* (Cambridge, MA: Harvard University Press, 2002), 166. Important to note, too, is that many union locals never really engaged in reform bargaining and remained committed to the industrial model. Especially important examples of this include Detroit, Chicago, Baltimore, and Washington, D.C.

102. Albert Shanker, "Improving Big City Schools," *New York Times*, March 12, 1989.

103. Shanker, "Improving Big City Schools."

104. Albert Shanker, "State of the Union Address, AFT Convention" (August 1977), reprinted in *American Educator* 21, no. 1 and 2 (1997): 8.

105. Albert Shanker, "State of the Union Address, AFT Convention" (August 1992), in *American Educator* 21, no 1 and 2 (1997): 20.

106. Albert Shanker, interview by Marcia Reecer [n.d.], transcript, box 66, folder 53, SHANKER.

107. Albert Shanker, "Where We Stand: Looking Back," *New York Times*, December 17, 1995.

108. Shanker, interview by Marcia Reecer.

109. Kate Rousmaniere, "Teacher Unions in Popular Culture: Individualism and the Absence of Collectivity," *Working USA* 3, no. 3 (1999): 45.

110. Fred M. Hechinger, "Lessons in Teacher Power," *New York Times*, November 21, 1971.

111. "Albert Shanker = Teacher Power."

112. Raskin, "Shanker's Great Leap."

113. Alden Whitman, "The Rise and Rise of Albert Shanker," *New York Times*, January 15, 1975.

114. Nat Henoff, "Reply to Shanker," *New York Times*, November 12, 1972.

115. Reginald G. Damerall and Maurie Hillson, "The UFT Tells It Like It Isn't and Makes It Look Like It Is," *Phi Delta Kappan* 55, no. 6 (1974), 377–82, 380.

116. Albert Shanker, "Teacher Unionism: A Quiet Revolution."

117. Shanker, "Shanker Responds: The Way It Really Is," 387.

118. Albert Shanker, "Where We Stand: Looking Back."

119. Judith Gluck to Albert Shanker, January 14, 1986, box 97, folder 105, SHANKER.

120. Eleana Mullins to Albert Shanker, October 5, 1988, box 98, folder 26, SHANKER.

121. "Shanker Pledged Integration . . . and Kept His Word," *New York Amsterdam News*, March 17, 1973. For more on the protests, see Jonathan Rieser, *Canarsie: The Jews and Italians of Brooklyn against Liberalism* (Cambridge, MA: Harvard University Press, 1985); Podair, *The Strike That Changed New York*, 188–92.

122. (Mrs.) Adelaide Stowe, letter to the editor, *New York Amsterdam News*, July 14, 1973; see also L. Adams, letter to the editor, *New York Amsterdam News*, June 23, 1973. The one column Shanker published was entitled "A. Philip Randolph; April 15, 1889–May 16, 1979," *New York Amsterdam News*, September 1, 1979.

123. Deena Birnbaum to Albert Shanker, October 26, 1988, box 98, folder 27, SHANKER.

124. Steven A. Sohn to Albert Shanker, December 18, 1990, box 99, folder 8, SHANKER.

125. Frederick Lightfoot to Albert Shanker, December 19, 1990, box 99, folder 3, SHANKER.

126. John J. Curran to Albert Shanker, June 6, 1988, box 98, folder 22, SHANKER.

127. Leslie A. Hart to Albert Shanker, March 31, 1988, box 98, folder 20, SHANKER.

128. Abe Scherzwey to Albert Shanker, November 8, 1988, box 98, folder 27, SHANKER.

129. Michael Murantz to Albert Shanker, August 11, 1985, box 2, folder 5, AF.

130. Scott Widemeyer to Albert Shanker, January 23, 1986, box 4, folder 24, SHANKER. Widemeyer also recommended that Sandra Feldman, president of the UFT, be given four issues per year to appeal to the column's New York base.

131. Albert Shanker, "Talking a Walk down Memory Lane," *New York Times*, December 15, 1985.

132. Teresa Gloster to Albert Shanker, December 31, 1985, box 97, folder 104, SHANKER.

133. Albert Shanker, "Twenty Years (and 1000 Columns) Later," *New York Times*, December 16, 1990.

134. Shanker, "Shanker Responds," 385.

135. Amy Gutmann, *Democratic Education* (Princeton: Princeton University Press, 1987), 87.

136. See Gary Orfield and Susan E. Eaton, eds., *Dismantling Desegregation: The Quiet Reversal of Brown v. Board of Education* (New York: New Press, 1997); Daniel P. Mayer, John E. Mullens, and Mary T. Moore, *Monitoring School Quality: An Indicator's Report* (Washington, DC: National Center for Education Statistics, December 2000), 13.

CONCLUSION

1. Robert Slavin, interview by Hendrik Smith, *Making Schools Work with Hendrik Smith*, PBS, 2005. http://www/pbs/org/makingschoolswork/sbs/sfa/slavin.html.

2. Jonathan Kozol, *The Shame of the Nation: The Restoration of Apartheid Schooling in America* (New York: Crown Publishers, 2005), 85; Jonathan Kozol, "Still Separate, Still Unequal," *Harpers*, September 2005, 41–54.

3. See Harvey Kantor and Robert Lowe, "From New Deal to No Deal: No Child Left Behind and the Devolution of Responsibility for Equal Opportunity," *Harvard Educational Review* 76, no. 4 (2006): 474–502.

4. "Schools to Compete for Funding in Obama Reform Plan," *Online News Hour*, PBS, July 24, 2009. http://www.pbs.org/newshour/bb/north_america/july-deco9/duncan_07–24.html.

5. "Schools to Compete for Funding in Obama Reform Plan."

6. Arne Duncan, "Crossing the Next Bridge" (speech, Selma, Alabama, March 8, 2010).

7. Quoted in Daniel J. Losen, "Graduation Rate Accountability under the No Child Left Behind Act," in *NCLB Meets School Realities: Lessons from the Field*, ed. Gail L. Sunderman, James S. Kim, and Gary Orfield, 105–20, 109, (Thousand Oaks, CA: Corwin Press, 2005). See also Gary Orfield, ed. *Drop Outs in America: Confronting the Graduation Rate Crisis* (Cambridge: Harvard Education Press, 2004); Gary Orfield and Susan E. Eaton, eds., *Dismantling Desegregation: The Quiet Reversal of Brown v. Board of Education* (New York: New Press, 1996); Jennifer L. Hochschild, *The New American Dilemma: Liberal Democracy and School Desegregation* (New Haven: Yale University Press, 1984).

8. Wanda J. Blanchett, "Disproportionate Representation of African American Students in Special Education: Acknowledging the Role of White Privilege and Racism," *Educational Researcher* 35, no. 6 (2006): 24–28. See also Daniel J. Losen and Gary Orfield, *Racial Inequity in Special Education* (Cambridge: Harvard Education Press, 2002); Beth Harry and Janette K. Klinger, *Why Are So Many Minority Students in Special Education? Understanding Race and Disability in Schools* (New York: Teachers College Press, 2006); National Research Council, *Minority Students in Special and Gifted Education* (Washington DC: National Academy Press 2002); The Civil Rights Project, *Discrimination in Special Education* (Cambridge: Civil Rights Project, Harvard University Press, 2001).

9. Wilhelmina Bustamante, "Address Made at the Meeting of the Board of Education on April 6, 1950, in Re Item #26, Banning Teachers Union," box 2, folder 27, CB.

10. Louise Sundin, interview by Dan Golodner, April 30, 2007, transcript, p. 142, AFTOH.

11. Sundin, interview, 218.

12. In general, the lack of influence of teacher unions on NCLB policy can be read in their relative absence from many of the strongest scholarly accounts of the creation of the law. See, for example, Lawrence J. McAndrews, *The Era of Education: The Presidents and the Schools, 1965–2001* (Urbana: University of Illinois Press, 2006); Patrick J. McGuinn, *No Child Left Behind and the Transformation of Federal Education Policy, 1965–2005* (Lawrence: University of

Kansas Press, 2006); Maris Vinovskis, *From A Nation at Risk to No Child Left Behind: National Education Goals and the Creation of Federal Education Policy* (New York: Teachers College Press, 2009); Elizabeth H. DeBray, *Politics, Ideology, and Education: Federal Policy during the Clinton and Bush Administrations* (New York: Teachers College Press, 2006).

13. DeBray, *Politics, Ideology, and Education,* 149–51.

14. Terry M. Moe, "A Union by Any Other Name," in *Choice and Competition in American Education,* ed. Paul E. Peterson, 123–35, 123, 125 (Lanham, MD: Rowman and Littlefield, 2006). See also Myron Lieberman, *The Teacher Unions: How They Sabotage Educational Reform and Why* (New York: Encounter Books, 2000); Peter Brimelow, *The Worm in the Apple: How the Teachers Unions Are Destroying American Education* (New York: Harper Collins, 2003). These critiques are not new and have come not only from political conservatives but, in fact, have been made by unionists themselves. For an explanation of why Chicago Teachers Union leader Margaret Haley thought unions were insufficient for addressing social issues, see Lois Weiner, "Teachers, Unions, and Social Reform: Examining Margaret Haley's Vision," *Educational Foundations,* v. 10, no. 3 (1996): 85–96. For a contrasting argument about the productive influence of teacher unions on school reform, see Charles Taylor Kerchner, Julia Koppich, and Joseph G. Weeres, *United Mind Workers: Unions and Teaching in the Knowledge Society* (San Francisco: Jossey-Bass, 1997); Tom Loveless, ed. *Conflicting Missions? Teachers Unions and Educational Reform* (Washington, DC: Brookings Institution Press, 2000); Susan Moore Johnson, Niall C. Nelson, and Jacqueline Potter, *Teacher Unions, School Staffing, and Reform* (Cambridge: Harvard University Press, 1985); Charles T. Kerchner and Julia E. Koppich, *A Union of Professionals: Labor Relations and Educational Reform* (New York: Teachers College Press, 1993).

15. U.S. Department of Education, National Center for Education Statistics, *Schools and Staffing Survey,* Public School Data File, 2003–2004.

16. For examples of how teacher quality debates have entered public discourse, see Amanda Ripley, "What Makes a Great Teacher?" *Atlantic,* January/February 2010, 58–66; Elizabeth Green, "Building a Better Teacher," *New York Times Magazine,* March 2, 2010; and Evan Thomas and Pat Wingert, "Why Can't We Get Rid of Failing Teachers?" *Newsweek,* March 15, 2010, 24–27.

17. See Daniel P. Mayer, John E. Mullens, and Mary T. Moore, *Monitoring School Quality: An Indicator's Report* (Washington, DC: National Center for Education Statistics, December 2000); Christopher Jencks and Meredith Phillips, eds., *The Black-White Test Score Gap* (Washington, DC: Brookings Institution Press, 1998); Steven G, Rivkin, Eric A. Hanushek, and John F. Kain, "Teachers, Schools, and Academic Achievement," *Econometrica* 77, no. 2 (2005): 417–58

18. McAndrews, *The Era of Education,* 229.

19. For more on novice teachers in minority schools, see Heather G. Peske and Kati Haycock, *Teaching Inequality: How Poor and Minority Students Are Shortchanged in Teacher Quality* (The Education Trust, June 2006).

20. Vinovskis, *From A Nation at Risk to No Child Left Behind,* 227.

21. Daniel Weisberg et al., *The Widget Effect: Our National Failure to Acknowledge and Act on Differences in Teacher Effectiveness* (New York: National Teacher Project, 2009).

22. Recently AFT president Randi Weingarten has acknowledged that teacher evaluation systems are inadequate. As a result, the AFT has agreed to work with the federal government in developing a new model for the evaluation and promotion of public school teachers. See "Union Chief Seeks to Overhaul Teacher Evaluation Process" *New York Times,* January 13, 2010.

23. Kathryn M. Neckerman, *Schools Betrayed: Roots of Failure in Inner-City Education* (Chicago: University of Chicago Press, 2007), 181.

24. Linda Perlstein, *Tested: One American School Struggles to Make the Grade* (New York: Henry Holt, 2007), 39. The research on and criticism of high-stakes standardized testing is substantial. Especially helpful are Linda Darling-Hammond, "From 'Separate but Equal' to 'No Child Left Behind': The Collision of New Standards and Old Inequalities," in *Many Children Left Behind: How the No Child Left Behind Act Is Damaging Our Children and Our Schools*, ed. Deborah Meier and George Wood, 3–32 (Boston: Beacon Press, 2004); Stan Karp, "NCLB's Selective Vision of Equality: Some Gaps Count More than Others," in *Many Children Left Behind*, 53–78; Amy Stuart Wells, "No Accountability for Diversity: Standardized Tests and the Demise of Racially Mixed Schools," in *The Resegregation of the American South*, Jack Bogart and Gary Orfield, 187–211, (Chapel Hill: University of North Carolina Press, 2006); Sharon L. Nichols and David C. Berliner, *Collateral Damage: How High-Stakes Testing Corrupts America's Schools* (Cambridge: Harvard Education Press, 2007); Lorraine M. McDonnell, *Politics, Persuasion, and Educational Testing* (Cambridge: Harvard University Press, 2004); Wayne Au, *Unequal by Design: High-Stakes Testing and the Standardization of Inequality* (New York: Routledge, 2009); Gary Orfield and Mindy L. Kornhaber, eds., *Raising Standards or Raising Barriers? Inequality and High-Stakes Testing in Public Education* (New York: Century Foundation Press, 2001); Angela Valenzuela, *Leaving Children Behind: How 'Texas Style' Accountability Fails Latino Youth* (New York: SUNY Press, 2005).

25. George Madaus and Marguerite Clark, "The Adverse Impact of High-Stakes Testing on Minority Students: Evidence from One Hundred Years of Tests," in *Raising Standards or Raising Barriers? Inequality and High-Stakes Testing in Public Education*, ed. Gary Orfield and Mindy L. Kornhaber, 85–106, 96 (New York: Century Foundation Press, 2001).

26. Susan Moore Johnson, *The Workplace Matters: Teacher Quality, Retention, and Effectiveness* (Washington, DC: National Education Association, 2006), 17.

27. Dana Markow and Michelle Cooper, *The MetLife Survey of the American Teacher: Past, Present, and Future* (New York: MetLife, Inc., 2008), 27, 40.

28. Perlstein, *Tested*, 51.

29. Reports have shown that teachers in low-income schools often spend part of their income on supplies for students; this became a central argument in the Detroit Federation of Teachers 2006 strike. See Abby Goodnough, "Teachers Dig Deeper to Fill Gap in Supplies," *New York Times*, September 21, 2002; Donna Winchester, "Many Teachers Buy Supplies for Students," *St. Petersburg Times*, May 22, 2006; "Detroit Teachers Maintain Strike on Salary Issue," *All Things Considered*, National Public Radio, August 30, 2006. http://www.npr.org/templates/transcript/transcript.php?storyId=5738205.

30. These factors vary significantly from those that teachers in small private schools attribute to their decision to leave the profession, although their attrition rates overall are similar. See Richard Ingersoll, "Teacher Turnover and Teacher Shortages: An Organizational Analysis," *American Educational Research Journal* 38, no. 3 (2001): 499–534. For more on teacher attrition in minority schools see Eric A. Hanushek, John F. Kain, and Steven G. Rivkin, "Why Public Schools Lose Teachers," *Journal of Human Resources* 39, no. 2 (2004): 326–54.

31. Quoted in Richard M. Ingersoll, *Who Controls Teachers' Work? Power and Accountability in America's Schools* (Cambridge: Harvard University Press, 2003), 84, 89.

32. Steve Farkas et al., *Stand By Me: What Teachers Really Think about Unions, Merit Pay, and Other Professional Matters* (Public Agenda, 2003), 17–18.

33. Farkas, *Stand By Me*, 21.

34. Morgaen L. Donaldson, "Greater Expectations, Higher Demands," in *Finders and Keepers: Helping New Teachers Survive and Thrive in Our School*, ed. Susan Moore Johnson et al., 1–18, 3 (San Francisco: Jossey-Bass, 2004).

35. Julia E. Koppich, "The As-Yet-Unfulfilled Promise of Reform Bargaining: Forging a Much Better System between the Labor Relations System We Have and the Education System We Want," in *Collective Bargaining in Education: Negotiating Change in Today's Schools*, ed. Jane Hannaway and Andre J. Rotherham, 203–28, 216 (Cambridge: Harvard Education Press, 2006). 216.

36. Farkas, *Stand By Me*, 18.

37. See Paul LeMehieu et al., *Making a Difference: The National Writing Project's Influence over Thirty Years* (Berkeley, CA: National Writing Project, 2007); Ann Lieberman, "The National Writing Project: Commitment and Competence," in *Reconnecting Education and Foundations: Turning Good Intentions into Educational Capital*, ed. Ray Bacchetti and Thomas Ehrlich, 185–207 (San Francisco: Jossey-Bass, 2007); Ann Lieberman and Diane R. Wood, *Inside the National Writing Project: Connecting Network Learning and Classroom Teaching* (New York: Teachers College Press, 2007).

38. "Address Made at the Meeting of the Board of Education on April 6, 1950."

Selected Bibliography

Adickes, Sandra E. *Legacy of a Freedom School*. New York: Palgrave Macmillan, 2005.

Allen, George. *Undercover Teacher*. New York: Doubleday, 1960.

Angus, David L., and Jeffrey E. Mirel. *The Failed Promise of the American High School, 1890–1995*. New York: Teachers College Press, 1999.

Arnesen, Eric. "'No Graver Danger': Black Anticommunism, the Communist Party, and the Race Question." *Labor: Studies in Working-Class History of the Americas* 3, no. 4 (2006): 13–52.

Balkin, Jack M., ed. *What Brown v. Board of Education Should Have Said: The Nation's Top Legal Experts Rewrite America's Landmark Civil Rights Decision*. New York: New York University Press, 2002.

Banks, Cherry A. McGee. *Improving Multicultural Education: Lessons Learned from the Intergroup Education Movement*. New York: Teachers College Press, 2004.

Banks, James A., ed. *Multicultural Education, Transformative Knowledge and Action: Historical and Contemporary Perspectives*. New York: Teachers College Press, 1996.

Berlin, Isaiah. "Two Concepts of Liberty." In *Liberty: Incorporating Four Essays on Liberty*, ed. Henry Hardy, 166–217. Oxford: Oxford University Press, 2002.

Biondi, Martha. *To Stand and Fight: The Struggle for Civil Rights in Postwar New York City*. Cambridge: Harvard University Press, 2003.

Blanchett, Wanda J. "Disproportionate Representation of African American Students in Special Education: Acknowledging the Role of White Privilege and Racism." *Educational Researcher* 35, no. 6 (2006): 24–28.

Blascoer, Frances. *Colored School Children in New York*. New York: Public Education Association of the City of New York, 1915.

Board of Education of the City of New York. *Report and Recommendations of the Joint Committee on Maladjustment and Delinquency*. January 1938.

Brimelow, Peter. *The Worm in the Apple: How the Teachers Unions Are Destroying American Education*. New York: Harper Collins, 2003.

Brown, JoAnne. *The Definition of a Profession: The Authority of Metaphor in the History of Intelligence Testing, 1890–1930*. Princeton: Princeton University Press, 1922.

Burkholder, Zoe. "From 'Wops and Dagoes and Hunkies' to 'Caucasian': Changing Racial Discourse in American Classrooms During World War II." *History of Education Quarterly* 50, no. 3 (2010): 324–58.

Burstein, Paul. *Discrimination, Jobs, and Politics: The Struggle for Equal Employment Opportunity in the United States since the New Deal*. Chicago: University of Chicago Press, 1998.

Bush, Rod. *We Are Not What We Seem: Black Nationalism and the Class Struggle in the American Century*. New York: New York University Press, 2000.

Capeci, Dominic. *The Harlem Riot of 1943*. Philadelphia: Temple University Press, 1977.

Chapman, Paul Davis. *Schools as Sorters: Lewis B. Terman, Applied Psychology, and the Intelligence Testing Movement, 1890–1930*. New York: New York University, 1988.

The Civil Rights Project. *Discrimination in Special Education*. Cambridge: The Civil Rights Project, Harvard University Press, 2001.

Clark, Kenneth. "A Negro Looks at Black Power," *New York Post*, November 11, 1967.

Cole, Stephen. *The Unionization of Teachers: A Case Study of the UFT.* New York: Praeger Publishers, 1969.

Collins, Christina. *"Ethnically Qualified": Race, Merit, and the Selection of Urban Teachers, 1920–1980.* New York: Teachers College Press, 2011.

Commission on School Integration. *Public School Segregation and Integration in the North.* Washington, DC: National Association of Intergroup Relations Officials, November 1963.

Counts, George S. *Dare the School Build a New Social Order?* New York: Arno Press and the New York Times, 1969.

Cuban, Larry. *How Teachers Taught: Constancy and Change in American Classrooms, 1880–1990.* New York: Teachers College Press, 1993.

Damerall, Reginald G., and Maurie Hillson, "The UFT Tells It Like It Isn't and Makes It Look Like It Is." *Phi Delta Kappan* 55, no. 6 (1974): 377–82.

De Forest, Jennifer. "Tilting at Windmills? Judge Justine Wise Polier and a History of Justice and Education in New York City." *History of Education Quarterly* 49, no. 1 (2009): 68–88.

DeBray, Elizabeth H. *Politics, Ideology, and Education: Federal Policy during the Bush and Clinton Administrations.* New York: Teachers College Press, 2006.

Dodson, Dan. "Public Education in New York City in the Decade Ahead." *Journal of Educational Sociology* 34, no. 6 (1961): 274–87

Douglas, Davison M. *Jim Crow Moves North: The Battle over Northern School Segregation, 1865–1954.* New York: Cambridge University Press, 2005.

DuBois, Rachel Davis. *All This and Something More: Pioneering in Intercultural Education.* Bryn Mawr: Dorrance, 1948.

———. *Build Together Americans.* New York: Hinds, Hayden, and Eldredge, 1945.

Dudziak, Mary L. *Cold War Civil Rights: Race and the Image of American Democracy.* Princeton: Princeton University Press, 2002.

Etzioni, Amitai. *The Semi-Professions and Their Organizations: Teachers, Nurses, Social Workers.* New York: Free Press, 1969.

Evans, Sara M. *Personal Politics: The Roots of Women's Liberation in the Civil Rights Movement and the New Left.* New York: Vintage, 1980.

Fairclough, Adam. *A Class of Their Own: Black Teachers in the Segregated South.* Cambridge: Harvard University Press, 2007.

———. "The Costs of Brown: Black Teachers and School Integration." *Journal of American History* 91, no. 1 (2004): 43–55.

Farkas, Steve, et al. *Stand By Me: What Teachers Really Think about Unions, Merit Pay, and Other Professional Matters.* Public Agenda, 2003.

Fass, Paula. *Outside In: Minorities and the Transformation of American Education.* New York: Oxford University Press, 1989.

Feldstein, Ruth. "'I Wanted the Whole World to See': Race, Gender, and Constructions of Motherhood in the Death of Emmett Till." In *Not June Cleaver: Women and Gender in Postwar America, 1945–1960,* ed. Joanne Meyerowitz, 263–303. Philadelphia: Temple University Press, 1994.

Finn, Chester, and Diane Ravitch, eds., *New Schools for a New Century: The Redesign of Urban Education.* New Haven: Yale University Press, 1997.

Fischer, Louis, David Schimmel, and Cynthia A. Kelly. *Teachers and the Law.* New York: Longman, 1981.

Formisano, Ronald P. *Boston against Busing: Race, Class, and Ethnicity in the 1960s and 1970s.* Chapel Hill: University of North Carolina Press, 1991.

Freeman, Joshua B. *Working-Class New York: Life and Labor since World War II*. New York: New Press, 2000.

Freeman, Joshua B., and Steve Rosswurm. "The Education of an Anti-Communist: Father John F. Cronin and the Baltimore Labor Movement." *Labor History* 33, no. 2 (1992): 217–47

Friedman, Andrea. "The Strange Career of Annie Lee Moss: Rethinking Race, Gender, and McCarthyism." *Journal of American History* 94, no. 2 (2007): 445–68.

Friedson, Eliot. *Professionalism: The Third Logic*. Chicago: University of Chicago Press, 2001.

Frymer, Paul. *Black and Blue: African Americans, the Labor Movement, and the Decline of the Democratic Party*. Princeton: Princeton University Press, 2007.

Fultz, Michael. "The Displacement of Educators Post-Brown: An Overview and Analysis." *History of Education Quarterly* 44, no. 1 (2004): 11–45.

Gerstle, Gary. *American Crucible: Race and Nation in the Twentieth Century*. Princeton: Princeton University Press, 2001.

———. "The Protean Character of American Liberalism." *American Historical Review* 99, no. 4 (1994): 1043–73.

———. "Race and the Myth of the Liberal Consensus." *Journal of American History* 82, no. 2 (1995): 579–86.

Gilbert, James B. *A Cycle of Outrage: America's Reaction to the Juvenile Delinquent in the 1950s*. New York: Oxford University Press, 1986.

Gitlin, Todd. *The Whole World Is Watching: Mass Media and the Making and Unmaking of the New Left*. Berkeley: University of California Press, 1980.

Glendon, Mary Ann. *Rights Talk: The Impoverishment of Political Discourse*. New York: Free Press, 1993.

Goluboff, Risa L. *The Lost Promise of Civil Rights*. Cambridge: Harvard University Press, 2007.

Gordon, David T., ed. *A Nation Transformed? American Education 20 Years after a Nation at Risk*. Cambridge: Harvard Education Press, 2003.

Grant, Gerald, and Christine E. Murray. *Teaching in America: The Slow Revolution*. Cambridge: Harvard University Press, 2002.

Green, Elizabeth. "Building a Better Teacher." *New York Times Magazine*, March 2, 2010.

Greenberg, Cheryl L. *"Or Does It Explode?" Black Harlem in the Great Depression*. New York: Oxford University Press, 1991.

Guinier, Lani. "From Racial Liberalism to Racial Literacy: Brown v. Board of Education and the Interest-Divergence Dilemma." *Journal of American History* 91, no. 1 (2004): 92–118.

Gutmann, Amy. *Democratic Education*. Princeton: Princeton University Press, 1987.

Hall, Jaqueline Dowd. "The Long Civil Rights Movement and the Political Uses of the Past." *Journal of American History* 91, no. 4 (2005): 1233–63.

Harlem Youth Opportunities Unlimited, Inc. *Youth in the Ghetto: A Study of the Consequences of Powerlessness and a Blueprint for Change*. New York: HARYOU, 1964.

Haskell, Thomes, ed. *The Authority of Experts: Studies in History and Theory*. Bloomington: Indiana University Press, 1984.

Haskins, Jim. *Diary of a Harlem Schoolteacher*. New York: Grove Press, 1969.

Hechinger, Fred. "The City School—A Mixed Report Card," *New York Times Magazine*, June 14, 1964.

———. "Teachers Adopting a Militant Approach," *New York Times*, January 9, 1969.

Herman, Ellen. *The Romance of American Psychology: Political Culture in the Age of Experts*. Berkeley: University of California Press, 1995.

Hochschild, Jennifer L. *The American Dilemma: Liberal Democracy and School Desegregation*. New Haven: Yale University Press, 1984.

Hulbert, Ann. *Raising America: Experts, Parents, and a Century of Advice about Children.* New York: Random House, 2003.

Hunter, Evan. *Blackboard Jungle.* New York: Simon and Schuster, 1954.

Ingersoll, Richard M. *Who Controls Teachers' Work? Power and Accountability in America's Schools.* Cambridge: Harvard University Press, 2003.

Jackson, John P. Jr. *Social Scientists for Social Justice: Making the Case against Segregation.* New York: New York University Press, 2001.

Jackson, Walter A. *Gunnar Myrdal and America's Conscience: Social Engineering and Racial Liberalism, 1938–1987.* Chapel Hill: University of North Carolina Press, 1990.

Jacobson, Matthew Frye. *Roots Too: White Ethnic Revival in Post-Civil Rights America.* Cambridge: Harvard University Press, 2006.

———. *Whiteness of a Different Color: European Immigrants and the Alchemy of Race.* Cambridge: Harvard University Press, 1999.

Jencks, Christopher, and Meredith Phillips, eds. *The Black-White Test Score Gap.* Washington, DC: Brookings Institution Press, 1998.

Johanek, Michael, and John L. Puckett. *Leonard Covello and the Making of Benjamin Franklin High School: Education as if Citizenship Mattered.* Philadelphia: Temple University Press, 2007.

Johnson, Lauri. "A Generation of Women Activists: African American Female Educators in Harlem, 1930–1950." *Journal of African American History* 89, no. 3 (2004): 223–40.

———. "'Making Democracy Real': Teacher Union and Community Activism to Promote Diversity in the New York Public Schools, 1935–1950." *Urban Education* 37, no. 5 (2002): 566–87.

Johnson, Susan Moore. *The Workplace Matters: Teacher Quality, Retention, and Effectiveness.* Washington, DC: National Education Association, 2006.

Johnson, Susan Moore, Niall C. Nelson, and Jacqueline Potter, *Teacher Unions, School Staffing, and Reform.* Cambridge: Harvard University Press, 1985

Joseph, Peniel E. "The Black Power Movement: A State of the Field." *Journal of American History* 96, no. 3 (2009): 751–76.

———. "Dashikis and Democracy: Black Students, Student Activism, and the Black Power Movement." *Journal of African American History* 88, no. 2 (2003): 182–203.

———. *Waiting 'Til the Midnight Hour: A Narrative History of Black Power in America.* New York: Henry Holt, 2006.

Kahlenberg, Richard D. *Tough Liberal: Albert Shanker and the Battle over Schools, Unions, Race, and Democracy.* New York: Columbia University Press, 2007.

Kantor, Harvey, and Robert Lowe. "From New Deal to No Deal: No Child Left Behind and the Devolution of Responsibility for Equal Opportunity." *Harvard Educational Review* 76, no. 4 (2006): 474–502.

Karpinski, Carol F. *"A Visible Company of Professionals": African Americans and the National Education Association During the Civil Rights Movement.* New York: Peter Lang, 2008.

Kaufman, Bel. *Up the Down Staircase.* Englewood Cliffs, NJ: Prentice Hall 1964.

Kelley, Robin D.G. *Race Rebels: Culture, Politics, and the Black Working Class.* New York: Free Press, 1994.

Kerchner, Charles T., and Julia E. Koppich, *A Union of Professionals: Labor Relations and Educational Reform.* New York: Teachers College Press, 1993.

Kerchner, Charles Taylor, Julia Koppich, and Joseph G. Weeres, *United Mind Workers: Unions and Teaching in the Knowledge Society.* Jossey-Bass, 1997.

Kliebard, Herbert M. *The Struggle for the American Curriculum, 1893–1958.* New York: Routledge, 1995.

Kline, Wendy. *Building a Better Race: Gender, Sexuality, and Eugenics from the Turn of the Century to the Baby Boom*. Berkeley: University of California Press, 2001.

Klineberg, Otto. *Negro Intelligence and Selective Migration*. New York: Columbia University Press, 1935.

Kluger, Richard. *Simple Justice: A History of Brown v. Board of Education and Black America's Struggle for Equality*. New York: Vintage Books, 1975.

Korstad, Robert, and Nelson Lichetenstein. "Opportunities Found and Lost: Labor, Radicals, and the Early Civil Rights Movement." *Journal of American History* 75, no. 3 (1988): 786–811.

Kozol, Jonathan. *The Shame of the Nation: The Restoration of Apartheid Schooling in America*. New York: Crown Publishers, 2005.

———. "Still Separate, Still Unequal." *Harpers*, September 2005, 41–54.

Larson, Magali Sarfatti. *The Rise of Professionalism: A Sociological Analysis*. Berkeley: University of California Press, 1977.

Lasch-Quinn, Elizabeth. *Race Experts: How Racial Etiquette, Sensitivity Training and New Age Therapy Hijacked the Civil Rights Revolution*. New York: Norton, 2001.

LeMehieu, Paul, et al. *Making a Difference: The National Writing Project's Influence over Thirty Years*. Berkeley, CA: National Writing Project, 2007.

Levine, Daniel U. "The Need for Teacher Activist Roles among Teachers in Big City School Districts." *Journal of Secondary Education* 44 (March 1969): 122–28.

Lichtenstein, Nelson. *State of the Union: A Century of American Labor*. Princeton: Princeton University Press, 2002.

Lieberman, Ann. "The National Writing Project: Commitment and Competence." In *Reconnecting Education & Foundations: Turning Good Intentions into Educational Capital*, ed. Ray Bacchetti and Thomas Ehrlich, 185–207. San Francisco: Jossey-Bass, 2007.

Lieberman, Ann, and Diane R. Wood. *Inside the National Writing Project: Connecting Network Learning and Classroom Teaching*. New York: Teachers College Press, 2007.

Lieberman, Myron. *The Teacher Unions: How They Sabotage Educational Reform and Why*. New York: Encounter Books, 2000.

Losen, Daniel J. "Graduation Rate Accountability under the No Child Left Behind Act." In *NCLB Meets School Realities: Lessons from the Field*, ed. Gail J. Sunderman, James S. Kim, Gary Orfield, 105–20. Thousand Oaks, CA: Corwin Press, 2005.

Loveless, Tom, ed. *Conflicting Missions? Teachers Unions and Educational Reform*. Washington, DC: Brookings Institution Press, 2000.

Lukas, J. Anthony. "Nation's Teachers Using Rights Protest Methods." *New York Times*, September 11, 1967.

Lyons, John F. *Teachers and Reform: Chicago Public Education, 1929–1970*. Urbana: University of Illinois Press, 2008.

Maleska, Eugene. "White Teacher in Harlem." *High Points in the Work of the High Schools of New York City* 29, no. 5 (1947): 5–9.

Markow, Dana, and Michelle Cooper. *The MetLife Survey of the American Teacher: Past, Present, and Future*. New York: MetLife, Inc., 2008.

Markowitz, Gerald E., and David Rosner. *Children, Race, and Power: Kenneth and Mamie Clark's Northside Center*. Charlottesville: University of Virginia Press, 1996.

Markowitz, Ruth Jacknow. *My Daughter the Teacher*. Newark: Rutgers University Press, 1993.

Mayer, Daniel P., John E. Mullens, and Mary T. Moore, *Monitoring School Quality: An Indicator's Report*. Washington, DC: National Center for Education Statistics, December 2000.

The Mayor's Commission on Conditions in Harlem. *The Complete Report of Mayor LaGuardia's Commission on the Harlem Riot of March 19, 1935*. New York: Arno Press, 1969.

McAdam, Doug. *Freedom Summer.* New York: Oxford University Press, 1990.

McAndrews, Lawrence J. *The Era of Education: The Presidents and the Schools, 1965–2001.* Urbana: University of Illinois Press, 2006.

McGuinn, Patrick J. *No Child Left Behind and the Transformation of Federal Education Policy, 1965–2005.* Lawrence: University of Kansas Press, 2006.

Meier, Deborah, and George Wood, eds. *Many Children Left Behind: How the No Child Left Behind Act Is Damaging Our Children and Our Schools.* Boston: Beacon Press, 2004.

Moe, Terry M. "A Union By Any Other Name." In *Choice and Competition in American Education,* ed. Paul E. Peterson, 123–35. Lanham, MD: Rowman and Littlefield, 2006.

Montalto, Nicholas V. *A History of the Intercultural Movement, 1924–1941.* New York: Graland Publishing, 1982.

Moskowitz, Eva. *In Therapy We Trust: America's Obsession with Self-Fulfillment.* Baltimore: Johns Hopkins Press, 2001.

Murphy, Marjorie. *Blackboard Unions: The AFT and the NEA, 1900–1980.* Ithaca: Cornell University Press, 1990.

Myrdal, Gunnar. *An American Dilemma: The Negro Problem and Modern Democracy.* New York: Harpers and Row, 1944.

Naison, Mark. *Communists in Harlem during the Depression.* Urbana: University of Illinois Press, 1983.

National Commission on Excellence in Education. *A Nation at Risk: The Imperative for Educational Reform.* Washington, DC: Government Printing Office, 1983.

Neckerman, Kathryn M. *Schools Betrayed: Roots of Failure in Inner-City Education.* Chicago: University of Chicago Press, 2007.

Nelson, Adam R. *The Elusive Ideal: Equal Educational Opportunity and the Federal Role in Boston's Public Schools, 1950–1985.* Chicago: University of Chicago Press, 2005.

O'Connor, Alice. *Poverty Knowledge: Social Science, Social Policy, and the Poor in Twentieth-Century U.S. History.* Princeton: Princeton University Press, 2002.

Ogbar, Jeffrey O.G. *Black Power: Radical Politics and African American Identity.* Baltimore: Johns Hopkins Press, 2004.

Orfield, Gary. *Schools More Separate: Consequences of a Decade of Resegregation.* Cambridge: Civil Rights Project, Harvard University, July 2001.

Orfield, Gary, and Susan E. Eaton. *Dismantling Desegregation: The Quiet Reversal of Brown v. Board of Education.* New York: New Press, 1997.

Orfield, Gary, and Mindy L. Kornhaber, eds. *Raising Standards or Raising Barriers? Inequality and High-Stakes Testing in Public Education.* New York: Century Foundation Press, 2001.

Orleck, Annelise. *Storming Caesar's Palace: How Black Mothers Fought Their Own War on Poverty.* Boston: Beacon Press, 2006.

Palladino, Grace. *Teenagers: An American History.* New York: Basic Books, 1996.

Parrish, Richard. "The New York City Teacher Strikes: Blow to Education, Boon to Racism." *Labor Today* 8, no. 3 (1969): 30–33

Patterson, James T. *Brown v. the Board of Education: A Civil Rights Milestone and Its Troubled Legacy.* Oxford: Oxford University Press, 2001.

———. *Grand Expectations: The United States, 1945–1974.* New York: Oxford University Press, 1996.

Pellicano, Roy C. "New York City Public School Reform: A Line Teacher's View." *Phi Delta Kappan* 62, no. 3 (1980): 174–77.

Perlstein, Daniel H. *Justice, Justice: School Politics and the Eclipse of Liberalism.* New York: Peter Lang, 2004.

————. "Teaching Freedom: SNCC and the Creation of the Mississippi Freedom Schools." *History of Education Quarterly* 30, no. 3 (1990): 297–324.

Perlstein, Linda. *Tested: One American School's Struggle to Make the Grade.* New York: Henry Holt, 2007.

Peske, Heather G., and Kati Haycock, *Teaching Inequality: How Poor and Minority Students Are Shortchanged in Teacher Quality.* The Education Trust, June 2006.

Podair, Jerald E. *The Strike That Changed New York: Blacks, Whites, and the Ocean Hill-Brownsville Crisis.* New Haven: Yale University Press, 2002.

Public Education Association. *The Status of the Public School Education of Negro and Puerto Rican Children in the City.* New York: Public Education Association of New York City, October 1955.

Raskin, A.H. "He Leads His Teachers Up the Down Staircase." *New York Times,* September 3, 1967.

————. "Shanker's Great Leap," *New York Times,* September 1, 1973.

Ravitch, Diane. *The Great School Wars: A History of the New York City Public Schools.* Baltimore: Johns Hopkins Press, 2000.

————. *Left Back: A Century of Battles Over School Reform.* New York: Simon and Schuster, 2000.

Redefer, Frederick L. "The Importance of Teacher Morale." In *Problems and Practices in New York City Schools,* 14–22. New York: New York Education Society for the Experimental Study of Education, 1957.

Report on the Harlem Project by the Research Committee: A Project Sponsored Jointly by the New York Foundation and the Board of Education of the City of New York, September 1943-June 1945. New York: Board of Education of the City of New York, December 1947.

Reyes, Luis O. "The Aspira Consent Decree: A Thirtieth Anniversary Retrospective of Bilingual Education in New York City." *Harvard Educational Review* 76, no. 3 (2006): 369–400.

Rieser, Jonathan. *Canarsie: The Jews and Italians of Brooklyn Against Liberalism.* Cambridge: Harvard University Press, 1985.

Ripley, Amanda. "What Makes a Great Teacher?" *The Atlantic,* January/Februrary 2010, 58–66.

Roberts, Gene, and Hank Klibanoff. *The Race Beat: The Press, the Civil Rights Struggle, and the Awakening of a Nation.* New York: Alfred A. Knopf, 2006.

Rofes, Eric E., and Lisa Stulberg, eds. *The Emancipatory Promise of Charter Schools: Towards a Progressive Politics of School Choice.* Albany: State University of New York Press, 2004.

Rossinow, Douglas C. *Visions of Progress: The Left-Liberal Tradition in America.* Philadelphia: University of Pennsylvania Press, 2007.

Rousmaniere, Kate. *City Teachers: Teaching and School Reform in Historical Perspective.* New York: Teachers College Press, 1997.

————. "Teacher Unions in Popular Culture: Individualism and the Absence of Collectivity." *Working USA* 3, no. 3 (1999): 38–46.

Ryan, James E. *Five Miles Away, A World Apart: One City, Two Schools, and the Story of Educational Opportunity in Modern America.* New York: Oxford University Press, 2010.

Santiago-Santiago, Isaura. "Aspira v. Board of Education Revisited." *American Journal of Education* 95, no. 1 (1986): 149–99.

Schierenbeck, Jack. "Opporunities Lost and Found: The Incredible Life and Times of (Miss) Layle Lane." *American Educator* 24, no. 4 (2000): 4–19.

Schmidt, Christopher W. "The Children of Brown: Psychology and School Desegregation in

Midcentury America," in *When Science Encounters the Child: Education, Parenting, and Child Welfare in 20-th Century America*, ed. Barbara Beatty, Emily D. Cahan, and Julia Grant. New York: Teachers College Press, 2006.

Schneider, Erich C. *Vampires, Dragons, and Egyptian Kings: Youth Gangs in Postwar New York*. Princeton: Princeton University Press, 1999.

Schrecker, Ellen. *Many Are the Crimes: McCarthyism in America*. Princeton: Princeton University Press, 1999.

Scott, Darryl Michael. *Contempt and Pity; Social Policy and the Image of the Damaged Black Psyche, 1880–1996*. Chapel Hill: University of North Carolina Press, 1997.

———. "Postwar Pluralism, *Brown v. Board of Education*, and the Origins of Multicultural Education." *Journal of American History* 91, no. 1 (2004): 69–82.

Selig, Diana. *Americans All: The Cultural Gifts Movement*. Cambridge: Harvard University Press, 2008.

Shaffer, Robert. "Multicultural Education in New York City during World War II." *New York History* 77, no. 3 (1996): 301–32.

Shanker, Albert. "Improving Big City Schools." *New York Times*, March 12, 1989.

———. "Looking Back," *New York Times*, December 17, 1995.

———. "Minority Group Members Gain More as Union Members," *New York Times*, June 20, 1971.

———. "Obstacles on the Road to Accountability," *New York Times*, March 28, 1971.

———. "Shanker Responds: The Way It Really Is." *Phi Delta Kappan* 55, no. 6 (1974): 383–87.

———. "State of the Union Address, AFT Convention" (August 1977). Reprinted in *American Educator* 21, no. 1 and 2 (1997): 8.

———. "State of the Union Address, AFT Convention" (August 1984). Reprinted in *American Educator* 21, no. 1 and 2 (1997): 26.

———. "State of the Union Address, AFT Convention" (August 1992). Reprinted in *American Educator* 21, no. 1 and 2 (1997): 20.

———. "Teacher Unionism: A Quiet Revolution," *New York Times*, October 28, 1973.

Sherry, Michael S. *In the Shadow of War: The United States Since the 1930s*. New Haven: Yale University Press, 1995.

Sitkoff, Howard. "Racial Militancy and Interracial Violence." *Journal of American History* 58, no. 3 (1971): 661–81

Skrentny, John D. *The Minority Rights Revolution*. Cambridge: Harvard University Press, 2002.

Smith, Mark C. *Social Science in the Crucible: The American Debate over Objectivity and Purpose, 1918–1941*. Durham: Duke University Press, 1994.

Solomone, Rosemary C. *Equal Education Under Law: Legal Rights and Federal Policy in the Post Brown Era*. New York: Palgrave Macmillan, 2000.

Stern, Sol. "Scab Teachers." In *Confrontation at Ocean Hill-Brownsville: The New York School Strikes of 1968*, ed. Maurice R. Berube and Marilyn Gittell, 180–81. New York: Praeger, 1969.

Sugrue, Thomas J. *Sweet Land of Liberty: The Forgotten Struggle for Civil Rights in the North*. New York: Random House, 2008.

Syrkin, Marie. *Your Schools, Your Children: A Teacher Looks at What's Wrong with Our Schools*. New York: L.B. Fisher, 1944.

Taylor, Clarence. *Knocking at Our Own Door: Milton A. Galamison and the Struggle to Integrate New York City Schools*. Lanham, MD: Lexington Books, 2001.

The Teacher's Handbook: A Guide for Use in the Schools of the City of New York. 4th ed. New York: Department of Education of the City of New York, January 1, 1928.

Teachers Union of the City of New York. *A Proposal to Establish an Experimental School Within the Public Schools System of the City of New York.* New York: Teachers Union of the City of New York, 1924.

Thomas, Evan, and Pat Wingert, "Why Can't We Get Rid of Failing Teachers?" *Newsweek*, March 15, 2010, 24–27.

Tyack, David B. *The One Best System: A History of American Urban Education.* Cambridge: Harvard University Press, 1974.

Tyack, David, Robert Lowe, and Elizabeth Hansot. *Public Schools in Hard Times: The Great Depression and Recent Years.* Cambridge: Harvard University Press, 1993.

Urban, Wayne J. *Gender, Race, and the NEA: Professionalism and Its Limitations.* New York: Routledge, 2000.

———. *Why Teachers Organized.* Detroit: Wayne State University Press, 1982.

Urofksy, Melvin, ed. *Why Teachers Strike: Teachers' Rights and Community Control.* Garden City, NY: Anchor Books, 1970.

U.S. Department of Education, National Center for Education Statistics. *Schools and Staffing Survey.* Public School Data File, 2003–2004.

VanDeburg, William L. *New Day in Babylon: The Black Power Movement and American Culture, 1965–1975.* Chicago: University of Chicago Press, 1992.

Vinovskis, Maris A. *From a Nation at Risk to No Child Left Behind: National Education Goals and the Creation of Federal Education Policy.* New York: Teachers College Press, 2009.

Weiner, Lois. "Teachers, Unions, and School Reform: Examining Margaret Haley's Vision." *Educational Foundations* 10, no. 3 (1996): 85–96.

Weisberg, Daniel, et al. *The Widget Effect: Our National Failure to Acknowledge and Act on Differences in Teacher Effectiveness.* New York: National Teacher Project, 2009.

Wells, Amy Stuart. "No Accountability for Diversity: Standardized Tests and the Demise of Racially Mixed Schools." In *The Resegregation of the American South*, ed. Jack Bogart and Gary Orfield, 187–211. Chapel Hill: University of North Carolina Press, 2006.

Westbrook, Robert B. *John Dewey and American Democracy.* Ithaca: Cornell University Press, 1991.

Wilder, Craig Steven. *A Covenant with Color: Race and Social Power in Brooklyn.* New York: Columbia University Press, 2000.

Zieger, Robert. *For Jobs and Freedom: Labor in America Since 1865.* Lexington: University Press of Kentucky, 2007.

Zimmerman, Jonathan. "Brown-ing the American Textbook: History, Psychology, and the Origins of Modern Multiculturalism." *History of Education Quarterly* 44, no. 1 (2004): 46–69.

Zitron, Celia Lewis. *The New York City Teachers Union, 1916–1964.* New York: Humanities Press, 1968.

Index